ARCHITECTURAL
MODEL BUILDING

fb

ARCHITECTURAL MODEL BUILDING

TOOLS, TECHNIQUES, AND MATERIALS

ROARK T. CONGDON

Fairchild Books
New York

Executive Editor: Olga T. Kontzias

Assistant Acquisitions Editor: Amanda Breccia

Editorial Development Director: Jennifer N. Crane

Development Editor: Michelle Levy

Assistant Development Editor: Sigali Hamberger

Editorial Intern: Emily Spiegel

Associate Art Director: Erin Fitzsimmons

Production Director: Ginger Hillman

Associate Production Editor: Andrew Fargnoli

Copyeditor: Susan Hobbs

Cover Design: Andrea Lau

Cover Art: Zimmer Gunsul Frasca Architects LLP

Text Design: Renato Stanisic

Library of Congress Catalog Card Number: 2009930987

ISBN: 978-1-56367-773-1

GST R 133004424

Printed in the United States of America

CH13, TP09

Contents

Extended Contents

Foreword

by Ross King

The Roman historian Suetonius tells the story of how Julius Caesar destroyed a newly completed house that had been built for him, at vast expense, on his estate at Nemi. Even though Caesar had witnessed the construction of the villa from the foundation upward, the finished product did not meet with his approval. For the Renaissance architect Leon Battista Alberti, there was a valuable lesson to be learned from this episode: "For this reason, I will always recommend the time-honored custom, practiced by the best builders, of preparing not only drawings and sketches but also models of wood or any other materials" (pp. 33 – 34).

All architects today would agree with Alberti. Behind virtually every great building is an architectural scale model of the sort he advocated. It is probably safe to assume that in 448 BCE, when a competition was held in Athens for the war memorial planned for the Acropolis, the sculptor Phidias constructed some kind of three-dimensional model to showcase his design and sway Pericles and his fellow Athenians. Likewise, one of the biggest building projects of the 21st century—the development of the World Trade Center site in Lower Manhattan—began in December 2002 when nine architectural models went on public display at the Winter Garden in the World Financial Center in New York.

Architectural models combine practicality and detailed craftsmanship with an artistic flair. Many great architects—Brunelleschi, Bramante, Michelangelo, François Mansart—originally trained as goldsmiths, painters, or sculptors. Some of them lavished great artistry (and great sums of money) on their models. A number of surviving examples, such as Antonio da Sangallo the Younger's for St. Peter's in Rome, or Sir Christopher Wren's "Great Model" for St. Paul's in London, are works of art in themselves. The former is 26 feet in length and took a carpenter six years to build. The latter featured small details, such as statues on the parapets, believed to have been commissioned by Wren from Grinling Gibbons, the greatest woodcarver in history.

The materials and techniques of model making have changed over the centuries. Wood, pasteboard, and stone have made way for laser-cut styrene and even (as the models at the Winter Garden revealed) holograms and sophisticated computer animation. But the impetus remains the same: to solve design problems, inform and impress patrons and the public, and win commissions. The need for skill, ingenuity, and imagination likewise remains. In what follows, Roark Congdon presents a clear step-by-step account of this process and of the methods and materials that can be used to achieve what Alberti calls "a clearer and more certain idea" of the building in question.

Ross King is the author of three books on Italian history and art: *Brunelleschi's Dome: How a Renaissance Genius Reinvented Architecture* (2000); *Michelangelo and the Pope's Ceiling* (2002); and *Machiavelli: Philosopher of Power* (2007). He has also published two novels as well as *The Judgment of Paris* (2006), a study of French Impressionism.

Preface

Architectural Model Building: Tools, Techniques, and Materials was written in order to present the inexperienced or student model maker with simple instructions, illustrations, exercises, and practical applications; all of which were designed to develop the skills necessary to build professional quality models. Unlike in Great Britain, the United States has few colleges or universities that offer courses that focus solely on the teaching of model building theories and techniques. Rather, certain techniques may be introduced as smaller units of broader courses.

Oftentimes, through the process of trial and error, students learn these processes on their own. In addition to this being a useful textbook for an architectural model making course, the information presented herein is intended to supplement courses for a variety of disciplines, including Interior Design, Landscape Architecture, Furniture Design, Industrial Design, Engineering, Lighting Design, and Theater and Stage Set Design. Introductory courses in Fine Arts that stress three-dimensional fundamentals would benefit from this as well. Finally, the nonacademic interested reader or hobbyist will find this information useful and simple to understand.

This book is divided into three distinct parts. Part 1 consists of Chapters 1 through 6, and begins by presenting the reader with a brief history of the use of models. The subsequent chapters offer tips on how to prepare an area for model making, and which tools to purchase. Even the most experienced model maker or designer will benefit from Chapter 4, "Planning a Model," before they begin their next project.

In Part 2 of this book, Chapters 7 through 11, students are introduced to presentation strategies and fundamental construction techniques. They will hone their physical model making skills by following a logical progression of exercises and examples. The materials introduced in each chapter—paper-based products, foam board, balsa wood, and basswood—become, in that order, progressively more difficult to work with. New techniques are introduced using the simplest of materials, thus giving the reader confidence in the fundamental techniques. To gain confidence working with a new, more demanding material, the reader will be asked to practice the simple techniques learned in earlier chapters.

Each material will demand that you make subtle changes in the primary techniques. The demonstrations and exercises are provided to assist you in perfecting those techniques.

In Part 3, Chapters 12 and 13, advanced learners will have the opportunity to fine-tune their techniques and add realistic detail. Working with mixed media and representing real-life materials is the rewarding and challenging conclusion to this textbook.

In addition to supplying the student with basic how-to information, this book also provides instructions on shortcuts, and tips on avoiding common mistakes in passages that display the Learn from the Pros icon. A glossary defines key terms, which are **boldfaced** throughout the text. The photographs make the hands-on lessons easy to grasp. Chapter Review and Practice offers carefully considered critical thinking questions as well as hands-on practice for the beginning to intermediate model maker. Advice from the Pros box (pp. 43–45) reinforces the lessons in an engaging format.

As you know, architectural models can be visualized in many different ways. Rough sketches in the design phase help inspire. Measured drawings can help communicate early ideas to clients. CAD programs are used to start seeing models in three dimensions. Appendix A shows the basic shapes used in the models you see photographed in this book. These were created using Google SketchUp.

The aim is to help visual learners conceive of all aspects of the three-dimensional model in ways they might not have seen in the photographs. The templates provide alternative forms of learning and visualizing the three-dimensional model.

In the field of three-dimensional modeling, the range of physical possibilities, topics, processes, and mediums is far too broad to be covered in entirety in one book. Indeed, materials such as styrene, and advanced techniques that utilize acrylics or wood, and processes such as mold making, casting, and computer-aided physical modeling are related topics of interest, covered in a handful of other books.

Acknowledgments

This book would not have been possible without the help of the following:

Model makers, thank you all for your generous donation of time, expertise, and studio visits: Scott Jennings of Scott Jennings Model shop, sorry about falling on that model; Tomoko Briggs of Zimmer Gunsul Frasca Architects LLP; Jason Hanner of Box Shop models and Weber Thompson, hand model and master of the museum board; Alec Vassiliadis of Sound Models Inc., thanks for the beautiful images and great stories; Lois Gaylord, hand model and model maker extraordinaire; Richard Armiger of Network Modelmakers, thanks for spinning such great yarns over fine British cuisine; William Zimmerman of William Zimmerman Architects, Go Dawgs; Sophie Hong of Tiscareno Architects; Timothy Richards; Roger Newell; and Keith Day of Modelbuilders Supply for the charts in Chapter 4.

Thanks to student model makers: Breanna Wucinich; Laura Osterman; Tyler Schaffer, Go Cougs!; and Lauren Jacobs.

Thanks to the following architecture firms: Zimmer Gunsul Frasca Architects LLP, with a special thanks to Leslie Morison, Jill Sandess, Tomoko Briggs, John Chau, Gustavo Lopez, Michelle Mills, Clint Diner, and Allyn Stellmacher; Owens Richards Architects, with special thanks to Tom Mulica; Stuart Silk Architects; Weber Thompson Architects, with special thanks to Joe Kolmer and Jason Hanner; William Zimmerman Architects; Olsen Sundberg Kundig Allen; Zeroplus Architects, with special thanks to Josh Brevoort and Lisa Chun; Castanes Architects; special thanks to Amber Murray; Roger Newell, AIA; Tiscareno Architects; special thanks to Sophie Hong, Aaron Swain, and Jim Cade; and Sullivan Conard.

For their generous donations of tools and images, I would like to thank: Bosch; Dremel; Alvin Tools; Dakota Art; FoamWerks; Farwest Materials; Walla Walla Foundry; Mervin Manufacturing; Lib Tech; and The Snowboard Connection.

Photographers, thank you for your time and expertise: Carrie Kapp of Punchlist Design; Andrew Putler; and Galen Hirss, and the rest of the Aspen crew—thanks for the season, losing that box of pens, level 1 move.

Museums and such: The Seattle Architecture Foundation, with special thanks to

Tracy Victory-Rosenquest, Steve Harvey, Eriko Kawamura, Sidney Dobson, Roberta Miner, Scott Jennings, and Stephen Willis; Duomo Museum in Florence, Italy; Grazie Mille Guiseppe Giari; Seattle Art Museum, Seattle, Washington; Special thanks to Natasha Lewandroski; The Victoria and Albert Museum, London, England; St. Paul's Cathedral, London, England; Foster White Gallery—thank you for donating the use of your space for the Seattle Architecture Foundations Model Exhibitions, year after year; and Gunnar Nordstrom Gallery.

Thanks also to the following individuals: Ross King, thank you for not only writing the foreword to this book, but for your generous donation of quotes and answers to my many questions. Thank you for writing such great books. Jack Dollhausen, thank you for not only teaching me how to sculpt, but teaching me how to teach. George Lucas, for making *Star Wars: A New Hope.* If it weren't for that movie, I may have paid attention in school growing up. As a result, my life would have taken a very different path. Bob Dylan, for writing "All Along the Watchtower," and Jimi Hendrix for perfecting it.

Thank you also to John Merner, Gunnar Nordstrom, Chris Bruce, Keith Wells, Shelly Yapp, Virginia Anderson, Jill Crary, Kathy Ankerson, Katherine Bicknell, The Wheel, Pamela Lee, Tom Hull, Cousin Laurel, Tom Barrack, Ramona and the rest of the staff at Palazzo Pecci Blunt in Rome, Contessa Simonetta Brandolini D'Adda and the Friends of Florence, Chris Berkstresser, Tim Doebler, Kexp.org, Jason Lascau, John Logic, Dan Crandall, Pete Saari, Jim Dine, Auguste Rodin, Marcel Duchamp, Fillipo Brunelleschi, Alexander Calder, Built to Spill, the various crews at Stevens Pass, Aspen Snowmass, and Mount Baker.

Special thanks to Michelle Levy, Olga Kontzias, Erin Fitzsimmons, and everyone at Fairchild Books!

Of course, I would be a terrible son if I didn't thank my parents for all they have done. I would also like to thank them in advance for (hopefully) lending me the money I have not asked for yet in order to pursue another graduate degree.

Materials Needed by Chapter

The following list indicates the materials mentioned in each chapter, and are recommended to have handy to complete Chapter Review and Practice. Part 1 of the text is preparatory. In Part 2, beginning with Chapter 7, students embark on learning and practicing model building techniques. Materials needed to execute advanced techniques, to create presentation quality and realistic models, are also included here.

CHAPTER 7

#11 blades (limitless amount)
Architect's scale
Bevel cutting tool
Burnisher
Cardboard
Chipboard
Craft knife

Double-stick tape
Drafting paper
Drafting pencils with B and 4H lead
Drafting tape or dots
Floor plan from a previous project
Foam board
Graphite transfer paper
Metal straightedge
Museum board in 1/32" and 1/16" thickness (2 ply and 4 ply)
Mylar or acetate sheets (four 8½" × 11")
Nail file
Paper towels
Retractable knife with snap-off segments
Sandpaper in a variety of grits (180–220 grit)
Sewing pins
Small strip of wood measuring 1/2" × 1/2" × 3"

Sobo or Tacky Glue
Spray adhesive
Triangles (a variety of them)
Try square or a contractor's combination square
T square
Tweezers
Utility knife, preferably retractable, with extra blades
Vellum or tracing paper
Vinyl cutting mat

Optional
Pounce wheel

CHAPTER 8

#11 blades (limitless amount)
Architect's scale

Burnisher
Cardboard
Chipboard
Compass
Craft knife
Double-stick tape
Drafting compass
Drafting paper
Drafting pencils with B and 4H lead
Foam board
Drafting tape or dots
Four 8$\frac{1}{2}$" × 11" Mylar or acetate sheets
Graphite transfer paper
Hobby clamps
Illustration board
Metal straightedge
Museum board in $\frac{1}{32}$" and $\frac{1}{16}$" thickness (2 ply and 4 ply)
Nail file
Paper towels
Retractable knife with snap-off segments
Sandpaper in a variety of grits (180–220 grit)
Sewing pins
Sobo or Tacky Glue
Spray adhesive
Triangles (a variety of them, including an adjustable one)
Try square or a contractor's combination square
T square
Tweezers
Utility knife, preferably retractable, with extra blades

Vellum or tracing paper
Vinyl cutting mat
Wire cutters
Wood (small strip: $\frac{1}{2}$" × $\frac{1}{2}$" × 3")

Optional
Acrylic and watercolor paints
Cups to hold water
Markers (a variety of them)
Mat board cutting system (straightedge integrated with a bevel and straight cutter; Logan is recommended)
Paint brushes (a variety of them)
Spray paints (a variety of them)

CHAPTER 9
#11 blades (limitless amount)
Architect's scale
Burnisher
Cardboard
Cardstock
Chartpak Graphic Tape, white, $\frac{1}{16}$" and $\frac{1}{8}$" widths
Chipboard
Craft knife
Double-stick tape
Drafting compass
Drafting tape or dots
Drafting paper
Drafting pencils with B and 4H lead
Foam board
Elevation drawings of four-panel windows

Graphite transfer paper
Hobby clamps
Hobby drill, Dremel Moto-Tool, or electric drill
Metal straightedge
Museum board in $\frac{1}{32}$" and $\frac{1}{16}$" thickness (2 ply and 4 ply)
Mylar or acetate sheets (four 8$\frac{1}{2}$" × 11")
Nail file
Paper towels
Retractable knife with snap-off segments
Sandpaper in a variety of grits (180–220 grit)
Scissors
Sewing pins
Small strip of wood $\frac{1}{2}$" × $\frac{1}{2}$" × 3"
Sobo or Tacky Glue
Spray adhesive
Triangles (a variety of them, including an adjustable one)
Try square or a contractor's combination square
T square
Tweezers
Utility knife, preferably retractable, with extra blades
Vellum or tracing paper
Vinyl cutting mat

Optional
Mat board cutting system (straightedge integrated with a bevel and straight cutter; Logan is recommended)

CHAPTER 10

- #11 blades (limitless amount)
- Architect's scale
- Burnisher
- Chipboard
- Craft knife
- Double-stick tape
- Drafting compass
- Drafting tape or dots
- Drafting paper
- Drafting pencils with B and 4H lead
- Foam board
- FoamWerks L clips and T clips
- FoamWerks Straight/Bevel Cutter and replacement blades
- FoamWerks Tape
- Graphite transfer paper
- Hobby clamps
- Hobby drill, Dremel Moto-Tool, or electric drill
- Metal straightedge
- Mylar or acetate sheets (four 8½" × 11")
- Nail file
- Paper towels
- Rabbet foam board cutter, either by FoamWerks or Alvin
- Retractable knife with snap-off segments
- Sandpaper in a variety of grits (180–220 grit)
- Scissors
- Sewing pins
- Small strip of wood ½" × ½" × 3"
- Sobo or Tacky Glue
- Spray adhesive
- Triangles (including an adjustable one)
- Try square or a contractor's combination square
- T square
- Tweezers
- Utility knife, preferably retractable, with extra blades
- Vellum or tracing paper
- Vinyl cutting mat

Optional

- FoamWerks Channel Rail with the Straight and V-Groove Cutter Attachments
- FoamWerks Circle Cutter
- FoamWerks Freestyle Cutter
- FoamWerks Hole Drill
- Mat board cutting system (straightedge integrated with a bevel and straight cutter; Logan is recommended)

CHAPTER 11

- #11 blades (limitless amount)
- Architect's scale
- Balsa wood in widths of 4" × 1/16" and 1/8"
- Balsa-wood stripper
- Balsa wood in strips of 1/4" × 1/16" and 1/8"
- Basswood in widths of 4" × 1/16" and 1/8"
- Basswood in strips of 1/4" × 1/16" and 1/8"
- Burnisher
- Craft knife
- Double-stick tape
- Dowels (variety of them)
- Drafting compass
- Drafting paper
- Drafting pencils with B and 4H lead
- Drafting tape or dots
- Engineer's square
- Graphite transfer paper
- Hobby drill, Dremel Moto-Tool, or electric drill
- Hobby clamps
- Metal straightedge
- Mini clamps
- Miter box
- Mylar or acetate sheets (four 8½" × 11")
- Nail file
- Paper towels
- Razor plane
- Razor saw and miter box
- Retractable knife with snap-off segments
- Sandpaper in a variety of grits (180–220 grit)
- Scissors
- Scroll saw
- Sewing pins
- Small strip of wood ½" × ½" × 3"
- Sobo or Tacky Glue
- Spray adhesive
- Triangles (variety of them)
- Try square or a contractor's combination square
- T square
- Tweezers
- Utility knife, preferably retractable, with extra blades
- Vellum or tracing paper
- Vinyl cutting mat

Optional
- Acrylic and watercolor paints (a variety of them)
- Band saw
- Corner clamps
- Cups to hold water
- Dremel Moto-Tool
- Dremel Scroll Saw
- Electric drill
- Markers (a variety of them)
- Micro table saw
- Micro miter saw
- Paint brushes (a variety of them)
- Palm sander
- Spray paints (a variety of them)

CHAPTER 12
- #11 blades (limitless amount)
- Acrylic cement
- Arylic sheets (two 8½" × 11", one ¹/₁₆" thick and one ⅛" thick)
- Architect's scale
- Balsa wood in strips of ¼" × ¹/₁₆" and ⅛"
- Balsa wood in widths of 4" × ¹/₁₆" and ⅛"
- Basswood in widths of 4" × ¹/₁₆" and ⅛"
- Basswood in strips of ¼" × ¹/₁₆" and ⅛"
- Burnisher
- Cardboard
- Cardstock
- Chipboard
- Craft knife
- Double-stick tape
- Dowels (a variety of them)

- Drafting brush
- Drafting compass
- Drafting pad, sometimes called a Skum-X pad
- Drafting paper
- Drafting pencils with B and 4H lead
- Drafting tape or dots
- Flat Grey automotive primer
- Foam board
- Graphite transfer paper
- Hobby clamps
- Hobby drill, Dremel Moto-Tool, or electric drill
- Linoleum knife
- Metal straightedge
- Museum board in ¹/₃₂" and ¹/₁₆" thickness (2 ply and 4 ply)
- Mylar or acetate sheets (four 8½" × 11")
- Nail file
- Paper towels
- Razor saw and miter box
- Retractable knife with snap-off segments
- Sandpaper in a variety of grits (180–220 grit)
- Scissors
- Sewing pins
- Sheet of cork (⅛")
- Small strip of wood ½" × ½" × 3"
- Sobo or Tacky Glue
- Spray adhesive
- Triangles (a variety of them, including an adjustable one)
- Try square or a contractor's combination square

- T square
- Tweezers
- Utility knife, preferably retractable, with extra blades
- Vellum or tracing paper
- Vinyl cutting mat

Optional
- Acrylic and watercolor paints (a variety of them)
- Band saw
- Corner clamps
- Cups to hold water
- Dremel Moto-Tool
- Dremel Scroll Saw
- Electric drill
- Feather
- Markers (a variety of them)
- Micro miter saw
- Micro table saw
- Paint brushes (a variety of them)
- Palm sander
- Spray paints (a variety of them)

CHAPTER 13
- #11 blades (limitless amount)
- 12–16 gauge wire
- Acrylic cement
- Acrylic sheets, (two 8½" × 11", one ¹/₁₆" thick and one ⅛ thick)
- Adjustable triangle
- Architect's scale
- A piece of furnace filter

Balsa wood in strips of 1/4" × 1/16" and 1/8"

Balsa wood in widths of 4" × 1/16" and 1/8"

Basswood in strips of 1/4" × 1/16" and 1/8"

Basswood in widths of 4" × 1/16" and 1/8"

Burnisher

Cardboard

Cardstock

Chipboard

Craft knife

Double-stick tape

Dowels (a variety of them)

Drafting compass

Drafting paper

Drafting pencils with B and 4H lead

Drafting tape or dots

Dried plants or twigs, such as yarrow

Foam balls of various sizes

Foam board

Graphite transfer paper

Hobby clamps

Hobby drill, Dremel Moto-Tool, or
   electric drill

Inexpensive chopsticks

Linoleum knife

Metal straightedge

Museum board in 1/32" and 1/16" thickness (2 ply and 4 ply)

Mylar or acetate sheets (four 8 1/2" × 11")

Nail file

Paper towels

Razor saw and miter box

Retractable knife with snap-off segments

Sandpaper in a variety of grits (180–220 grit)

Scissors

Sewing pins

Small strip of wood 1/2" × 1/2" × 3"

Sobo or Tacky Glue

Spray adhesive

Triangles (a variety of them)

Try square or a contractor's combination
   square

T square

Tweezers

Utility knife, preferably retractable, with
   extra blades

Vellum or tracing paper

Vinyl cutting mat

Wire cutters

Optional

Acrylic and watercolor paints (a variety of
   them)

Band saw

Corner clamps

Cups to hold water

Dremel Moto-Tool

Dremel Scroll Saw

Electric drill

Feather

Markers (a variety of them)

Micro table saw

Micro miter saw

Paint brushes (a variety of them)

Palm sander

Scale figures or vehicles

Spray paints (a variety of them)

PREPARATION

PART 1

A Brief History of the Architectural Model

1

OBJECTIVES

- *Understand how the model has been used by designers over the centuries*
- *Understand how techniques and outcomes of model building have changed over time*
- *Apply your knowledge of historical model making to your current ideas and projects*

This chapter presents a brief overview of the history and use of the architectural model. It will also introduce you to the different types of models and their specific applications.

It is impossible to say for certain when the first architectural model was made. Some of the oldest surviving models were produced in Egypt, circa 3,000 BCE. Egypt was an empire obsessed with the afterlife. Pharaohs built elaborate underground tombs, **mastabas,** and

pyramids that contained treasures they wanted to take with them to the afterlife. In addition to containing their earthly remains and possessions, these tombs "had hundreds of small, brilliantly painted, wooden scale models located in almost every chamber" (Smith, 2004, p. 1). Small, scaled-down versions of soldiers, pets, boats, buildings, and servants—everything the Pharaoh would need could be found in these chambers. The wood or terra cotta models fulfilled a specific, religious, or magical function quite different from our western ideals of representation. By merely having a replica of something, it ensured the deceased access to it for all of eternity.

Greek architecture evolved from the architecture of earlier, neighboring Mediterranean and Middle Eastern civilizations of

Egypt, Minoa, and Mycenae. The Greeks began using models not as objects, but as a part of their design process. Classical Greek architecture followed a rigid set of rules and conventions. Sometimes this eliminated the need for scale models in the design or building process. However, models made from wood, wax, brick, or plaster were still used as tools to "convince patrons or panels of judges of the virtues of their particular designs" (King, 2000, p. 7).

The Greeks' fascination with optics also necessitated the construction of full-size, wooden models, known to the ancient Greeks as **paradeigma**. It is often difficult to judge the effect a certain form or pattern will have on the viewer when it is in a reduced scale. Greek architecture, especially that of the later Hellenistic era, was extremely detailed. Sometimes, for example, a full-scale wooden model of a Corinthian column, complete with an ornate capital, **fluting,** and **entasis** may have been be created and placed into the position that a marble column was later to occupy. This would allow them to make aesthetic decisions based on the model, and leave no doubt in the minds of the craftsmen as to exactly what was required.

The Romans were the ancient world's greatest imitators and innovators. Because many Roman architects were actually Greek by birth, it should come as no surprise that much of what we call classical Roman architecture is appropriated and modified classical Greek architecture.

The arch, not utilized by the Greeks, is the symbol of Roman architecture. However, it is actually an invention of a neighboring people known as the Etruscans. Although the Etruscans are credited with inventing the arch, it was the Romans who realized its potential. It was the Roman invention of a waterproof concrete that allowed them to surpass the engineering achievements of the earlier civilizations to which they were indebted. The Romans created an architecture uniquely their own by combining the arch and its relatives—the barrel vault and dome—with classical forms derived from the Greeks.

The Roman architectural theorist Vitruvius was quick to point out that because Roman architecture no longer followed the regimental canons laid down by the Greeks, this newfound freedom necessitated the use of models as a tool for communicating various designs (Smith, 2004, p. 17). Like the Greeks before them, detail models were commonplace, usually sculpted in wax and then later cast in plaster. Although very few of these remain, a handful can be found at the Archaeological Museum in Rome. As the Roman Empire slowly declined, the technologies they utilized were forgotten as Europe slipped into the Dark Ages.

As the first millennium drew to a close, the church slowly began to realize that the anniversary of their savior's death would not bring about the end of the world. Because life on this earth proved to be somewhat more permanent than they had previously believed, they began to invest more time and money in churches and cathedrals. No longer simple basilica forms, the twelfth- and thirteenth-century cruciform churches were built using new styles and techniques. These Romanesque and Gothic buildings did not use architects per se, but rather master builders. Models were commonly used to convey information about the master builder's design to both clients and construction personnel alike.

Models were also used to test the feasibility of new designs or construction techniques. In 1296, Arnolfo di Cambio created a model of the Florence cathedral. The model later collapsed under its own weight, and is now lost to us (King, 2000, p. 6). It was common to build large reference models of semi-permanent materials directly on the building site. For example, Ross King writes in his book *Brunelleschi's Dome* that in 1390, there existed a brick and plaster model of San Petronino (Bologna, Italy), which was nearly 60 feet long.

In 1418, a competition was announced in Florence, Italy. It called for, among other things, someone to design a dome that could cover Arnolfo di Cambio's cathedral. In the following months, over a dozen ornately fashioned models were created and submitted to the church and city fathers in charge of the competition (King, 2000, p. 11). Some of these models can still be viewed today in the Museum of the Duomo in Florence (see Figures 1.1 and 1.2).

Eventually the contest was won by Fillipo Brunelleschi, a man who would be described by contemporary standards as an architect. This man, the **capomaestro,** or boss of all bosses, was a brilliant engineer, watchmaker, goldsmith, and sculptor. A gigantic model of Brunelleschi's design was actually fabricated by Neri di Fioravanti. This model served as a guide throughout the construction process. This model was so large that several people could fit inside it, and after it was no longer needed as a reference for the builders, it was converted into a Renaissance version of a **honey bucket** (King, 2000, p. 119).

Numerous models were created for use during the construction. Ross King (2000) writes:

> Because of the complexity of Fillipo's design, the stone masons had difficulty understanding how exactly the stones were to be cut and then fitted together. The enterprising *capomaestro* therefore made other, less conventional models for them to follow. A number of these were made from wax and clay, and some he even carved from *rape grandi,* large turnips that the Florentines ate in winter (p. 72).

In the early sixteenth century, Michelangelo was charged with the completion of the Farnese Palace, begun by Antonio da Sangallo the Younger. Michelangelo deviated from the classical rules of architecture by increasing the height of the top story and creating a cornice that was in proportion to the entire building, as opposed to the top story. To prove to his skeptics that his composition would be effective; he created a 15-foot-tall, 1:1 scale wooden model that was to be hoisted into place atop the palace. The model was extremely large; critics claimed the walls of the palace would still need to be shored up to support it. After the model was in position, those same critics were silenced because Michelangelo's theory of proportion proved to be correct.

The most famous of Sangallo's projects that Michelangelo took over was his design for St. Peter's in Rome. Michelangelo created two designs for the dome of St. Peter's. A wooden model of his unused scheme can still be seen today in the Vatican museum.

Three hundred years later, we come to the work of the Spanish architect Antonio Gaudí. His church, the Sagrada Familia, in Barcelona, is still under construction. The construction is primarily based not upon plans or elevations, but reproductions and fragments of plaster models that he created roughly one hundred years ago.

As creating construction drawings of his naturalistic designs was nearly impossible, Gaudí spent a great deal of time building plaster models to pass on a clear vision of his

FIGURE 1.1 (Left). Fillipo Brunelleschi's wooden model for the dome of Santa Maria Del Fiore, Florence, Italy. *Opera di Santa Maria del Fiore. Photographer: Nicolo Orsi Battagnli.*

FIGURE 1.2 (Right). The remaining portion of Brunelleschi's wooden model for the lantern on the Duomo, Florence, Italy. *Opera di Santa Maria del Fiore. Photographer: Nicolo Orsi Battagnli.*

design to succeeding generations of builders. When funds for the construction of the cathedral would periodically dry up, Gaudí would pass his time creating more models, refining his design, and drawing inspiration from organic forms, which he emulated and incorporated into his designs. Unfortunately, many of his original plaster models were destroyed during the Spanish Civil War.

Today, visitors to the Sagrada Familia can view a large portion of the model shop. In the 1950s, the cathedral had two model makers and one assistant. Today the model shop has thirteen full-time employees casting and carving plaster, cataloguing and restoring fragments of original models, as well as carving full-size columns, etc. **Molds** are made from the full-size plaster columns. The design is then cast in artificial stone and put in place. This contemporary paradeigma is then used as a model from which the actual stone column is carved.

In 1956, Eero Saarinen began designing the Trans World Airlines (TWA) terminal at JFK Airport. In his attempt to design a building that would capture the drama and movement inherent in air travel, he and Kevin Roche conceived of a design so complicated it was necessary to develop it through the use of models, as opposed to drawings. In his book *Eero Saarinen,* Antonio Roman describes the process:

The Beaux-Arts tradition—from which many of today's architects would not be completely detached—placed emphasis on drawing. Nearly every design was supposed to begin with plans from which the models could subsequently be made. The TWA project constitutes a unique case in contemporary architecture, perhaps the first one documented in which the inverse procedure was followed: first they built the models and then they used the small structures to elaborate drawings" (2002, p. 46).

Several finished models were produced by professional model makers before the first design drawing was made.

Before pursuing his father's field of architecture, Saarinen trained as a sculptor. For him, "tactile interaction with his design was an essential part of the creative process" (Roman, 2002, p. 46). Evidence of this interaction and its influence on his designs is best illustrated in what historians have coined the "Grapefruit Story." Kevin Roche's firsthand description reads: "Eero was eating breakfast one morning and was using the rind of his grapefruit to describe the terminal shell. He pushed down its center to mimic the depression that he desired, and the grapefruit bulged. This was the seed for the four bulges of the shell" (Roman, 2002, p. 50). Like Fillipo Brunelleschi, another sculptor turned architect, Saarinen found food stuffs to be a palatable medium for model making.

In 1957, the final model for the TWA building was built at a 1:25 scale (1" = 2'-0").

The immense size of the model made it simple for them to add, remove, and manipulate elements of the building while retaining a clear view of the structure as a whole. It was common for a design meeting to take place in the model shop where new shapes would be developed, created, and tested directly on the model. This allowed designers to encounter and solve problems before they even approached the drawing board (Roman, 2002, p. 51). (See Figure 1.3.)

These pristine working models were essential communicative mediums among clients, staff, engineers, and designers. It was also a "perfect tool for simulating interior spaces and the effects that space and light would have on the passengers using the terminal" (Roman, 2003, p. 53). The use of the model as a preliminary design tool continued to inform Saarinen's process for the remainder of his career.

Sydney Pollack's 2006 documentary, *Sketches of Frank Gehry,* offers us an impressive glimpse of Gehry's design development, driven by a technologically improved version of the process pioneered by Saarinen some fifty years earlier.

In one of the opening scenes, Gehry sits at a large table with partner Craig Webb, the two of them musing over a study model. As Gehry attempts to communicate his vision by using obtuse expressions like "crankier!" Craig sculpts the model by frantically adding and subtracting from the abstract mass using nothing more than scissors, scotch tape, and occasionally crinkled silver cardstock.

The workspace is shown filled with pristine wooden site and massing models into which his brightly colored **maquettes** are inserted, removed, replaced, and refined. Gehry's models are created using "two or three scales at once" because he wants to keep his "focus on the building and not on the model as an object" (*Sketches of Frank Gehry,* film by Sony Pictures, 2006).

Unlike Saarinen, the Gehry partnership is able to use the computer as yet another medium for model making. Design development models are scanned and digitized into two-dimensional computer representations that create physical plans. The digitized plans are then modified based on the building requirements. When a modification occurs in one medium, the change is then explored in the next. This back and forth relationship between drawings and models is constant, fuels creativity, and is a major influence on the sculptural appearance of the finished buildings. For Gehry, everything begins with the model. The addition and utilizations of new technologies is something

FIGURE 1.3 Eero Saarinen's TWA Terminal, New York International (now John F. Kennedy International) Airport, New York, circa 1962. *Photographer: Balthazar Korab Copyright Balthazar Korab Ltd.*

that facilitates, but does not change, his basic creative process.

Gehry is not alone in his use of the model as a design tool. Many contemporary firms, such as Zimmer Gunsul Frasca Architects LLP (ZGF), use similar practices (see Figures 1.4, 1.5, 1.6, and 1.7). In an interview with the author, John Chau, principal designer at ZGF, offered a brief description of how models fit into their design process:

The purpose of the Fifth + Columbia study models was two-fold: (1) to document thoughts and ideas generated during the development and evolution of the design, and (2) to explore potential design directions. The study models were used to evaluate design concepts and their capability to integrate form, structure, function, and sensitivity to the urban site and adjacent historically significant structures. The notion that the form of the building can achieve a sense of grace, movement, and balance while deferring to the scale of adjacent buildings was the intent of these studies. The final presenta-

FIGURE 1.4 Fifth + Columbia study models. The models in the foreground are made from simple materials such as foam and paper. As the design becomes more refined, so do the materials used to explore the forms. *Architects/model makers: Zimmer Gunsul Frasca Architects LLP.*

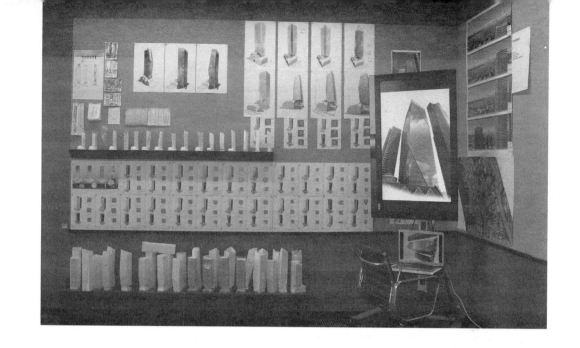

FIGURE 1.5 (Top Right). Models are one of many design tools used by contemporary architects. Here you can see not only physical models, but also digital models and drawings. *Architects/photographers: Zimmer Gunsul Frasca Architects LLP.*

FIGURE 1.6 (Bottom Left). A series of massing explorations focuses on three design directions: (A) curved, (B) canted, and (C) faceted. The three directions were evaluated based on the potential to create a building with a unique architectural expression that revealed an integrated structural approach. *Architects/photographers: Zimmer Gunsul Frasca Architects LLP.*

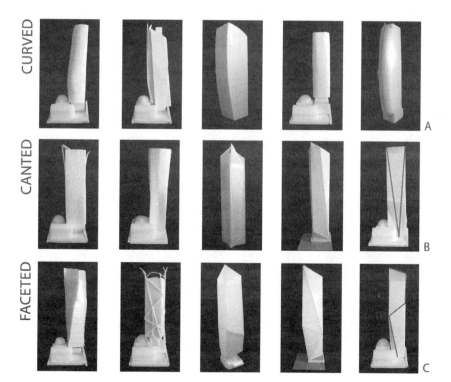

CURVED

CANTED

FACETED

A

B

C

FIGURE 1.7 (Bottom Right). Formal explorations into the opportunities presented by the favored faceted design scheme from Figure 1.6. The creation of balance can be achieved through the proportional arrangement of mass about an axis that is not symmetrical or static. *Architects/photographers: Zimmer Gunsul Frasca Architects LLP.*

tion model illustrates the favored faceted scheme that resulted from this exploration process (personal communication, 17 February 2009).

Although contemporary architecture takes different forms and uses different design-enhancing technologies, the role of the model as a tool remains much the same. The architectural model has always been, and continues to be, a tool for design, a tool for instruction, and, most importantly, a tool for communication.

KEY TERMS

capomaestro

entasis

fluting

honey bucket

maquettes

mastabas

mold

paradeigma

Chapter Review and Practice

1. How was a paradeigma *useful in visualizing the final form of a building?*

2. *Research Vitruvius. How many books on architecture did he write?*

3. *Research the following question: When did working drawings begin to replace models as "construction documents"?*

4. *List five advantages that models have over construction drawings. List five advantages of creating construction drawings in conjunction with architectural models.*

5. *How do you think computer-based simulations will affect the use of physical models in the next five years? The next twenty years? The next fifty years?*

Model Types and Their Uses

2

OBJECTIVES

- *Learn about the different model types*
- *Be able to choose a model type based on your presentation aims*

This chapter offers a brief overview of the types, functions, and terminology of various models used in the architectural fields. Much like music, the precise categorization of a model is difficult. For example, an artist who falls under the broad umbrella of hip-hop may also freely sample elements of rock, soul, or jazz in any given work. The terminology and types of models are not mutually exclusive. Just because you are building a study model does not preclude you from creating a scale model and a massing model. The aforementioned study model may, in turn, be displayed upon a site model. The information covered here will assist you in your quest to find a method to best express your ideas.

SCALE MODELS

James Stevens Curl has written a wonderful *Dictionary of Architecture* in which the term **scale** is defined as: "1. In architecture, the proportions of a building or its parts with reference to a module or unit of measurement. 2. In architectural drawing, the size of the plans, elevations, sections, etc., in relation to the actual size of the object delineated" (2005, p. 587).

At its simplest, the term **scale model** refers to the size of a three-dimensional representation of an object, which follows the second *Dictionary of Architecture* definition. With the exception of the roughest of study or diagram models, nearly every model made will fall under the blanket term of scale model.

Throughout this textbook, we will focus on the many uses of the scale model as a vehicle to develop and evaluate architectural designs. The final goal is to communicate the appearance of new construction before it is built.

STUDY MODELS

The term **study model** most often refers to a quickly fabricated model, constructed early in the design process. The purpose of a study model is to aid in design development, rather than to illustrate a finished product. Other, Latin terms for these types of models that have found their way into common usage include *maquettes,* **concetti,** and **bozetti.**

Many students cringe when asked to do a study model. This is often because they feel that this is just busy work an instructor requires them to do, as opposed to something that will ultimately help them during their design process. There really is no substitute for the creation of a three-dimensional object when it comes to visualization. Next time you hear the old adage "it looked good on paper," ask yourself if there was a model involved. Several subsections of study models exist, but they can be boiled down to two basic categories.

WORKING MODELS

Also known as development, primary, sketch, concept, or massing models (see Figures 2.1, 2.2, 2.3, and 2.4), working study models are most often employed early in the design process. These models assist in the visualization of basic design concepts. They can aid in establishing relationships between positive and negative spaces (solids and voids). They can also illustrate the relationships between a proposed structure and the existing site's adjacent buildings and topographical features. At their most simplified they can be used much like a bubble diagram, a method of charting relationships of objects and spaces in the preliminary phases of design. A **concept model** can be as simple as samples of the proposed

building materials juxtaposed with materials already present on the site. The UBC conceptual model shown in Figure 2.1 was made to communicate influences in the work of zero plus architects, who work specifically with gravity, time, and pattern in addition to the endless inspiration found in nature. It was exhibited at the Emily Carr Museum in Vancouver. The materials are: acrylic, steel, magnifying glass, polyurethanes, rubber dip, found objects, and honeycomb cardboard. Despite the useful qualities of this type of model, it is wise to avoid sharing the cruder versions of these models with clients because they may mistake your loose ideas for a lack of craftsmanship.

Notice how the design evolves with each consecutive study model. In the third study model (Figure 2.4), the initial gesture of the first study model remains; however, the spaces and formal qualities of the architecture begin to refine themselves. Notice also the change of materials. By using a thicker material and placing the model on a well crafted base, the model appears more important and permanent. This particular model could be utilized not only as a design tool but also for use in discussions with the clients.

INDUSTRY MODELS

Also known as **secondary** or **rough massing models,** **industry models** represent the next step in the design process. Although by no

means final, the models in Figure 2.5 are useful in depicting slightly more specific areas of the design. As a result of the increased specificity, a more accurate scale must be employed. Consider also the verisimilitude or accuracy of the materials used to construct the model, and their relationship to those proposed for the actual building project.

This secondary model type is an excellent tool for working out interior, framing, or construction details, showing sectional views of the building and the relationship between

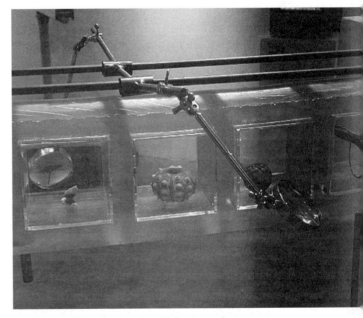

FIGURE 2.1 This conceptual model was made to communicate influences in the work of zero plus architects, who work specifically with gravity, time, and pattern, in addition to endless inspiration found in nature.
Model makers and photographers: Josh Brevoort, Lisa Chun, Chad Schneider, and Chad Downard of zero plus architects.

FIGURE 2.2 (Top Left). Burke-Watson Beach House, Pacific Beach, Washington. An early study model. Materials: chipboard, tape, and glue. *William Zimmerman, William Zimmerman Architects.*

FIGURE 2.3 (Top Right). The model evolves. *William Zimmerman, William Zimmerman Architects.*

FIGURE 2.4 (Opposite). Final massing study model, with revised roof forms and window proportion study. The initial gesture of the first study model remains; however, the spaces and formal qualities of the architecture begin to refine themselves. *William Zimmerman, William Zimmerman Architects.*

the proposed design and the existing site. They tend to be made at a larger scale than the earlier developmental models.

Study models are usually fabricated out of cardboard, museum board, illustration board, foam core, mat board, chipboard, foam, or cardstock. The earlier the stage of design, the less permanent the adhesive you should use. For example, it is much easier to disassemble and modify a study model held together by masking tape and sewing pins than one that has been glued or duct taped together. Figure 2.6 illustrates an even earlier version of the design shown in Figures 2.2, 2.3, and 2.4. The rough model is akin to a thumbnail sketch, bubble diagram, or a sculptor's maquette.

Plan Ahead at the Start

Take your time when constructing the base. A well-built base and a better-crafted model of the contours or existing buildings can save you time during the presentation phase. Selective detail in the topographic or site model, such as scale figures or cars, well-crafted edges, and consistency of materials can look professional despite the speed at which it was built.

FIGURE 2.5 Although by no means final, these models are useful in depicting slightly more specific areas of the design. *Architects: ZGF. Photographer: Carrie Kapp, Punchlist Design.*

FIGURE 2.6 It is much easier to disassemble and modify a study or sketch model that is held together by drafting tape and sewing pins than one that has been glued or duct taped together. *William Zimmerman, William Zimmerman Architects.*

Think About Permanency in Later Phases of Your Study Model

Some parts of your design may never change—columns, central core, site plan, and so forth. After your design has been finalized, you may be able to use select portions of your study model in your presentation model. Better yet, construct your study models so that rougher detailed areas can be removed, easily rebuilt, and replaced. This will save precious time and materials as your deadline nears (see Figure 2.7).

Blueprints and Spray Mount Are a Model Builder's Best Friend

Affixing design drawings (plans and elevations) to your board surface, cutting them out, and assembling them together is a quick way to visualize the spatial qualities of your design. This works well for both interior and exterior models (see Figure 2.8).

Interior Models

Interior models are used to illustrate the relationships between the functions and scale of various interior spaces, to show furnishings, and to highlight the effects and composition of different nonstructural or finish materials. Interior models have a distinct advantage over a single, fixed-point perspective rendering, in the sense that nearly all the relationships between a room's components can be seen in a single glance. An interior model can easily clarify the character of a room and is an excellent tool for showing the amount and sources of light. The acoustical properties of rooms can also be tested using specialized interior models. An interior model is the most accurate way to clarify

FIGURE 2.7 Notice how two different massing models of ZGF's Fifth + Columbia model were able to be easily inserted and removed from the context model. *Architects and photographers: Zimmer Gunsul Frasca Architects LLP.*

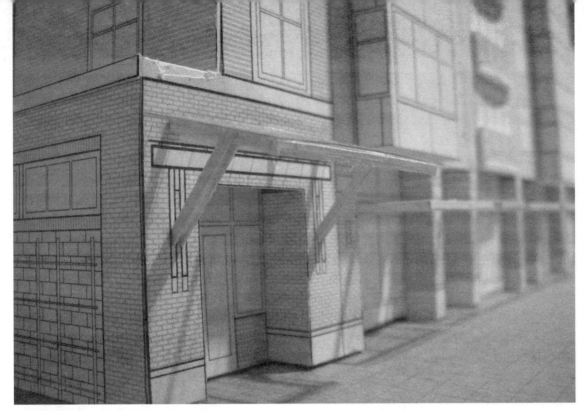

FIGURE 2.8 This study model was for a multifamily residence over retail spaces located on Queen Anne Hill, Seattle, Washington. Affixing design drawings (plans and elevations) to your board surface, cutting them out, and assembling them together is a quick way to visualize the spatial qualities of your design. *Architects: Tiscareno Associates. Model by Shane Herzer.*

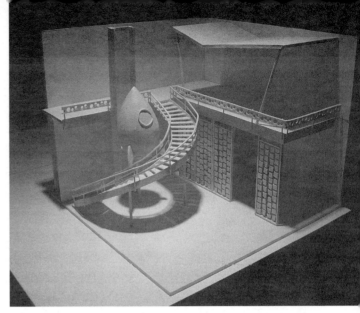

FIGURE 2.9 This all-white model highlights the formal and spatial qualities and retro styling of this gallery space. *Student designer/model maker: Breanna Wucinich.*

FIGURE 2.10 Notice how certain interior portions of the building façade and sidewalk are fabricated in concert with the exterior model. *Student model maker: Laura Osterman.*

and experience the three-dimensional effect of a room's various design features. These qualities cannot be accurately checked on a working drawing.

There are two basic types of interior models, the first of which does not reproduce the exterior or possibly even adjacent rooms. This type is made exclusively for interior studies (see Figure 2.9).

The second type is basically one in which certain interior portions of the building are fabricated in concert with the exterior model (see Figure 2.10).

As previously mentioned, lighting is an intangible design element that can be most easily described and experimented with in an interior model (see Figures 2.11, 2.12, and 2.13).

In Figures 2.11 and 2.12, this portion of Olson Sundberg Kundig Allen Architects model of the Frye Art Museum addition highlights the behavior of the natural light, illustrates the formal qualities of the space.

FIGURE 2.11 (Top Left). Daylight model by Owens Richards Architects. *Owens Richards.*

FIGURE 2.12 (Top Right). This model highlights the behavior of the natural light, as well as illustrates the formal qualities of the space. Frye Art Museum, Seattle. *Olson Sundberg Kundig Allen Architects.*

FIGURE 2.13 (Opposite). This model, seen from above, shows not only the effects of daylight on the gallery space, but the relationship between the interior and exterior. *Olson Sundberg Kundig Allen Architects.*

The behavior and control of natural light is of paramount importance in museum design.

Think about Scale

Most interior designers create models between $1/4" = 1'-0"$ and $1/2" = 1'-0"$ scale. The larger the scale, the more accurately the interior details can be portrayed. Remember, a bold color on a small wall will give you quite a different effect when it is in the model form than when painted on your client's actual wall. The same goes for patterns and materials.

Point of View

Think about how you will present your interior model. Common ways of viewing interior models include the use of a removable or open roof, or a fold-down or open wall. Some models can open down the center, like a book. Should you be working with a scale of $1" = 1'-0"$ or larger, it is possible to cut an opening in the bottom so that the viewer's head can actually enter the model from the inside. Open exterior walls can be viewed from the outside. These and other strategies for effective presentation techniques will be discussed in Chapter 4.

Careful consideration must be given when building a lighting model. Try to limit the amount of "light pollution" entering your model through the viewing portals. Think

FIGURE 2.14 This model highlights the HVAC systems, structure, and the interior spaces of the building it represents. *Model maker: Scott Jennings. Architect: Zimmer Gunsul Frasca Architects LLP.*

about the natural light provided by windows and doors, and ascertain whether these portals are sufficient points from which to view the interior.

SECTION MODELS

A **section model** is used for much the same purpose as a section drawing. These are created by cutting through the surface or any part of the model to show the interior or profile. This type of model will show the "elevation" of the interior rooms, while simultaneously showing the overall form of the building as well as the relationship of the sectioned rooms to the building itself. Carefully cut building sections can also be used to illustrate construction or connection details. One advantage of section models is their ability to leave a façade intact while simultaneously revealing the character of several interior spaces and highlighting construction details. Section models are an excellent choice when building symmetrical objects and transportation models, such as ships, submarines, trains, planes, and automobiles (see Figure 2.14).

PRESENTATION MODELS

Presentation models are also categorized as finished models and are customarily employed after the final design stage. Detail, craftsmanship, and communication with the client are the goals of presentation models. These are often made of the same monochromatic materials, thus emphasizing the building's spatial characteristics and the effects of light and shadow upon it. Should you want to emphasize a difference in surfaces, contrasting materials such as balsa wood and foam board may be employed in the same model. Mirrors, sheets of acrylic, and a variety of adhesive backed vellums can be used to emphasize reflective qualities of different materials.

Interior presentation models can be monochromatic when illustrating foot traffic patterns or formal relationships between the three-dimensional spaces. Conversely, an interior presentation model can have the detail of a dollhouse should you want to isolate a certain elevation such as a façade or display wall, or focus on schemes such as materials and/or lighting. More on the pros and cons of dollhouse realism will be discussed in Chapter 3. Depending on the budget or scope of the project, full-scale mock-ups can be created to fully communicate the design to the client. These prototype interiors are really more theater or set design than model building, but in the case of chain businesses, hotel rooms, and certain building details, this is a viable option,

should the budget allow! In Figure 2.15, you can see the final presentation model of the Fifth + Columbia building. (Refer to Figures 1.4, 1.5, 1.6, 1.7, 2.5, 2.6, 2.7, and 2.8 to see how models were utilized as design tools.) "One of the key design considerations for the Fifth + Columbia Tower was to respect and enhance the adjacent historical structures and surrounding urban streetscape. Thus, the final presentation model illustrates the complimentary relationship between these elements" (Jill Sandess, ZGF). See the color insert for more examples of presentation models.

Although this tip concerns all model types, it is especially relevant when creating a presentation model. The thickness of materials you select must relate to the scale of your model. For example, at 1" = 1'-0" scale, a typical exterior wall would need to be constructed 1/8" thick; thus, a logical choice for your wall material would be 1/8" foam core.

Site Models

A **site model** is a three-dimensional scale representation of the context for your building or project. Other terms for, and varieties of, site models include **contour models, topographic models,** or **context models. Raised** or **bas relief** are slightly more esoteric terms that

FIGURE 2.15 The final presentation model of the Fifth + Columbia building. *Model maker: Scott Jennings. Architect: Zimmer Gunsul Frasca Architects LLP.*

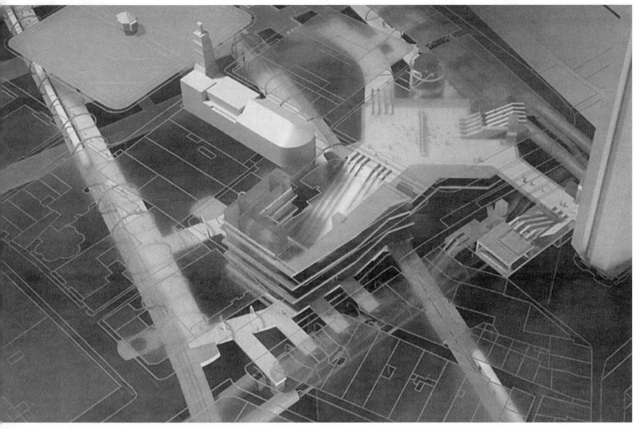

FIGURE 2.16 An early proposal for new Crossrail and London Underground stations at Tottenham Court Road. A context model is a necessary tool for visualizing your design's impact on, and relationship to, its surroundings. *Model maker: Richard Armiger, Network Modelmakers, London, England. Photo by Andrew Putler Photography www.andrewputler.com.*

ing features of the built environment such as streets, sidewalks, and adjacent structures. A context model is a necessary tool for the visualization of your design's impact on, and relationship to, its surroundings. In Figure 2.16, notice how Richard Armiger of Network Modelmakers chose to subtly include the surrounding infrastructure of the Tottenham Court Road Station, London, England.

SPECIAL USE MODELS

The category of special use models is one that is rapidly being replaced by computer generated models. This category is not one that the student of architectural design is likely to engage with in academic settings. Nonetheless, a brief outline of specialized models and their uses should be included here.

Complicated constructions such as shells, domes, and load-bearing frames, and the effects of natural and man-made forces upon them elude precise mathematical calculation. Thus, the only way to accurately judge, say, the effects of a one-hundred-year storm, earthquake, or flood is to use a scale model in specialized chambers, such as wind tunnels, heat chambers, and firing ranges. Often the materials used in models cannot be the same as in the actual construction, hence appropriate materials with equivalent strength and weight must be found.

Before Boeing introduced their Computer Aided Three-dimensional Interactive Appli-

can (rarely) refer to a topographic site model. Site models often contain scale-imparting elements known as **entourage.** Examples of entourage include scale figures, automobiles, or foliage. See Chapter 14 for more information on entourage.

A contour model is one that represents the shape of existing or proposed natural features of the surrounding area such as earth and water. A contour or topographical model is usually represented by an earthtone material such as corrugated cardboard in a study model, or cork or masonite in a presentation model.

A context model includes topographical features with the addition of other exist-

cation (CATIA) program into the offices of architects, complicated, free-form buildings by architects such as Saarinen, Gaudí, and Gehry had to be created in model form first. Subsequent design drawings were developed thereafter.

Acoustical test models, usually 1:10 scale, have greatly reduced the need for post-construction adjustments in materials. Special microphones and recording devices allow nearly exact measurements of the acoustic conditions of the finished spaces.

MASSING MODELS

Massing models, or solid/void models are simplified versions of the overall form of your building or surrounding buildings. The lack of openings, details, and voids allow massing models to be quickly and easily constructed. The houses and hotels used in Monopoly are good examples of massing. Massing models are a good choice for small-scale studies, and for illustrating existing structures on a site model. Figures 1.15 and 1.16 are examples of two designs for ZGF's Fifth + Columbia building. Both of these study models are surrounded by massing models.

STRUCTURAL MODELS

Structural models focus more on how a building is constructed, as opposed to its aesthetic or formal character. Structural models focus on elements such as the framing or truss systems, connection details, or, in larger scales, can also be used for structural tests. A section model is an example of the combination of structural and interior models.

Detail models can fall under the category of structural models, but can also be created to illustrate things such as molding connections, and areas where two or more nonstructural materials meet. Although Figure 2.14 shows a section model, it also illustrates, to a certain extent, the structure of the building.

You have just been given a brief overview of the types, functions, and terminology of various models used in the various design fields. Remember, the terminology and types of models are not mutually exclusive, and there is never any single correct answer to the question of what type of model you should make. The information you have just covered will assist you as you move forward in this book and discover the variety of methods available to help you to best express your ideas.

KEY TERMS

bas relief
bozetti
concept model
concetti

context models
contour models
detail models
entourage
industry models
interior models
massing models
presentation models
raised
rough massing models
scale
scale model
secondary models
section models
site model
structural models
study models
topographic models
working models

Chapter Review and Practice

1. *What are study models used for?*
2. *What are presentation models used for?*
3. *The houses and hotels in the game Monopoly are what type of models?*
4. *Can you list five types of special use models?*
5. *Can you list five reasons to use a section model?*

Interior Models

OBJECTIVES

- *Learn what distinguishes interior models from other types of models*
- *Be able to choose the type of model best suited for your project's goals*

The best way to fully understand the true volume of an interior space is to create a scale model. Your choice of model type, construction, and materials depends on the model's purpose. More often than not, the purpose or goal of an interior model is to portray, as accurately as possible, the materials and items that inhabit the space. This demand for increased detail and realism is the reason why interior models tend to be of a larger scale than pure exterior or landscape-integrated architectural models. Furthermore, it is not at all uncommon to merely focus on a vignette or specific area, completely ignoring adjacent spaces or the exterior altogether.

STUDY MODELS

Study models are used to illustrate, visualize, or explore spatial relationships between spaces or objects in space. The models in Figures 3.1 and 3.2, by Alec Vassiliadis for NBBJ, are of a courtroom interior. The model was built to ensure that there were clear lines of sight between the users of the space. In addition to this model, a 1:1 mock-up was created. The increased scale removed all doubt as to the lines of sight among the users of the space. Of primary concern was the view from the judge and jury toward the witness stand. The witness is purposefully left exposed so that body language cues, such as wringing hands and fidgeting, cannot be hidden.

Study models are used as a design development tool. They are excellent for exploring the psychological or compositional effects of interior spaces, furniture layout, or exploring the juxtaposition of nonstructural materials. They are particularly useful as a tool for designing compact areas such as kitchens, bathrooms, closets, furniture prototypes, and more. Figure 3.3 shows a foam board model of the temporary exhibition space at the Seattle Art Museum; it is used for exhibition planning. Small-scale versions of the artwork are reproduced and put in place to fully understand the formal, spatial, visual, and psychological impact of the art on the viewer. Issues such as visitor capacity, flow, access,

FIGURE 3.1 This courtroom model was built to ensure that there were clear lines of sight between the defendants, judges, jury, and legal counsel. *Architect: NBBJ. Photographer/model maker: Alec Vassiliadis, Sound Models, Inc.*

FIGURE 3.2 This is an alternate view of the courtroom in Figure 3.1. *Architect: NBBJ. Photographer/model maker: Alec Vassiliadis, Sound Models, Inc.*

egress, and evacuation procedures can also be more fully explored when using a design development model. This model was made from foam board and museum board. The floor was created using color copies of the existing gallery floor.

Interior daylight models are useful for studying environmental factors, such as how the sun's rays will penetrate a building during different seasons. (Refer to Figures 2.13 and 2.14.)

PRESENTATION MODELS

Interior presentation models tend to be the most realistic, as well as the largest scale, of any architectural presentation models. This large scale facilitates not only the visualization, but the use of many actual material finishes. Models such as these can be high-dollar items commissioned by developers and created by professional model makers. They can also be created solely to be reproduced in a photograph. The model in Figure 3.4 leaves no doubt as to the qualities or scale of the space, or the material selections of the proposed interior:

> This is Fred Hutchinson Cancer Research Center, by ZGF. It was a large model, 1/2" = 1' scale, about 3 square feet in size. We used a lot of materials. The exposed structural material was a painted polystyrene because a great deal of it had to be formed into a curve. The stair treads

were basswood, the railings were a photocopy on Mylar. The office walls were acrylic with a mat board overlay for the spandrels. The floors were also a photocopy over Gatorfoam. The model was built to help with the visualization of the spiral stairs and how the bridges connected to the floors. This model was intended to be a working model, so the only show was from the view you see. The back side was very much pieced together with lots of tape. I had to build this model in pieces so it would fit out

FIGURE 3.3 This foam board model of the temporary exhibition space at the Seattle Art Museum is used for exhibition planning. *Model maker Seattle Art Museum. Photographer: Roark T. Congdon (author).*

my shop door (Scott Jennings, from Scott Jennings Model Shop, personal communication, Jan 21, 2009).

Lighting models can be combined with presentation models as well. (Refer to Figures 2.13 and 2.14.)

Presentation Furniture
Furnishings, appliances, and even doors, windows, and stairs can be purchased online from model supply shops such as Model Builders Supply (www.modelbuilders supply.com/home.php) and 4D Model Shop (www.modelshop.co.uk).

How Much Is Too Much?
Or, how much is just enough? Think about your focus. Are you are designing a space or decorating it? Designers are more likely to be focusing on spatial relationships or qualities such as layout, flow, lines of sight, or function. If only a portion of your finishes are too realistic, they may distract viewers from your intended focus.

INTERIOR MODELS
Interior models generally range in scale from 1/8" = 1'-0" to 1" = 1'-0". Due to the larger scale, even the simpler interior models will have a comparatively high level of detail; craftsmanship and neatness are essential. The smaller scale should be used in cases such as

an exterior model with a removable roof. The small scale is good for showing relationships of spaces, but a poor choice if you want to emphasize details. Many details that are considered essential in larger scale models can be eliminated at a 1/8" = 1'-0" scale. The smaller the scale, the less essential the details, and the more abstract the model becomes.

Most dollhouse materials are at 1:1 scale (1" = 1'-0"), but prefabricated interior objects such as chairs and the like are fairly easy to obtain at 1/2" = 1'-0" scale as well. The question of scale is really a question of detail. For example, at 1/2" = 1'-0" scale, most details can be easily represented. However, the more details you add, the more time it will take and the more expensive it will be. Most dollhouse materials are at 1:1 scale, but prefabricated interior objects such as chairs are fairly easily obtainable at 1/2" = 1'-0" scale as well. Many details that are considered essential in larger scale models can be eliminated at a 1/8" = 1'-0" scale. Creating interior models at 1/4" = 1'-0" scale is rarely a good idea. This particular scale is large enough that you could theoretically include most of a room's details, but so small that it would be especially difficult to actually make them.

FIGURE 3.4 This model leaves no doubt as to the qualities of the space, the scale of the space, as it relates to humans, or the material selections of the proposed interior. *Model maker and photographer: Scott Jennings.*

When it comes to detail, if it is too small to be cut out with a craft knife, it should be left off the model.

Scale of Interior Walls
Make sure you choose a material that is the correct thickness for your interior walls and partitions. Although students tend to gravitate toward foam board, it is not typically a good choice for interior walls at a scale of less than 1/2" = 1'-0".

Goals of Interior Models
- To illustrate as accurately as possible the true volume of the space.
- To showcase the three-dimensional properties, plan, furniture layout, and so forth of the space, often from above.
- To impart an idea of the ceiling height, and its effect on the space.
- To illustrate, as accurately as possible, the composition and effects of a designer's material, color, furnishing, object, and lighting choices.

The interior model is the primary model type used by set, theater, and stage designers to communicate the ideas.

PRESENTATION STRATEGIES
There are several strategies for creating interior models. The following are a few common presentation techniques.

Open Top
The use of an **open top model** is a good strategy when creating a large model, be it in scale or actual size. Open top models are good at showing the relationship of the interior to all the existing walls as well as the exterior and surrounding landscape. These are also useful for multi-story models. Floors can be stacked one atop the other and built in a manner so they are easily removed, clearly showing relationships between the two levels. Another similar strategy involves the use of a breakaway roof. Ensure that you build your roof of durable material because it will be handled often (see Figure 3.5).

FIGURE 3.5 Open top models are good at showing the relationship of the interior to all the existing walls as well as the exterior and surrounding landscape. Jones Residence, Whidbey Island, Washington. *William Zimmerman Architects.*

FIGURE 3.6 By removing one corner and a portion of the floor, it is possible to simultaneously showcase the building's interior and exterior forms, as well as give a general idea of the building's structure. *Model by Richard Armiger, Network Modelmakers, London. Collection of the Victoria and Albert Museum, London.*

FIGURE 3.7 A vignette model can be integrated into an elevation drawing. *Zimmer Gunsul Frasca Architects LLP.*

flat presentation is to create a **low relief** of something like a bar or commissioned artwork and attach it to a presentation board (see Figure 3.7).

Fold Out Model

The **fold out model** is basically two open façade models constructed in such a manner so as to reveal itself along an axis, like a book. Each "page" is a diametrically opposed façade model. The model can be closed to show a complete exterior model as well (see Figures 3.8, 3.9, and 3.10).

Fold Down Model

The **fold down model** type is typically constructed without a ceiling. Particularly useful in square or rectangular study models, walls can be folded up or down to provide up to a 360-degree view of the space.

Whack-a-Mole Model

If the model is of sufficient scale, it is possible to build an enclosed model with a hole in the base large enough for a person's head to fit through, referred to as a **whack-a-mole model.** This gives an excellent impression of the true sense of space. This strategy was employed by Sir Christopher Wren's model of St. Paul's Cathedral in London

Open Façade

By removing what is referred to as the *fourth wall,* one can get a good idea of a single interior space, or progression of spaces along that wall, as they relate to the structure of the building. It is acceptable to remove more than one wall. All or part of the ceiling can be included in **open façade models.** The inclusion of a removable ceiling is a great strategy for lighting models (see Figure 3.6).

Vignette

A **vignette** generally highlights a single wall or detail of an interior model. Think of it as a small-scale window display. An excellent way to integrate models into an otherwise

FIGURE 3.8 (Top Left). This large model opens up along its axis.
Designer/ photographer: Tyler Schaffer.

FIGURE 3.9 (Bottom Left). Tyler Schaffer's model as it opens along the central axis.

FIGURE 3.10 (Top Right). This is a backlit interior view of the model shown in Figures 3.8 and 3.9. Views such as this would not be possible if the model did not open.

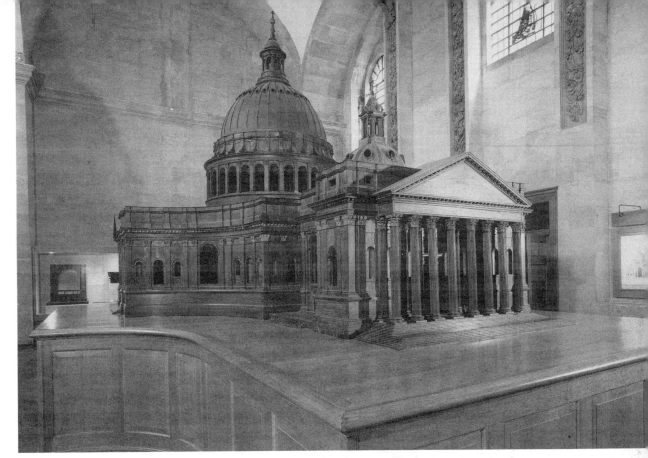

FIGURE 3.11 Model of St. Paul's Cathedral proposed by Sir Christopher Wren, London, 1674. *Photo: ©Sampson Lloyd. Permission granted by St. Paul's, London.*

(see Figure 3.11). This model, which is approximately 16 feet long, is hollow with a fully detailed interior.

Transparent Models

Transparent models are particularly useful for displaying spaces as they relate to other spaces on adjacent floors. Transparency can be one or all walls, ceilings, or floors. A quick and moderately inexpensive way of showing this juxtaposition is to print your plan onto a transparency and then attach the transparency to cut acrylic or another transparent material. Transparent floor slabs can be spaced using black or white painted dowels, or, as shown in Figure 3.12, acrylic rods. The figure shows a model of the Providence Medical Center in Everett, Washington. In email correspondence with the author, Jill Sandess of ZGF explained the reasoning behind using such a model (February 21, 2009):

> The study model for a new 680,000 SF, eleven-story acute care tower, was used to help nurses and other hospital staff visualize vertical and horizontal program connections and circulation. It was built so that it could be quickly reconfigured to evaluate of a variety of options and program adjacencies.

Whenever possible, try to create a model that can be both viewed from above to highlight the space planning (see Figure 3.13), and viewed at eye level to help the viewer experience the true volume and impact of a space (review Figures 3.1 and 3.2).

FURNITURE

Always save the furniture from any model you make. Having a collection of scale furniture to draw from will save you countless hours. Be on the lookout for dollhouse furniture, interesting shapes, and appropriately sized fabric samples. Dollhouse furnishings can oftentimes be taken apart, painted, and reassembled into new furnishings.

It is extremely rare to make model furniture from a single medium. A piece of furniture will almost always involve the use of wire, wood, and fabric together. You

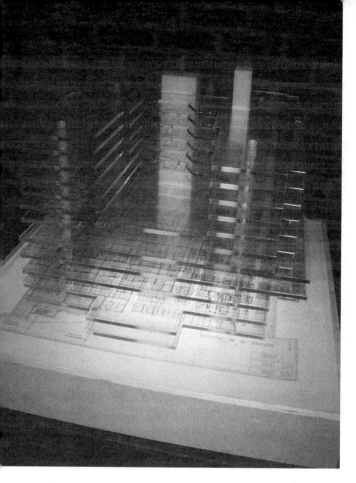

FIGURE 3.12 This transparent model was used to help the hospital staff visualize vertical and horizontal program connections and circulation. *Architect/model maker: Zimmer Gunsul Frasca Architects LLP.*

Moveable Walls and Furniture

The best way to secure moveable objects such as walls, partitions, or furnishings is to place a piece of lightweight metal, such as tin, below your floor. Simply attach or integrate tiny vinyl magnets to the bottom of your moveable objects, and *voila!* Test this method before going through the effort of adding magnets to everything.

If magnets are not a possibility, make your floor from foam board, at least 1/2-inch thick. Using a hobby drill, create holes in the bottom or feet of your moveable objects. Using a dab of glue, insert something (headless pins, filed dowels, kebab skewers, etc.), sharp side out, into the holes.

This is also a useful technique for keeping permanent freestanding objects, such as toilets or pedestal sinks, in place while the glue dries it to the floor.

Always make any moving parts out of sturdy material because they will be handled often.

may occasionally be required to use soldered metals or acrylics as well. A single piece of well-crafted furniture may require the same amount of time and money as an entire model. Remember, when it comes to models, something that stands for or signifies furniture may be an effective representation, especially at a small scale (see Figure 3.14).

FIGURE 3.13 The federal courthouse model as seen from above. Alternative views of this model by Alec Vassiliadis are shown in Figures 3.1 and 3.2. *Photographer/model maker: Alec Vassiliadis, Sound Models Inc.*

Furniture Study Models

The design of furniture is one of the most difficult and time-consuming processes in the field of interior design. Furniture design courses could require several study models at a small scale, roughly 1" = 1'-0". As the designs for a particular piece of furniture are refined, the scale is increased, and the materials become more permanent.

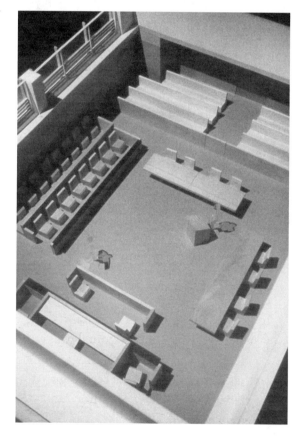

When the scale reaches 1:1, I require two models from my students. The first is built from inexpensive materials such as foam board. This is generally the last place to make final aesthetic or construction refinements before creating a final design, or full-scale prototype. These are generally constructed from wood, steel, or other permanent materials because they will have to perform as "actual" furniture. Oftentimes the 1:1 study model can be disassembled and used to create a template for the final piece.

Remember, creating a scale model—even a rough study model—is the best way to explore the juxtaposed shapes and volumes of a complex interior space. The choices of model type, construction, and materials are dependent upon the model's audience and purpose. In this chapter, you have been introduced to several presentation strategies that should assist you in your model choice.

FIGURE 3.14 Small-scale furniture, toilets, and, yes, even the kitchen sink can be found at architectural model suppliers. Notice the variety of sizes (scales) in this image.

KEY TERMS

fold down model
fold out model
interior daylight models
low relief
open façade(s)
open top
transparent models
vignette
whack-a-mole model

The early mock-ups are generally made from cardboard, chipboard, foam board, or cardstock, tape, and white glue. Study models made from these materials tend to be rough, and focus on conveying the formal qualities or function of the object in question. Refined study models are often created using basswood or balsa wood.

As the scale increases, the material, by necessity becomes stronger. Models built at a scale greater than 1" = 1'-0" tend to use foam board or wood in areas where strength is a factor.

Chapter Review and Practice

1. List ten uses for interior models.

2. Find five sources for interior model components, such as furniture. Share them with the class, and compile a master list.

3. How could Google SketchUp be used in making interior models, specifically as a tool for representing materials?

4. List five things to consider when choosing a scale for an interior model.

5. List five strengths as well as five limitations of interior models.

6. Match each limitation, mentioned in the previous question, with a strategy that would enable the model to achieve its goals.

7. List and define seven interior model presentation strategies.

Planning a Model

4

OBJECTIVES

- *Learn to pair a model's intent with the best procedures for construction*
- *Ask the right questions to be well prepared before you start building a model*
- *Learn about different types of models, and how to think them through from concept, to design, to construction*
- *Learn how to create a budget based on use, scale, level of detail, techniques, and materials*

This chapter will address questions of the model's use, detail, budget, and construction techniques. It will address planning considerations, such as scale, use, and acquisition of materials, and the planning of construction techniques based on considerations mentioned in earlier chapters.

MODEL USES

"How should I do the model?" This is a question often raised by students. In reality, they are not asking how, specifically, to build or construct the model. What they are really asking is a series of questions all wrapped up into one. To answer this seemingly simple yet extremely complex question, start with this one: *How should I plan the model?*

When planning to build a three-dimensional model, consider the model's use, the level of detail required, the budget available, and the materials and techniques that will best suit your model.

PLANNING CONSIDERATIONS

In the first sentence on the first page of his 1970 book, *Architectural and Interior Models: Design and Construction,* Sanford Hohauser suggests considering four of the six following questions before starting a model:

1. *Use* (Hohauser). What is the model going to be used for? Is it a design tool, or a presentation tool? Who is the audience for your model—peers, instructors, clients, potential investors? What materials do you want to represent? What is the concept behind your design, and how do you want to represent that? Will it be photographed? Will it be displayed? How long is it intended to last?

2. *Scale*. At what scale can you build the model that will help you reach your goals most effectively?

3. *Detail* (Hohauser). How much detail does the model need to have? What is the

minimum amount of detail that must be shown? Is there enough time and money to get your model to this level of detail? Will you be building a model of your entire project, or will a smaller vignette suffice?

4. *Budget* (Hohauser). In terms of both time and money, how much of each should you allot for the model? What are the disadvantages to fabricating your model quickly and cheaply? If more time and money are spent on your model, what other uses might the model serve?

5. *Construction Techniques* (Hohauser). What techniques will need to be employed to do the job as economically as possible? What skills, tools, materials, and amount of space will be needed? Are these readily available?

6. *Materials*. What materials do you want to represent? What model building materials do you have access to? What materials are you comfortable and confident using? How will the materials you choose to work with be interpreted? Are they realistic in terms of color and texture, or are they noncommittal, such as white mat board? What are the advantages and disadvantages of each material?

Whenever possible, discuss your project with the most knowledgeable employee you can find at your local art store. It is not at all uncommon to find employees there with undergraduate or even graduate degrees in art or design related fields. Many choose to work just a few hours a week to get a great discount on supplies. Chances are they have already done projects similar to yours and can help to expedite your shopping Try to avoid special orders; there is always a chance that what you need will be backordered, discontinued, lost, or hijacked.

If you are having difficulty garnering information from your local art store, call the company directly and ask for a sales representative. You will never find someone so learned about a product as one whose job it is to sell it. Sales representatives are fully versed in a product's uses, strengths, and weaknesses. If you want to know how to cut, adhere, or paint an object, simply call the manufacturer and ask. If you describe to them what you want to do, they will provide you with a product to help you meet your goals!

In the previous chapter, we discussed a variety of different model types and their uses. The model type you decide on will help you to address the aforementioned questions. The reverse is also true: the previous questions will help you to decide what type of model you will need to create.

Remember, no single model can address every issue of your design. Think about a presentation that combines different model types at different scales. You are encouraged to present drawings in conjunction with your models (refer to Figure 1.5).

Use

What materials do you want to represent? The scale of your model will greatly affect the manner in which you choose to represent materials. In interior models, actual materials or finishes that you believe will have the greatest impact on a potential space should most likely be used. For example, vinyl flooring or tile can be used for the floor. Textile samples can be utilized to sheathe furnishings and for window treatments. Color copies of carpet or wood flooring can be placed on the floor of your model. Real paint can be sprayed or airbrushed onto wall surfaces. The actual stain can be utilized on balsa or basswood. For representing concrete, actual cement or pigmented plaster can be used as well. When using the actual materials in an interior model, it aids greatly in showing their conceptual or compositional relationships. This is something that a material board or collage might otherwise fail to do as effectively. Exercise caution when representing carpet. A color copy of carpet mounted to the floor portion of an interior model will be much easier to work with than actual carpet.

However, if you are working on a 1:1 scale, or are creating a prototype, the actual materials most likely should be used. In the

1997 PBS documentary, *I.M. Pei: First Person Singular,* Pei is seen using full-size fittings created from the actual materials to judge how the scale, materials, and forms of the details would affect the overall composition of his building. Full-scale mock-ups that utilize the actual materials of apartments or condominiums are commonplace in the showrooms of high-end condominiums or hotel chains. They also sometimes are wired with lighting for effect.

What is the concept behind your design, and how do you want to represent it?

How well will your model illustrate concepts such as space, form, order, light, contrast, material combinations, composition, proportion, pattern, environment, color, and texture?

Although there are no magic formulas for answering these questions, being aware of them will often put you on the road to answering them. If you remain cognizant of the questions, it will be easier to manipulate your model along the way to emphasize the qualities you want to express.

How will the model be used? Frank Gehry Partner is famous for its utilization of models as a design tool. Study models, or design development models, are generally constructed quickly and made from nonprecious materials such as paper or cardboard.

If your model is intended to be used as a presentation tool, you must first think about your audience. To whom will you be presenting this model? As a general rule, instructors and students of art and architecture can more easily visualize spatial and material concepts than the layperson. Another general rule of thumb: the less familiar the individual is with the processes of architecture, the more realistic and detailed the model will need to be to better convey your vision.

Many presentation models are created using botanical detail and are created for the purpose of selling the design either to potential clients or investors. Presentation models are costly, both in terms of time and money. However, the cost of a presentation model can quickly be offset by an early sale of a condominium unit, or the reception of a commission or project.

Will your model be photographed?

Will your model be displayed? If so, factors such as the length of time and where it will be displayed must be taken into account. Paper-based materials tend to fade over time or when exposed to natural sunlight. Wood and plastic models tend to fare better than their paper-based counterparts. Is your model delicate? If so, will it need to be displayed in a transparent case, or can it be displayed as is? How will your model be illuminated? How important is the viewer's orientation to the model? At what level should your model be displayed? Do you need to create a pedestal for it? Can it be hung on the wall? If the model has removable parts, in what stage is it best displayed?

Think about how your final model will be displayed and then build a solid, suitable presentation base. Consider the shape and proportion of your base as it will relate to your final model.

Scale

Often, my response to a student's question "How should I make my model?" is yet another question—"What do you mean?" More often than not, the next question they pose is "Well, what scale should it be?"

The answer to the dilemma of scale lies in a myriad other questions, such as: What type of model are you going to be making? Table 4.1 lists a few model types and some recommended scales. If Table 4.1 is not specific enough for your needs, refer to Table 4.2.

How detailed is your model going to be? For example, at $1/2" = 1'-0"$ scale, most details can be easily represented; however, this will most likely add time and expense to your model. Many details that are considered essential in larger scale models can be eliminated at $1/8" = 1'-0"$ scale. The smaller the scale, the less essential the details, and the more abstract the model becomes.

A good rule of thumb is if it cannot be easily cut out with a craft knife, it is too small and can be left out. Be wary

TABLE 4.1 MODEL TYPES AND SUGGESTED SCALES

Model Type(s)	Suggested Scale(s)
Concept models	No concrete scale
Topographic, landscape, or site models	1/16"–1'-0" or 1:200 up to 1/32"–1'-0" or 1:500
Building models	(1:50–1:200 or 1/32"–1'-0") note 1/4"–1'-0" scale is 1:48
Commercial designs	1/8":1'-0" or 1:100
Residential designs	1/4"–1'-0" or 1:50
Interior or detail Models	(1/8"–1'-0" to 1:1 ratio)*

* Most dollhouse materials are at 1" = 1'-0" scale, but prefabricated interior objects such as chairs, etc. are fairly easily obtainable at ½" = 1'-0" scale as well.

when working at 1/4" = 1'-0". If the scale is 1/2" = 1'-0" or larger, it is simple to cut out details. If the scale you are working at is 1/8" = 1'-0" or smaller, it is acceptable to omit most details. If it is at 1/4" = 1'-0", it is large enough that the details can be seen, but small enough that it is extremely difficult to cut them out. The smaller the model, the less detail it will contain. The first details to disappear are the smaller ones, such as door handles. As the scale decreases further, the various textures begin to disappear. The last details to be omitted tend to be smaller projections, molding, and window detail.

TABLE 4.2 POPULAR SCALES

Scale	Ratio	Use Comments	Finished Materials Available
1" = 100 ft.	1:1200	Overall development sites.	Cars, trees, houses, base materials.
1:1000	1:1000	Overall development sites.	Cars, trees, houses, base mtrls, airliners.
1" = 80 ft.	1:960	Overall development sites.	Cars, trees, houses, base materials.
1" = 60 ft.	1:720	Housing, commercial development sites.	Cars, landscape, base materials, houses.
1:500	1:500	Housing, commercial development sites.	Vehicles, l'scape materials, houses, people.
1" = 50 ft.	1:600	Housing, commercial development sites.	Cars, l'scape, base mtrls, houses, airliners.
1" = 40 ft.	1:480	Housing, commercial development sites.	Cars, house, boats, l'scape, mt'ls, st. furn, figs.
1:400	1:400	Multiple housing, commercial developments.	As above.
1/32" = 1 ft.	1:384	Multiple housing, commercial developments.	As above.
1:300	1:300	Multiple housing, commercial developments.	Few specific items.

1" = 20 ft.	1:240	Commercial and industrial projects.	Vehicles, boats, figs, airliners, st. furn, L'scpe.
1:250	1:250	Commercial and industrial projects.	As above plus fences & specific items.
1:200	1:200	Commercial and industrial projects.	As above. Popular scale.
1/16" = 1 ft.	1:192	Commercial and industrial projects.	As above.
1:150	1:150	Commercial and industrial projects.	Cars, figures. Not a popular scale.
3/32" = 1 ft.	1:144	Commercial and industrial projects.	As above.
1" = 10 ft.	1:120	Houses, commercial & industrial projects.	As above.
1:100	1:100	Houses, commercial & industrial projects.	Popular scale, most items avail. + interiors.
1/8" = 1 ft.	1:96	Houses, commercial & industrial projects.	As above.
1:75	1:75	Rarely used.	No specifics.
1:50	1:50	Houses, interiors, small comm & ind projects.	Popular scale, best avail. + interior items.
1/4" = 1 ft.	1:48	Houses, interiors, small comm & ind projects.	As above.
3/8" = 1 ft.	1:32	Primarily for engineering process modeling.	Everything for engineering models.
1:25	1:25	Engineering, interiors, sets, sections.	Wide range of all items. Popular scale.
1/2" = 1 ft.	1:24	Engineering, interiors, sets, sections.	As above.
1:20	1:20	Interiors, study sections.	Some figures, no other specifics.
1" = 1 ft.	1:12	Dollhouse/Miniaturist, study sections.	Everything except major trees.
1:12	1:12	Dollhouse/Miniaturist, study sections.	As above.

Source: modelbuilderssupply.com/pdf/model_making.pdf ©2005 by Keith Day.

Make sure the plans of your model are at the same scale as the model you intend to build. Using the same scale for both your model and your plans will make it easier for you to plan the model, understand and anticipate unusual or difficult details, and transfer measurements from one medium to the other. This is especially useful for determining the thickness of materials you will need to use for walls, windows, floors, and more.

What Materials Do You Want to Represent?

What materials do you plan to use for the model? Do the dimensions of your construction materials lend themselves to your project? Is your project larger than 32" × 40"?

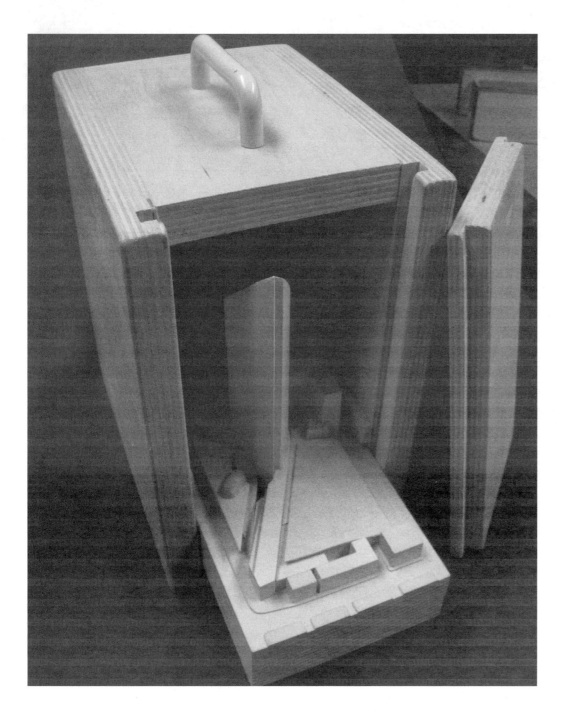

How do you plan on connecting the separate pieces needed to create a single object?

Do You Want to See Inside?

How important is the relationship between the interior and the exterior? For example, it is probably a good idea to build a residential model with a removable roof. In a larger building, however, it might suffice to merely make the plan visible through openings in the model.

How Important Is This Project?

The scale, materials, and the craftsmanship of the model will all say something about not only the designer, but the importance of and the attention they have given to the project. How much (visual) impact will the scale you choose have on your viewers? In a conversation with the author (December 17, 2008) Alec Vassiliadis, a model maker, recounted the following story: The 8-inch-tall model and the box that contains it (see Figures 4.1 and 4.2) were planned and built to be a cohesive whole. When the architect arrived at the client's office, he said nothing about the exquisitely crafted box that he placed in the center of the long, empty

FIGURE 4.1 This model was integrated into a carrying case. *Photographer/model maker: Alec Vassiliadis, Sound Models Inc.*

meeting table, itself made of a beautiful hardwood. As he began to speak, he would casually slide the box partially open, only to shut it again. Each time he did this, it served to heighten the sense of excitement, mystery, and anticipation as to what was in the box. Before he finished the talk, he excused himself and went to the restroom, leaving the small, mysterious box sitting on the table. When he returned, he found that the clients, like children on Christmas Eve, were unable to contain themselves. They had opened the box and removed the model, around which they huddled as if it were a campfire. This small model managed to dominate the immense boardroom and captivate its viewers. When it comes to scale, bigger is not always better; remember, there are always a multitude of factors that one should consider.

How Will You Transport It?

Will it fit through the door of your studio? Will it fit through the door of your house? Will it fit through your client's door? Can you fit it into your car? Can it be carried onto an airplane? If so, will it fit under the seat in front of you? How many times will you need to transport it?

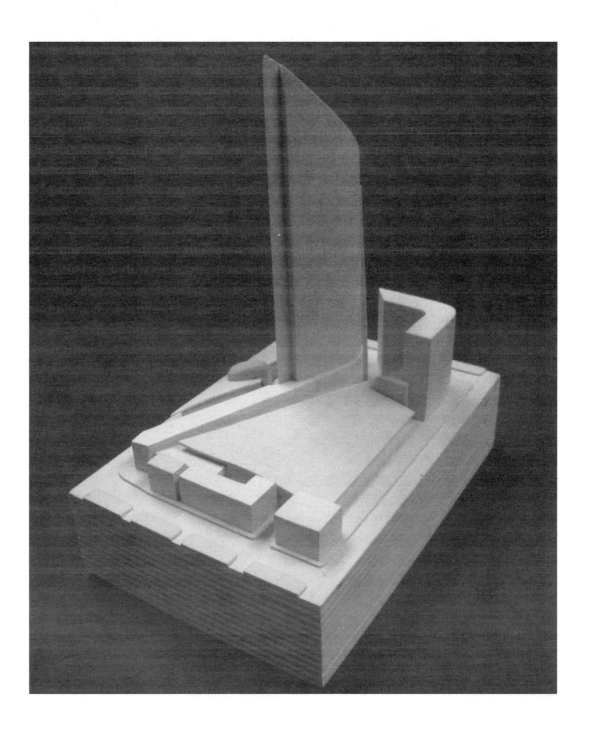

FIGURE 4.2 The exquisite craftsmanship of this small model made a big impact on the architect's clients. *Photographer/model maker: Alec Vassiliadis, Sound Models Inc.*

Detail

How much detail does the model need to have? Another way to pose this question is: How much can you abstract your original concept yet still effectively communicate your design to your audience? The more detailed your model, the less effort will be required to visualize the final product; however, too much detail, or being too specific as to the material choices of the final design in the early phases of the project, can cause problems with the client as well. For example, unnecessary verisimilitude at an early stage can distract an audience's focus from the design, or design development, which should be the goal of an early model.

What Is the Minimum Amount of Detail that Must Be Shown?

Massing models, topographic models, and site models tend to be more abstract than interior presentation models. When it comes to interior presentation models it is possible to utilize too much detail. When the realism approaches that of a dollhouse, it is possible for the viewer to focus not on the quality or concept of the design, but on the craftsmanship of the model. When the model becomes an object as opposed to a representation of an object, you may have gone too far. As a rule of thumb, the higher the level of detail, the more clearly you will be able to communicate your ideas to the client. If your

model is too realistic, however, you run the risk of the client rejecting it outright because it may seem like there is no flexibility in a seemingly finalized plan. By using abstract materials that bear no true relation to the final project, it is possible to communicate the essence of your project without committing to any specific materials. A pitfall that comes with the utilization of premade or dollhouse accessories is the financial cost. Although your model will almost certainly be impressive, the costs involved can very quickly skyrocket.

Is There Enough Time and Money to Get Your Model to this Level of Detail?

It is essential that your entire model share a consistent amount of detail or abstraction. Exceptions to this would be placing a presentation model of a proposed building in a massing model that shows the context into which the proposed building would fit. The contrast between the levels of detail would be an effective means of highlighting your proposal. Conversely, if you choose to finish all the buildings in a context model in a similar color, texture, and material, it does help to fit the proposed structure into its intended context.

If you lack the time or finances to finish your model to the level of detail you require, consider the following: Will you be building a model of your entire project, or will a smaller

vignette suffice? Consider a smaller scale, simplified, monochromatic model that represents the entire project, supplemented by larger scale, more detailed vignettes such as door and window details, stair details, or any specialty object such as railings or cabinetry.

When simultaneously showing models of different scales and levels of detail, consider how you will unify these models into a cohesive whole. Elements such as color, materials, and unified bases can effectively unify otherwise disparate objects. Placing objects with disparate scales on the same base is not recommended. It tends to confuse the viewer and look like you made a mistake in your measurements.

Budget

How much time and money should you allot for the model? Too many times I have seen students and professionals alike being penny smart and pound foolish. If your main concern is to fabricate something as cheaply as possible, you are going to produce a cheap looking model.

Once again, consider the model's purpose. What are the potential advantages and disadvantages of your investment, in terms of time and money? What do you stand to gain by going the extra mile? Exactly what do you gain in terms of time saved by using a more expensive, quicker technique or material? What do you stand to lose by expediting your process, cutting corners, or using lesser quality materials or cheaper, more time-consuming processes? How long is your model intended to last? A rule of thumb is the cheaper the materials, the shorter the lifespan of the model.

Think about the financial value of your time, and the amount of money you may or may not save by doing things "on the cheap." For example, if you save a dollar by not buying a full-size sheet of material yet spend 45 minutes "Frankensteining" something together, you have probably not used your time very wisely. In addition to wasting your time, you may have compromised the structural or aesthetic integrity of your project.

Go with what you know. The time to experiment with a new material or technique is during your spare time, *not* the night before a project is due. If it is essential to utilize a new technique, try to do so under the tutelage of someone who has experience working with the techniques or materials in question.

Costs of Materials
This list of fabrication materials ranges from least expensive to most expensive:

- paper
- cardboard

- cardstock
- chipboard
- foam board
- mat board
- polystyrene
- balsa wood
- basswood
- MDF (medium density fiberboard)
- plywood
- Plexiglas or acrylic
- aluminum
- brass
- copper

Construction Techniques
What techniques will need to be employed to do the job as economically as possible? What skills, tools, materials, and amount of space will be needed? Are the materials needed for these techniques readily available? The techniques and materials discussed in the later chapters should provide ample information for most students and enable them to construct quickly and economically any study, conceptual, or moderately abstracted model.

Before starting any model, be certain that the tools and materials are readily available, and you are working in a technique with which you have had prior experience. There is a time and place for experimentation, and it is not when you are faced with a deadline.

This chapter has addressed a variety of questions pertaining to the model's use, detail, budget, and construction techniques. Critical to a successful model are planning considerations, such as scale, use, and acquisition of materials, and the planning of construction techniques based on considerations mentioned in Chapters 2 and 3.

Chapter Review and Practice
1. *What does the quality of your model say about you as a designer?*
2. *Who are the correct audiences for a study model?*
3. *What are six things to consider when planning a model?*

In-Class Project
Assume you have an 1,800-square-foot, two-story, mixed-use space. The lower floor should contain a bookstore with a small coffee stand, and the upstairs should be an office space. Each unit is required to have separate ingress/egress as well as restrooms. Based upon the scenarios following this exercise, answer these questions:

1. Based upon your list of six planning considerations above, rank the planning

considerations for this space in order of importance. Defend your choices.

2. What do you think are the goals of this model? Explain your choices.
3. What scale will you choose, and why?
4. How important is it to represent the built environment into which your building is placed?
5. What type of model are you going to create—study model, presentation model, open top, sectional model, massing model, or other? Explain your choices.
6. What materials would you choose to use for this project, and why?
7. Will the model require any supplemental information?

Scenario One

You are given 72 hours to present four possible solutions to your design to the partners at your firm.

Scenario Two

You have two weeks to present your preliminary design to the client, who is, incidentally, unable to read a floor plan. Of primary concern to your client is the effect of natural light on the interior spaces, particularly the seating/reading areas of the bookstore, and the overall aesthetic feel of the interior space and finishes. Furthermore, your client has expressed concern regarding the loading and unloading of foodstuffs and books as it relates to customer parking.

Scenario Three

You have nearly completed your design process. At 4 PM, you receive a call from the same client. They would like you to present a model to some potential investors tomorrow at 11 AM. You have two other people on your design/model making team. Answer the In-Class Project questions 1–7. Include a time-table/planning guide as to who will be doing what on the model and when. How are you going to ensure that the model is not only finished on time and that everything fits together, but that it has a cohesive look as well?

BOX 4.1 ADVICE FROM THE PROS

Scott Jennings
Architectural Model Maker and Owner,
Scott Jennings Model Shop
Seattle, WA

1. Always know where your fingers are when cutting material.
2. Understand why you are building the model.
3. Know the characteristics of the material you are using. What glues should you use? How does the material cut? Does it accept paint? Does it expand and contract? Build the model as if you were assembling a full-scale building; understand how the structure works.
4. Always have Unglue or a sharp knife handy in case your fingers adhere to the model.
5. Only use sharp tools.
6. Some woods and plastics are toxic when cut—research your material.
7. Use the right tool for the job—if it seems wrong, it probably is.
8. Never get the exact amount of material for a job: there will be waste and miscuts.
9. Make at least one extra of a unique part. Order or make more trees than you need.
10. Be sure that that your model will fit out the door and in your transportation.
11. Never assume that tools stay square.
12. Always make sure you are working on a client's model whenever they visit your shop.

Timothy Richards
Architectural Sculptor, Historic Models
Bath, United Kingdom

1. Go and see the building you intend to model.
2. Draw or sketch the main detail of the building.
3. In order to make a model, you need to know about the original building; it is not primarily about the model—it is about the building.
4. Plinths are important. They are the introduction before the main event—model makers do not pay enough attention to plinths.
5. If you have to make a cover, think carefully about its design and quality.
6. As usual, everything takes at least twice as long to do as you think it will.
7. Explain the purpose of your model clearly and ask for feedback so you're in agreement with the client regarding the final product.
8. Always get a deposit up front and lay out a schedule of payment.
9. A finished model is the sum of problems solved.
10. In most models it is the materials, and not the architecture, that comes to the fore.
11. Buildings are much like people.

Jason Hanner
Architectural Model Maker, Architect,
and Owner of Box Shop
Seattle, WA

1. Plan ahead.
2. Always keep the thickness of the material in mind.
3. Use only as much glue as you need—more isn't better.
4. Wash your hands frequently (particularly if working with white material).
5. Change your blade often.

Tomoko Briggs
Architectural Model Maker, Zimmer
Gunsul Frasca Architects LLP
Seattle, WA

1. Think about options for materials. Will your model contain wood, plexiglas or both? Depending on the materials used, models will look different and serve different purposes.
2. Build a good base for the model—straight, flat, and sturdy.
3. Keep the blades sharp—change them often.
4. Measure twice, and think the outcome through before you make cuts.
5. Keep all of your fingers!!!

William Zimmerman
Principal Architect, William Zimmerman
Architects, and Lecturer, University
of Washington
Seattle, WA

1. Always take an inventory of your model materials beforehand and have them purchased and onhand before beginning.
2. Always use a sharp blade. Change blades frequently. Blades are cheap compared to the time involved in making a model.
3. The $1/8$-inch-thick material used for making one-foot increments in the site topography is usually not exactly $1/8$-inch thick. Somewhere in the making of the slope across a building exterior, this difference has to be compensated for, and should be planned for.
4. In late summer/early fall, be on the lookout for dried plants that can be harvested for free

and used as trees and shrubs for future model making.

5. Remember the scale model is an abstraction and should not be too realistic. Ask yourself what it is you are trying to achieve through the model. If it is an architectural model, it should not look like the attempted reality of a railroad model set.

6. Before planning the model, ask yourself who the audience is and that should tell you how detailed the model should be.

7. Be careful with accurate color and materiality because they never will look real. It is best sometimes to use abstract or plain representations that engage the imagination of the viewer.

Roger Newell, Architect
Seattle, WA

1. Determine what scale to use for the model. I usually build my models at $1/8" = 1'-0"$.

2. Collect all materials necessary, including extra materials to allow for errors while building.

3. Order outsourced materials early. For me, this includes the wood base, Plexiglas cover, and high-density foam contour base. Allow about two weeks for these materials to arrive.

4. Determine a base elevation for the building that will allow the model to set into the foam base. I never set my models on top of the contoured base, but opt to have them set into a base similar to the actual structure.

5. Determine how much of the site to include in the model in order to best illustrate the

architectural concept. Allow enough driveway space to include a vehicle outside the model to provide scale.

6. Determine how to show exposed structural members such as columns, beams, and trusses. Determine which materials will best show the structure, such as round PVC pipes for columns, and PVC or balsa wood for beams and trusses. Explore model train suppliers for materials.

7. Start with a clean cutting board and new blades. Previous cuts in the cutting boards can cause errors when making precision cuts.

8. Number and/or label all parts prior to cutting. Cut exterior building walls in order, starting at one corner and continuing around the building until you have returned to the original corner.

9. Start with the floors; then do the easy walls.

10. As you build, take the wall segments and fit them to the actual floor plan that was previously cut. Do not cut out all the walls at once. Work around the sides, cutting only the next one or two walls to be fitted.

Lois Gaylord, Freelance Model Maker
Seattle, WA

1. Keep your blade *sharp*! Either replace your blade frequently, especially when using X-Acto knives, or buy a set of small sharpening stones and use them frequently. This is cost effective when using scalpel blades.

2. Always make multiple passes when cutting by hand. Trying to cut through thick material in

one pass is a recipe for broken blades, over cuts, and other disasters.

3. Use only enough glue to do the job. Excess glue just makes a mess. Use the end of your 6" steel ruler to wipe off excess glue and then clean it with a paper towel. This keeps your clothes clean and fibers from your jeans off of the model.

4. Measure only when necessary. Cut pieces to fit what you have already built. For example, cut out a footprint (floor plan) of your building and then cut the wall lengths to fit the footprint.

5. Cut walls that have an angled top (follow the roof pitch) the full length of the wall. Shorten the straight walls to account for material thickness when making butt joint corners.

6. If possible, mark window and door placements directly off of plans. (Note: plans must be at the same scale as the model.)

7. Make a model of your model. If you are faced with a complicated form, such as a roof, mock it up in cardboard first. You can often use those pieces as templates to cut out the final pieces. This is especially helpful when making pieces that have to fit into a model that is already built.

8. When building a model where the interior is shown, build the exterior walls first. Then the interior walls can be butted up to the exterior walls avoiding the possibility of the exterior wall either bowing out because the interior wall was too long, or gaping because it was too short.

Alec Vassiliadis
Owner, Sound Models Inc., Former Model Shop Foreman, NBBJ Architects and Model Maker for the Sculptor Sir Anthony Caro

1. Do whatever you can to reduce stress while you work, especially when using machines, or even when just putting things together. Music, food, regular breaks, and laughter all help. Any mounting stress will cause you to make mistakes, which, in turn, raises stress levels—injury is close behind.

2. Leaving things where you can find them is also a biggie. What's worse than spending time and energy looking for your knife, measuring stick, or that piece you just cut? I am always forgetting where I put things, so consequently I use at least a half dozen rulers and a few knives when I am building models.

3. Never allow anyone to distract you, especially when you are on power tools—all it takes is a moment of inattention to get hurt.

4. Always use sharp tools. Dull ones are imprecise and take more of your energy to use—this exponentially raises the chances of making mistakes or getting hurt.

5. A good cleanup is worth doing in the middle of the day as well as at the end; you end up finding some of the stuff you misplaced, and it helps to regulate and clear up your thinking about the model that you are building.

6. Ask about different ways of doing things, even ones you are familiar with. You may learn something new.

7. When making multiples of something, cut a few additional spare copies—nice to have if you mess one of them up. Also, build your collection of items for use in future models.

8. Try to cut the material and not yourself.

9. When using cutting motions (chisels, knives, even hammers) *always* cut away from yourself, then away from your work. Try to envision the cutting path of your tool if it were to get away from you and act accordingly.

10. If and when you do get hurt, drop everything you are doing and sit or lie down on the floor. You have about three or four seconds before shock hits you. You may faint, and standing can really make the situation much worse. Get some help in whatever way you can. If you are working with other people, keep an eye on each other. If you are working alone (not a good idea), have someone check on you very regularly.

11. Really love what you do.

Richard Armiger
Owner, Network Modelmakers
London, England

The three key questions every good artist asks are:

1. What is it you're trying to achieve?
2. Did you succeed?
3. Was it worth it?

For a model maker, these can translate as:

1. What is the story? (Hopefully, selling a lot of dicey, over-hyped apartments/offices).
2. Did you succeed? Was your story clear? Inspiring?
3. Was it worth it? (Monetarily; creatively; efficiently. Did you use the best technique for the story you were meant to tell?)

These two have never failed me:

1. Measure twice.
2. Cut once.

Your Workspace

5

OBJECTIVES

- *Recognize the features that combine to create an efficient workspace*
- *Understand the importance of proper tool, material, and project storage*
- *Understand the most pertinent safety concerns*

This chapter presents an overview of typical features of a model maker's workshop. Having a space set aside specifically for the creation of your models will contribute not only to the quality of the model, but the experience of model making itself. For me, there are very few things more pleasurable in life than the experience of closing the door (in effect, shutting out the world), turning up the stereo, and setting to work on one of my many projects.

Ideally, your workspace is a separate building on your property, or a rented "studio" separate from your home. More than likely you will have to make do with a dry garage, basement, attic, or spare room in your house; these can all be easily converted into a studio or workspace. Perhaps you are a starving college student, and you will be making models in your dorm or bedroom.

PRIMARY FEATURES OF A GOOD WORKSPACE

Regardless of your room size or shape, a few components that all good workspaces share are:

- Lighting
- Multiple work surfaces
- Humidity—better yet, dryness
- Sturdy and secure storage space
- Ventilation

Lighting

Having the proper lighting is essential for your creative space. I remember learning about the importance of studio lighting in my very first undergraduate sculpture course. I was told, and still believe, that one should create work with the same lighting conditions under which it will eventually be viewed (or photographed). If you are building an architectural model, consider the actual building's relationship to the path of the sun during the different seasons and time of day. Consider also where the model will be presented. Will it be seen in a public space, the client's office, a foyer in your school?

FIGURE 5.1 A quality model shop will ideally have good ventilation, lots of natural light, and plenty of durable work surfaces. *Scott Jennings Model Shop.*

of different lengths to the flange enables me to place the bottom of a typical drafting or swing arm lamp in the top of the pipe. Using this pipe base is an inexpensive way to both raise the level of your light source, and increase the ambient light on your work surface and project (see Figure 5.1).

Multiple Work Surfaces

You can never have too much work surface. Too much work surface really means not enough work! First of all, have at least two separate surfaces upon which you can work, one for cutting (minimum 32" × 40") and a second for the construction of your model. If possible, a third table used exclusively for gluing is truly a luxury. Have a surface where you can walk around as many sides as possible. Consider the utility and popularity of the kitchen island. In fact, the same principles that make a good kitchen also make a good workspace. Sufficient preparation space is vital in both of these instances. If space allows, consider placing a smooth, hollow-core door atop a couple of sawhorses. Many collapsible sawhorses allow you to attach power strips to them. This is an excellent way to bring power to your work areas (see Figure 5.1).

Desk lamps are designed to aid in the illumination of specific areas without causing glare. When placing task lighting, think about how much ambient light is available from different sources. Does it change throughout the day? Using only task or desk lights will strain your eyes due to the contrast between the lit and unlit portions of your work surface. I prefer to have two or three swing arm lamps available to me. I usually mount one on each side of my table, and a third I place nearest to where I am sitting. Mounting a 1/2-inch **floor flange** to my flat work surface and attaching 1/2-inch pipes

Humidity—Better Yet, Dryness

Due to the fragile nature of the many paper-based products used in model construction, having a clean, cool, dry space to store materials and models is essential for the longevity and quality of both. I have lost track of how many times I have seen a student's model attacked by mold, warped by humidity, or otherwise disfigured by the heat of an automobile's rear window.

As a prototyper, I worked with a wide variety of silicones and urethanes. These required specific temperature-controlled environments. Sometimes a steel cabinet with a heat lamp would suffice; other times, entire rooms were dedicated to storage of these materials.

Sturdy and Secure Storage Space

The storage in your workspace will take on a number of different shapes and forms. Efficient storage solutions are essential for keeping an organized studio. The search for a single misplaced tool can translate into countless hours of wasted time. Organization is the key to success.

Tool Storage

When storing tools, a rolling machinist's or mechanic's cart is an excellent solution for smaller hand tools. The portability of these units makes them an excellent choice, should your shop contain more than one worksta-tion. Neatly storing tools or equipment in adjustable, overhead shelves or cupboards helps to ensure that they will stay in prime condition. Peg board is an excellent choice for wall material because it will accept a wide variety of hangers that can keep anything from hammers to hardware off the floor and in plain sight. Drawing an outline of a device in the place where it is to be hung is an excellent way to keep track of tools, especially if you are working in a shared environment. Never store tools with unsheathed blades in a drawer—it is dangerous and will damage the blades. Think outside the box when it comes to finding storage solutions. Check out kitchen, medical, and restaurant supply retailers for unique solutions to your storage needs.

Material Storage

One of the most efficient ways to build a model is to minimize the amount of time you spend searching and shopping for materials. Having a well-organized stock of materials close at hand is an excellent way to save both time and money. My shop is filled with items I may only use once a year. If that one time is at 3:00 AM, six hours before a deadline, rest assured I am happy I made space for it.

When it comes to material storage, first and foremost, keep your materials off the floor! There is no point in storing something if it is going to be moldy, warped, cracked, or otherwise disfigured by the time you get around to using it. If you are using a space with a concrete floor, moisture can quite often "wick up" through the floor and find its way to your materials. *Never, ever, store paper-based or any other type of material that reacts with water (plaster, cement, grout, etc.) on a concrete surface.* Store similar materials, or materials that tend to be used in conjunction with each other, in the same vicinity. Common sense should prevail when storing materials; although you may eventually make a plaster mold from a clay model, do not store the two together. Clay must usually be kept damp, and plaster must always be kept dry.

Concerning the storage of cardboard, mat board, illustration board, or foam board, there are two schools of thought—vertical or horizontal storage. A vertical rack or series of racks can save space, and is also excellent for keeping your materials organized. The drawback of such a system is that, in time, the boards can begin to bend and distort under their own weight. Vertical storage is a common solution in many art supply stores and frame shops. The rapid turnover of their inventory ensures that the boards will stay in pristine condition. Large flat shelves, flat files, or other means of horizontal storage are great for keeping the materials flat, but they can often be difficult to keep organized. Other drawbacks include scuffing from dragging materials against one another; warping, denting, and distorting can result from resting larger sheets upon smaller ones. Another drawback is the large amount of floor space needed (minimum 32" × 40"). A flat file is a fair, albeit expensive, compromise when it comes to board storage. The top of a flat file can be utilized as a sturdy work surface. They are often built on casters—when it comes to items in your workshop, portable is nearly always better than permanent.

Lumber can be stored on a sturdy, permanent rack. The key word is sturdy. Do not build a rack out of one-by-twos and expect it to hold two-by-fours. Place a long piece of lumber on the floor between the wall and some sturdy benches for storage of your larger sheets of wood (MDF, plywood, hardboard). Acrylic, balsa, and basswood can be stored vertically, or in a flat file, depending on the material size. Small- to medium-sized mailing tubes can be used to store dowels, rods, and various strips of wood.

One or more sets of small drawers or bins can be used to store tiny items such as nuts, bolts, blades, small items you have made but aren't ready to use, or various items used for entourage. Be certain that you have at least one sturdy bookshelf for these drawers and bins, as well as for books and periodicals (see Figure 5.2).

Project Storage

Longevity of the model is always an important consideration, and as discussed in Chapter 4 should always be taken into consideration before construction begins. Regardless of your storage capability, as soon as your model is complete, it should be photographed or otherwise documented.

Work-in-Progress Storage

There is no magic solution when it comes to storing a work in progress. Adopting a flexible storage solution such as the use of industrial grade, adjustable shelves are always a good option. Individual plywood, MDF, or melamine bases, either custom-made for each model or a quiver of boards cut slightly

FIGURE 5.2 Look to retail shops for inspiration when it comes to storage. *Scott Jennings Model Shop.*

FIGURE 5.3 Always keep your old models. They are a great way to revisit thoughts or concepts you may have had years earlier. *Architect: William Zimmerman.*

below the dimensions of your shelves, facilitates the transportation of your project across the shop or across town (see Figure 5.3).

Good Ventilation

Many products you'll find useful are to be used with adequate ventilation. At the very least, have a window or two you can open from time to time. Whenever using any aerosol-based material, use a spray booth equipped for just such a purpose. If you do not have access to a spray booth, *go outside!* For more on ventilation requirements, see the sections on workspace safety, ventilation, sound, and dust later in this chapter. Ventilation considerations will be mentioned in conjunction with the information in later chapters dealing with various materials. It is safe to assume that anything that sets, dries, cures, or sprays has a toxic element to it. Installing a couple of fans in your window—one to bring clean air in and a second to evacuate the existent air—is an inexpensive way to improve air circulation in your shop.

SECONDARY FEATURES OF A GOOD WORKSPACE

The following are not necessary, but helpful to have:

- A sink
- Access to an outdoor space (weather permitting)
- Natural light, preferably northern exposure
- Numerous power outlets
- Room for expansion

A Sink

Small shops do not necessarily require running water. In such a shop water will still need to be used from time to time for acrylic painting and the like. Having a sink down the hall or a few bottles of water on hand will usually suffice. In a larger space, or in a space where you will be mixing plaster and the like, or have frequent need to wash your hands, a sink soon becomes indispensable. A slop sink is an excellent piece of equipment in larger shops.

Access to Outdoor Space (Weather Permitting)

Access to an outdoor space (preferably covered) is a luxurious addition to one's working environment. This usually provides improved ventilation during the warmer months, and can provide a safer place when working with more toxic materials. If your exterior space is clean and covered, a work surface on wheels can be rolled outside. This is a good way to judge the effects of daylight on your model. When working outside, consider your materials: How does prolonged exposure to sunlight affect them? Will a sudden gust of wind propel your project or materials skyward?

Natural Light, Preferably Northern Exposure

This was touched on a few times earlier in the chapter. Having access to natural light reduces your need for excessive task lighting. Ideally, your shop would have a skylight with a northern exposure; this will provide a consistent light throughout the day (Figure 5.1).

Numerous Power Outlets

A good rule of thumb is to provide two outlets for each work surface. Nearly all of the tools we will be discussing in this book run on 110-volt, 60-cycle alternating currents. When working with power tools, use three-pronged plugs. Do not use more than one power tool at a time on a single outlet. Power tools tend to overload circuits much more easily than home appliances. Use only heavy-duty extension cords, especially for power tools and halogen lamps.

Many shops have power strips that run the length of the room or workbench. Outlets are usually placed about 18 inches apart, and between 18 and 24 inches above the workbench. Consider how many circuits are running through your shop. Plan the placement of workspaces so that more than one tool may be used at a time without blowing a fuse. Having the overhead lights on an electrical circuit that is separate from outlets ensures adequate lighting should you blow a fuse.

Room for Expansion

One should always anticipate the need for additional storage, projects, and technologies. I know of very few shops, firms, or even museums where the amount of material or project storage was not underestimated. As you become more involved in activities such as the ones discussed in this textbook, you will also require more tools and materials, and will create larger projects. Artist-type lofts or workspaces are available for rent in many cities. When renting a studio or the like, consider the neighboring spaces. How often do they come available? Does the building offer short-term rentals? This is always a great option should you need to facilitate a single, short-term project. When thinking about expansion, consider your shop's proximity to rentable storage units. Are you on the ground floor with a loading dock? Are you on the fourth floor of a building with no elevators? Finally, consider your ceiling height, the size of your door, and the dimensions of the circulation spaces in your building. On more than one occasion, beautifully crafted objects have had to be partially dismantled (or worse) in order to get them out of the space in which they were created.

THE BARE MINIMUM: A STUDENT WORKSPACE AT HOME

If you are a student working on some of your first models, I strongly encourage you to take my advice and allocate a private space for building your models. I have seen many a roommate relationship deteriorate rapidly over possession of the dining room table. A typical solution to this problem for dormitory dwellers involves elevating one's bed roughly 5 feet above the floor. This opens up some space for drawing tables, computer workstations, a variety of work surfaces, and maybe even a comfy chair. Conversely, having the foot of your bed under part of a work surface is also a viable option. The space between the top of a door and the ceiling is often wasted space that could be used for storage.

SMALL SPACES

A shop of roughly 100 square feet can accommodate a variety of needs. Bear in mind, the layout of your shop will depend primarily on the types of models you will be creating. A room of this size can comfortably accommodate two work surfaces, small and large shelving for storage, a computer workstation, and a drawing surface. If you plan to work with elementary materials such as artist boards, foam board, papers, and balsa wood, a space of this size will be more than adequate. When it comes to the

design or layout of my own studio, I consider the different tools and machines I will be using and the amount of useable space each item will require.

LARGER SPACES

If you are fortunate enough to have access to a one- or two-car garage, a space of roughly 10 by 20 feet or even 20 by 20 feet, you should be able to accommodate nearly all the tools and processes we will be discussing in this book.

A larger shop will allow you to build a myriad of model types, using materials such as wood, acrylic, and a variety of foams. If you space plan properly, you should also be able to accommodate some mold making and **casting** processes as well. Bear in mind, if you plan on working with molds, a sink becomes more of a necessity than a luxury. A shop of this scale will begin to resemble that of a serious sculptor or woodworker.

When space planning a larger shop, it is essential to think in terms of workstations and workflow. Imagine that you will be building a model from basswood and acrylic. A model of this type will need a sturdy base of 3/4-inch plywood, MDF, or the equivalent. One of the first accessible tools in your shop should be a table or ripsaw. That way you can cut down your base and place the remaining sheet in a storage space, hopefully also located near the entrance to the shop. Your base can then be placed on one of your

worktables. The next step in your process would be to trim your basswood or Plexiglas, which would be done with your table saw, miter saw, or scroll saw. Scrap pieces can then be stored, discarded, or recycled, whereas the cut pieces can be placed on the work surface. Some people prefer to work on projects in the center of the room and surround themselves with smaller workstations, whereas others prefer to work on the final model in the rear of the shop. When planning a shop, I always consider the size of the materials I am working with first and the amount of dust and debris each process creates second. If possible, try to divide larger shops into actual rooms. Separate into clean and dirty sections. I would not suggest placing a tool that generates sawdust next to an area that necessitates a clean environment, such as painting or the workbench used for creating a finished model.

Workbenches, Tables, Desks

If money is no object, by all means run out and buy a new workbench from your local home improvement center. These often come with overhead storage, drawers, and cabinets. Consider flexibility when it comes to choosing a work surface. Drafting tables can serve double duty in a smaller space. Do not use your drafting table for cutting because it will then be useless as a drawing surface (see Figure 5.4).

Circulation, Anthropometrics, Ergonomics

If possible, make sure all of your work surfaces are at the same height, usually 36 inches. Having all work surfaces the same height allows for numerous combinations, especially if one or more of your tables is on wheels. A 24-inch gap is an acceptable width between tables, but a 36-inch space between two work surfaces actually provides you with room to "work" as opposed to just circulate.

If you will be using wall shelves over 7 feet tall, having a step stool or light-duty ladder nearby is extremely handy. Using heavy-duty hooks to hang the ladder out of your way is a great space saver.

WORKPLACE SAFETY

All shops should have a list of safety rules posted where everyone can see them. Eye and ear protection should be readily available, not just for those using the shop but for those visiting as well. Safety concerns will be mentioned where appropriate throughout this book. In addition, here is a list of rules that should always be followed in any shop environment:

- Know the rules of your particular shop.
- Eye and ear protection should be worn at all times, especially when working with

tools that throw dust, sparks, or other shrapnel.

- Know where the first aid kit is located and ensure that it is always stocked.
- Keep your shop as neat and clutter free as possible. Leave adequate floor space to move about freely and easily.
- Use only adequately sharpened tools. A dull blade or chisel will lead to the unsafe practice of using too much pressure to make a cut.
- Always consider your stabilizing hand in relation to your cutting hand. Keep your noncutting hand out of the path of the blade. Consider where the blade will be going; consider also where the blade *could* go.

Power Tool Safety

In addition to the previous guidelines, these safety considerations should always be followed:

- Always be familiar with the safe use and the inherent danger of power tools. If you do not know how to use a tool, *do not use it!*

- Loose clothing, jewelry, and long hair must be removed or tucked away. Beware the strings on your hooded sweatshirt. Should they be caught in a table saw blade, you will meet with disastrous results.
- Clamp loose boards in place before cutting them with hand tools or using a drill press.
- Always have a tight grip on your hand tools before operating them.
- Use push sticks or keep fingers a minimum of 4 inches away from table saw blades.
- Always use blade guards.

Ventilation and Dust

It is universally suggested that processes that produce any type of dust—sawdust, plaster dust, dust from dried clay, etc.—be kept separate from areas where cleanliness is essential, such as painting and urethane casting. Painting should be done in a spray booth or outdoors. Most universities and commercial shops are equipped with specialized, well-ventilated areas for those processes.

There are many factors to take into account when planning a workspace. Regard-less of your space's size, try to organize it such that you can easily move from one task to the next without having to completely uproot your project. If at all possible, try to create a triangular work zone that utilizes three separate work surfaces: one for cutting, one for gluing, and the final one for actually constructing your model.

KEY TERMS

anthropometrics
casting
ergonomics
floor flange

Chapter Review and Practice

1. *How does lighting affect one's ability to perform certain tasks?*
2. *What is the effect of fluorescent vs. incandescent lighting on colors?*
3. *What are the advantages to having multiple work surfaces?*
4. *Investigate the similarities and differences between the layout and storage capabilities of a well-designed kitchen and a well-designed shop.*
5. *List seven safety guidelines to consider when working with power tools.*

Basic Tools and Their Uses

6

OBJECTIVES

- *Familiarize yourself with the essential tools used in architectural model building*
- *Learn the safest ways to use these tools*
- *Learn to choose the right tool for the model making function you want to execute*

It is entirely possible to create beautiful models of cardboard, foam core, paper, illustration board, chipboard, museum board, Bristol board, basswood, or balsa wood with minimal tools and materials. As your skills increase, different tools will be required. However, there are certain items you will need for nearly every project, including:

- X-Acto type knife (sometimes called a craft knife) and # 11 blades

- Utility knife (preferably retractable)
- Retractable blade knife with snap-off segments
- Single-edge razor blades
- Handheld mat cutter
- Hobby saw and miter box
- Balsa strippers
- Scissors
- Steel straightedge with cork backing
- Architect's and engineer's scales
- Drafting compass and artist's circle cutter
- Dividers
- Various drafting triangles
- Sewing pins
- A cutting surface of hardboard (masonite) or a vinyl cutting mat (recommended)
- Hobby clamps (small, quick-clamp variety with rubber pads)

- Burnisher
- T square and drawing board
- Caliper
- Tweezers
- Scissors
- Pencils of different hardnesses—4H, 2H, HB
- Contractor's combination square
- Pliers—long-nose and needle-nose
- Wire cutters
- Jeweler's screwdriver kit, or tiny screwdrivers from an eyeglass repair kit
- Jeweler's files
- Protractor
- Nail punch
- Adjustable triangle, or angle square
- Circle cutter
- Sanding block

- Sandpaper from 150 to 400 grit
- Tape measure
- Hair dryer
- Razor plane
- A variety of adhesives
- Graphic tapes
- Pressure-sensitive overlays
- A variety of paints

(See Figures 6.1, 6.2, 6.3, 6.4, and 6.5.)

KNIVES

These tools are discussed in depth in Chapter 7.

- Craft knife (oftentimes referred to as an X-Acto knife) and #11 blades
- Utility knife (preferably retractable)
- Retractable blade knife with snap-off segments

FOAM BOARD TOOLS

A variety of foam-board-specific tools will be introduced and demonstrated in the section on foam board models.

Single-Edge Razor Blades (No. 9 Blades)

These thin and sharp blades are usually used in conjunction with tools such as the rabbet

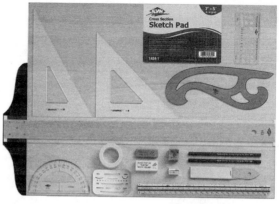

FIGURE 6.1 Various drafting tools are of use to the model maker—T squares, French curves, triangles, eraser shields, drafting pencils, erasers, scales, and sanding blocks. ©2009 Alvin & Company, Inc.

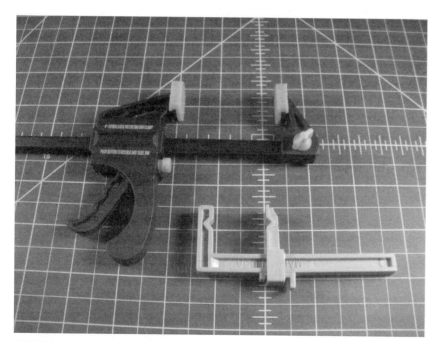

FIGURE 6.2 Hobby clamps can be like a second set of hands.

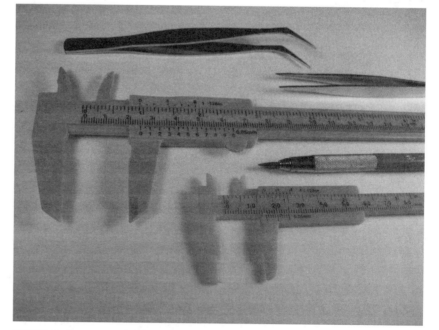

FIGURE 6.3 From top to bottom: tweezers, calipers, and drafting pencils.

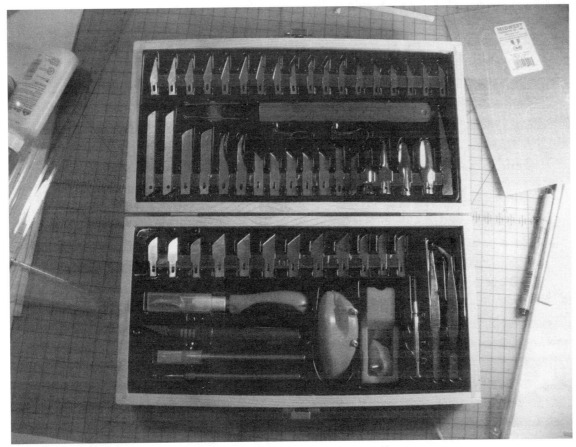

FIGURE 6.4 Starter sets are often available at hobby shops. This one contains more than enough for the student model maker.

FIGURE 6.5 Try squares are available in a variety of sizes.

foam board cutter, and handheld or table-mounted mat cutters.

The sharpness of these blades makes them extremely useful for trimming small amounts of material as well as for a variety of other miscellaneous tasks. The use of these blades will be elaborated upon in the later how-to sections. The cutting of fragile and thin materials can be accomplished by simply manipulating the blade with your thumb and forefinger. These are the sharpest of all the handheld blades and are extremely useful for cutting a variety of films.

Handheld Mat Cutter

A handheld mat cutter is extremely useful for perfectly straight 90- and 45-degree cuts in materials such as mat and foam board. Some mat cutters have adjustable depth and angle settings for the blade. This feature is ideal for **scoring** your paper or cardboard products. Some models have an attachable straightedge that usually ranges between 24 and 36 inches. Longer cuts will demand either a larger, fixed-position mat cutter, or a careful marriage of

oting blade is beyond all but the most skilled individuals.

Hobby Saw and Miter Box

A hobby saw may also be categorized as a razor saw. These saws normally contain 32 teeth per inch. With its thin blade, it is capable of making fine cuts in soft materials such as balsa and basswood without splitting or chipping the material. A razor saw is about one third the thickness of a coping saw (see Figure 6.7).

The miter box makes it possible to create perfectly vertical 45- or 90-degree cuts, and helps to alleviate splitting of the wood and ragged edged cuts. Additional features to look for include an integrated clamping system for holding different widths of material, and adjustable stops for **kerfs** and beveled channels, which are used to stabilize rods or tubing while cutting.

Scissors

With scissors, you definitely get what you pay for. Inexpensive scissors are fine for making maquettes or study models, but a small pair of sewing scissors will prove invaluable when cutting precise curves on materials such as acetate or cardstock. You may want a heavier version for cutting materials like cardboard,

separate cuts. Logan Graphic Products, Inc. produces an excellent system whereby you can mount a 45- or 90-degree cutter to a 24-inch straightedge (see logangraphic.com). The interlocking nature of this system ensures a straight cut. Other mat cutters, such as those made by Logan or Dexter, have features such as adjustable depths or cutting angles. Handheld cutters that do not utilize an integrated straightedge are much more difficult to control when it comes to producing a straight line (see Figure 6.6).

Circle Cutter

Many companies manufacture circle or compass cutters. These are used for making precise circular cuts. A swivel knife can accomplish much the same task as a circle cutter. Swivel knives are misleading. The skill required to make a clean cut using a tiny and piv-

light plastics, and thin vinyl, more commonly referred to as shears as opposed to scissors. Some manufactures produce a type of rolling scissor, which cuts paper using a single blade and bearings. When choosing scissors, look for features such as ergonomic handles, self sharpening, and stainless steel blades.

Steel Straightedge with Cork Backing

Ruler-type straightedges can be thin and flexible. Cork backing helps to eliminate slipping; it also elevates the steel and reduces smearing when inking. If your straightedge does not have a nonslip backing, I would suggest adding a piece of masking tape to help increase friction between your straightedge and the surface to be cut. Straightedges can be nearly one-eighth of an inch thick, and have beveled or straight edges. Use caution when using a straightedge of (unhardened) aluminum—the soft edges can easily be burred and will damage your blade (see Figure 6.8).

Architect's and Engineer's Scales

Triangular versions of both architect's and engineer's scales will be necessary. I would suggest having 12-inch versions, as well as a 4-inch miniature version. If you have the means, I would suggest buying a scale and cutting the end flush to the beginning of the

numbers. This will make it quicker and easier to measure in certain circumstances.

Drafting Compass

These are essential for drawing perfect circles larger than 2 inches in diameter. Introductory

sets are available that contain dividers and attachments necessary for inking.

Dividers

A divider looks a lot like a compass, but lacks the capacity to draw. Dividers are used to

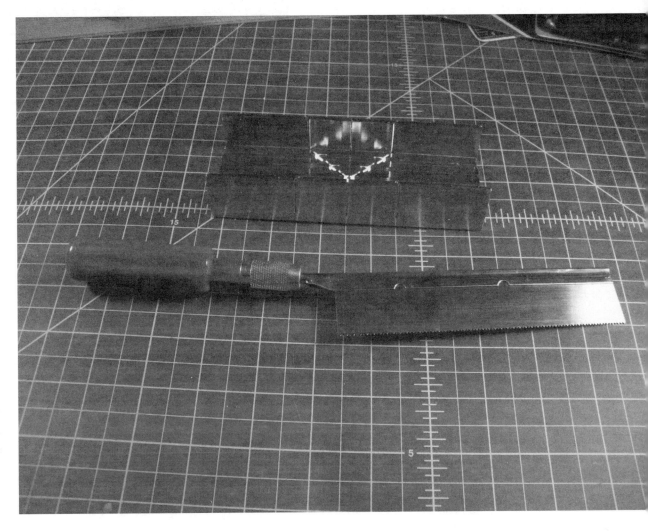

FIGURE 6.7 Razor saw and miter box.

measure hard-to-reach areas, and can also be used to transfer exact measurements quickly. Extremely useful are equal spacing dividers. These are designed for situations where exact spacing between numerous points is necessary.

Various Drafting Triangles
You should have a wide variety of sizes, especially small to medium. We will be utilizing both 30/60-degree, and 45/45-degree versions. Steel versions, although expensive, can prove to be extremely useful.

Sewing Pins or Straight Pins
These are great for tacking study models, using for support while gluing sets, or reinforcing awkward connections. Straight pins should have a flat head on them (suitable for building things) whereas sewing pins should have round plastic or glass heads for easier use while sewing. Depending on their placement, they can be left in, clipped, or pulled out of your model. Wire cutters are a more precise tool than long-nose or needle-nose pliers when it comes to cutting pins.

A Vinyl Composite Cutting Mat
These are self-healing and often reversible cutting surfaces. They come in a variety of sizes, from an 8½" × 11" version that includes holes for fitting into three-ring binders to 5' × 10' versions. These are made of a

FIGURE 6.8 Always label your tools! A cork-backed metal straightedge is absolutely indispensable to model makers.

synthetic composite that can be cut into, yet retain their smooth surface. Some manufacturers print a grid pattern and diagonals on the cutting surface. Some versions are reversible and have different colors on each side. Other mats are semi-transparent and can be used in conjunction with a light table. I would suggest a version between 24" × 36" and 36" × 48" to start with. Important: Never expose these mats to excessive heat or sunlight because they can warp, buckle, or otherwise lose their integrity. Vinyl cutting mats can be seen in the

background of most of the how-to shots in this book.

Hobby Clamps
Clamps (small, quick-clamp variety with rubber pads) are useful for attaching your work either to itself or your work surface. The quick-clamp varieties save precious time when working with fast-setting adhesives. Wider clamps are useful for holding perpendicular elements, such as four-sided boxes, in place (review Figure 6.2). Dremel manufac-

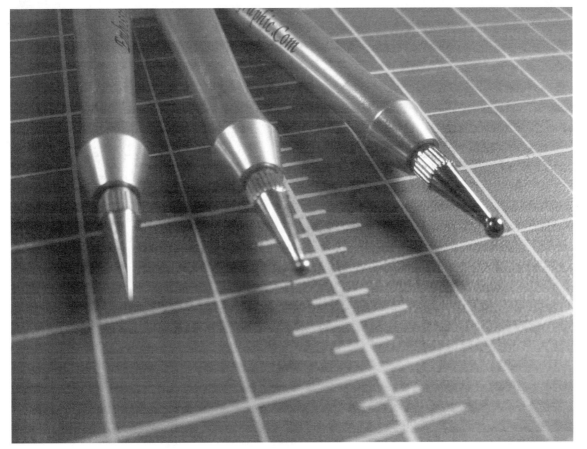

would suggest owning two or three sizes—small, medium, and large. A T square of hardened aluminum or steel is excellent for square cuts on stock materials (review Figure 6.1).

Parallel Rule and Drawing Board or Table

A setup similar to this reduces the need for a T square. A wire system on the underside of the drawing surface ensures that the straightedge remains parallel, regardless of where it moves on the board. Some parallel rules have steel, as opposed to plastic straightedges, which allows them to be used as a guide for cutting. Placing a steel straightedge flush against your parallel rule will accomplish the same thing. Always remember to put a piece of cardboard, mat board, or better yet, a self-healing vinyl cutting mat between the material you are cutting and the melamine surface of your drawing board.

Calipers

This is an extremely useful tool for obtaining and transferring exact interior or exterior measurements of objects. High-end models feature tempered steel and LCD screens, but inexpensive, plastic models are also available (review Figure 6.3).

tures a lightweight multi-vise in which the bar clamp can be attached to a base that swivels and tilts to nearly any position. A tool such as this can act like a third hand and can hold either your work or a rotary tool.

Burnisher

Burnishers were originally manufactured to apply press-on type for the graphics indus-try. They are extremely useful for disguising small cuts and fanned edges on surfaces such as mat board. Should you choose to apply press type to your model, they are useful (see Figure 6.9).

T Square and Drawing Board

T squares are commonly available in lengths of anywhere from 12 inches to 48 inches. I

Tweezers

Tweezers are ideal for use in hard-to-reach areas, or when handling small or delicate parts. When used in conjunction with a rubber band, they make excellent makeshift clamps for small or delicate parts (review Figure 6.3).

Pencils

Lead, or graphite, is categorized using the letters H or B. H indicates hardness; B indicates darkness. Thus a 6H lead is harder than a 2H, and as a result will leave a lighter line. A 6B pencil is softer than a 2B, and will leave a darker line. The softer, or darker, the lead, the more susceptible it is to smudging or smearing. Pencils with the nomenclature of F or HB have a fairly hard lead that can also be used to lay down a dark line or tone. A 4H lead is good for marking, holds its point longer, and does not smudge easily. It is an excellent choice for drawing on models (review Figure 6.3).

Contractor's Combination Square

A *combo square* is the term commonly used when referring to a machinist square, engineer's square, or a **try square**, sometimes spelled "tri-square" (review Figure 6.5). This is a nice alternative to a metal triangle. Many metal triangles are made from nonhardened aluminum and, thus, are not suitable for use when cutting. Combo squares are used to mark and measure wood. The word "square" refers to its capability to check the accuracy of right angles. Try can also be used as a verb, meaning to check a surface's straightness, or whether it is perpendicular to an adjoining surface. Do not assume that a combo square will always stay square.

Pliers

A variety of long-nose and needle-nose pliers should be on hand at all times. These are good for precision work, as well as selective demolition of model parts and extraction of pins.

Wire Cutters

Although the previously mentioned pliers may have built-in wire cutters, it is a good idea to have a separate pair for cutting in a confined space.

Very Small Screwdriver

Many of your models will utilize small screws, thus necessitating these tools. These are usually standard parts of a jewelry or eyeglass repair kit.

Jeweler's Files

These are useful for smoothing out or shaping small sheets of Plexiglas, basswood, or balsa wood.

Protractor

Protractors are used to plot and measure angles. They are available in plastic or steel. Although usually semicircular, they are also available in 360-degree versions.

Nail Punch

This tool will prevent wear and tear on your fingers when working with straight pins.

Adjustable Triangle or Angle Square

This is a useful tool for transferring or discovering odd angles either in plan or on your model. The adjustable nature of this triangle also makes it useful as a temporary support of inclined planes.

Sanding Blocks of Various Sizes and Shapes

A typical sanding block is designed to hold quarter sheets of sandpaper. The block acts as a flat backing to the paper, making it easier to achieve an even surface on the object you are sanding. When sanding tiny surfaces and/or objects, try placing the sanding block in a clamp and then moving the delicate object across the sandpaper. It is also possible to fashion your own block in nearly any size or shape. After making the block, sandpaper can be spray mounted to it.

Sandpaper from 150 to 400 Grit

The higher the number, or grit, the smoother the sandpaper, e.g., a 200 grit is smoother than a 180 grit. Have a wide variety of grits available for cleaning up edges and burrs, and for shaping soft materials.

Hair Dryer

This is useful for heat shrinking certain types of acetates, as well as for accelerating the drying of water-based paints and adhesives.

Balsa Stripper

A balsa stripper is a tool designed to accurately cut balsa or basswood sheets into identical strips, usually ranging from 1/8- to 1/2-inch wide. Using a balsa stripper is an economical alternative to buying precut strips of wood. (As shown in Figure 6.4, a balsa stripper is included in the kit.)

Razor Plane

A razor plane is useful for shaping and shaving balsa wood. This is a quicker and cleaner tool for roughing out large areas of balsa, but the final finishing should still be reserved for sandpaper. (As shown in Figure 6.4, a razor plane is included in the kit.)

ADHESIVES

Make sure you have the following adhesives, as well as some paper towels available.

- A **polyvinyl acetate (PVA)** white glue, such as Elmer's, Sobo, or Tacky
- Spray adhesive, preferably repositionable, such as 3M super 77
- Double-stick tape
- A glue or cement specifically for balsa wood

Super Glue

A couple drops will do. If you are unsure about bonding unlike materials together, this will often work. It is especially useful for bonding plastics, acrylics, or urethanes either to each other or to a different material. Bear in mind, Super Glue will slightly distort the surface of transparent materials. Plan ahead for some surface inconsistencies at the edges of transparent materials, and make sure these areas arc well disguised behind frames, mullions, etc. The technical name for Super Glue is cyanoacrylate.

Hot Glue

This glue is as fast as it is messy. Depending on the brand you purchased, glue stick refills can be easy or difficult to find. An obscure, cheap brand of glue gun may not be the best choice if you can never find glue for it. Hot glue is good in small doses for tacking parts in place while a different adhesive sets up. Models made with hot glue tend to look sloppy and unprofessional. Beware of the messy glue bridge or string that extends between the area you just glued and the tip of your gun; chances are it is going to end up somewhere you don't want it to. With the possible exception of study models, you should refrain from using hot glue. Although it is mentioned in its title, hot glue guns are HOT—be careful because it is extremely easy to burn yourself.

Airplane Glue, Model Glue (Cellulose-Based Glue)

This type of glue is normally sold in tiny tubes, is primarily used for wooden models, and can be purchased in most hobby shops. This is an excellent choice for bonding cardboard to cardboard. Be sure to use this in a well-ventilated area.

Spray Adhesive

Spray adhesive is an excellent choice for quickly laminating thin sheets of colored paper to your board, or board to board. Always use in a well-ventilated area, and always place the paper you will be spraying atop a clean sheet of paper. It is highly suggested you lay down a *clean* sheet of paper each time. The spray is sticky. Should any mist get on your project, it will attract dust, which can ruin a project's pristine appearance.

There are basically two types of spray adhesive available—a repositionable artist type adhesive, and a nonrepositionable type. I prefer 3M super 77 spray adhesive because it allows you to lift and reposition your materials in the first few moments after application, but then dries to a strong, permanent bond.

Archival Tape

Although it looks similar to masking or drafting tape, this is extremely strong and expensive. It is made to be used with archival documents and artwork as a hinge between the paper to be framed and the mat board. It will remain permanently attached for years to come, and will not damage **archival** material.

Double-Sided Tape

Double-sided tape is available as either a light-duty, thin, clear tape, or a thicker foam tape. The thinner tape is good for laminating two surfaces; the foam is good for use as padding in larger scale furniture models. This is different from double-stick tape.

Double-Stick Tape

This tape is commonly used in frame shops for the purpose of laminating two boards together. It is extremely strong, yet can be removed easily with a rubber cement eraser. It is basically a strip of rubber cement attached to a slightly wider strip of plastic, nonadhesive tape. It can be applied by cutting and laying individual strips onto a board and then removing the plastic strip. Double-stick tape guns are also available; these are similar to price guns that one would find in a supermarket. They simultaneously lay down the adhesive while removing the plastic strip.

Drafting Tape

Every student should already have a roll or two of drafting tape on supply. This is not as sticky as normal masking tape and is designed to be removed without peeling up or tearing fragile paper or board surfaces.

Duct Tape

What *can't* duct tape do? From scout-camp wallets to patching holes in Apollo 13, duct tape has been holding our planet together for nearly half a century. If it is good enough for NASA, it is good enough for us. Available in a wide variety of colors and grades, duct tape is a plastic- or vinyl-backed, fabric-lined tape combined with an extremely sticky adhesive. Many people do not realize this, but duct tape sticks much better to itself than it does to other surfaces. Nevertheless, if you are looking for something strong, this will work for you. It is a pretty unsightly tape; make sure you hide it from view in anything but a study model. It now comes in colors, including white; white may be your best choice if working with white board.

Masking Tape

Similar in appearance to drafting tape, masking tape is its stickier cousin. Bear in mind, masking tape is not as forgiving as drafting tape and should not be used as a temporary fix. It will definitely tear or otherwise damage the surface of nearly anything it comes into contact with. In an emergency, some of the tack can be removed from the tape by placing it on and lifting it off of your jeans. The more times you do this, the less tacky it becomes. Bear in mind, as it loses its power of adhesion, it also picks up a proportionate amount of lint, which it will then deposit on

your model. Masking tape is a good choice for use on models where it will not be seen. One caveat: Do not use masking tape on an archival model, e.g., a model that is intended to stick around for a few years. It damages the archival board it comes into contact with, and will eventually dry up and fall off.

Packing Tape

This is a clear, strong tape normally used on cardboard boxes for shipping. It normally comes in 2-inch widths. It is also available in a light brown. It is useful for temporary or utilitarian tasks that may be required of you, but not often used in the finished product.

Strapping Tape

Strapping tape is a clear-backed fiber reinforced tape with strength comparable to duct tape. It is available in widths of $1/2$ to 2 inches. Unlike duct tape, the fibers do not allow the tape to lengthen, stretch, or distort. I use strapping tape exclusively for holding plaster **mother molds** together.

Transparent Tape

Often called Scotch or invisible tape, this tape is useful for permanent constructions. It does not have high shear strength, and tears quite easily. Despite its name, it can still be seen, and should not be used where visible to the viewer. This is a great choice for cardstock study models.

Graphic Tapes

Graphic tapes are available in a variety of sizes (1/8 to 3 inches), colors, and textures. These can be used to great effect, especially when representing windows, mullions, door frames, and more on smaller scaled, international-style skyscrapers and the like. They are also useful for representing parking lot stripes, or similar landscape delineations.

Pressure-Sensitive Overlays

Pressure-sensitive overlays are available in a variety of colors and faux textures. They are usually semi-transparent.

A VARIETY OF PAINTS

Because color adds interest and depth to your models, you will find yourself wanting a variety of paints at the ready. What follows are short descriptions of some popular choices. Experiment and do further research to find your favorites.

Acrylic Paint

Acrylic is a water-based artist's paint, meaning you can clean it up with water. It is available in a variety of grades and sizes, and is useful for changing or adding an opaque color to your models.

Watercolor Paint

Watercolor is another type of water-based artist paint. Unlike acrylics, watercolors will create a semi-transparent glaze to whatever it is applied.

Spray Paint

Spray paint is useful when you want to apply a uniform coat to the surface of your model. Numerous types and finishes of spray paint are available. These include, but are not limited to, flat, gloss, primer, and textured. The type of spray paint you will need is completely dependent upon what you will be using it both on and for.

TOOL SAFETY

Whether you are just beginning as a model maker or are highly advanced, these rules always apply for safety and best results.

- **Always wear proper clothing:** Do not wear loose fitting clothing or jewelry that can get caught in moving machinery. Never wear open-toed shoes when working with sharp objects. Tie up and pull back long hair.
- **Always wear eye and ear protection:** Flying debris and loud noises are a constant danger in a shop environment.
- **Stay sober, stay safe:** Do not operate tools or machinery when fatigued or under the influence of alcohol or drugs, prescription or otherwise.
- **Avoid distractions:** Keep your mind on what you are doing. Stop work and turn off the tool when you are speaking to someone else. Never take your eyes off what you are doing.
- **Secure your work:** Clamp or otherwise secure your work to keep it from moving while you are cutting.
- **Keep your work area clean:** Keep your table and floor clear of scraps and other clutter. The more cluttered a space, the more likely accidents are to occur.
- **Use only properly functioning tools:** Never use a tool for something other than its intended use or if it is in disrepair. Always unplug power tools before performing any maintenance such as changing a blade.
- **Keep safety guards in place:** Do not remove a blade guard or any other type of safety guard from your equipment—it is there to keep you safe.
- **Use good blades:** Never use a blade that is cracked, warped, or otherwise damaged.
- **Know the tool before you use it:** If you don't understand how to safely use a tool, don't attempt to use it— it is just that simple.

HAND TOOLS

Before attempting to use any tools, not just the ones mentioned in this book, make sure you receive training in the proper and safe use of tools. Although reading this book is a great way to supplement your knowledge, it is no substitute for a hands-on safety lecture. Some hand tools you will find useful include:

- Linoleum knife
- Handheld glass cutter
- Screwdrivers
- Handheld twist drill
- Files
- Coping or jeweler's saw with a variety of blades
- Crosscut saw
- Miter box
- C-clamps and quick clamps
- Chisels
- Rasps
- Wrenches
- Model maker's plane
- A variety of different levels

Linoleum Knife

A linoleum knife is useful for scoring acrylic and other plastic laminates. The round, non-cutting edge is useful for adding linear textures to soft materials such as balsa wood or mat board.

Screwdrivers

Many of your tools will require periodic adjustment, often facilitated by the use of a screwdriver. Stock your shelves with both standard and Phillips head varieties.

Files

Files are useful for smoothing and shaping stiffer materials such as wood, metal, or plastics. Files are made differently depending upon whether you are working with wood or metal. Unlike sandpaper, files are hard and will not lose their shape when working with harder materials. This also makes them ideal for getting into small areas such as corners.

Coping or Jeweler's Saw with a Variety of Blades

This is an economical alternative to a band saw. A coping saw is designed for cutting curves in thin woods. Typically, the more teeth per inch the blade has, the tighter radius it can cut and the more fragile it is. It is best to store blades in their original packaging.

Crosscut Saw

Like the name implies, this saw is designed for use when cutting across the grain of wood. To ensure a clean, vertical cut, I would suggest using this saw in conjunction with a miter box.

Miter Box

This tool is used to create precise cuts, usually at a 45- or 90-degree angle in a board. It is a three-sided box, open at the top and ends.

Hammer

For model making, bigger hammers aren't necessarily better. A small, 10 oz. version

should be sufficient for most every need. An upholstery hammer is nice due to its low swing weight and double head. The thinner, streamlined head is magnetic in order to hold tiny upholstery nails.

C-Clamps and Quick Clamps

Have a variety of clamps available, including C-clamps and larger, multipurpose quick clamps, for a variety of applications. Common **throat sizes** (the part that does the actual clamping) range from 1/2 to 3 inches. When using clamps, be careful not to damage your work surface. Place a piece of cardboard or soft wood between your clamp and work surface to keep it pristine.

Chisels

Chisels will be used primarily for cutting away material on the surface of wood. A chisel will also be used to clean up castings.

Wrenches

An adjustable wrench with a jaw opening of 1/2 inch should suffice for most of your model making needs.

Model Maker's Plane

A model maker's plane is used after the wood is rough cut. Planing occurs before the sanding of your wood to a smooth finish. This particular type of plane can be used to plane flat or curved surfaces.

Bubble Levels

A bubble level is used to find the perfect vertical (plumb) or horizontal (level). This is also referred to as a spirit level.

PORTABLE POWER TOOLS

Although most tasks can be accomplished using only hand tools, the addition of power does tend to simplify and expedite things. A few common hand tools that you will find useful are:

- Rotary tool (Dremel, etc.)
- Cordless drill/driver
- Flashlight
- Palm sander

FIGURE 6.10 Dremel Moto-Tools are useful for sanding, grinding, and shaping wood and plastics. *Photograph courtesy of the Dremel brand, Mount Prospect, Illinois.*

- Soldering iron
- Jigsaw

Rotary Tool

A rotary tool is a small, handheld tool, similar to those used by dentists. Rotary tools accept a wide variety of rotary bits, commonly referred to as **burrs.** Other accessories can be used in conjunction with a rotary tool for sanding, polishing, carving, drilling, and cutting a variety of surfaces.

When choosing a rotary tool, look for one with high revolutions per minute (RPMs), a flexible shaft, and a variety of bits. Extremely helpful, but not necessary, are quick connect/disconnect features. Dremel, a brand name that is commonly misconstrued as the actual name of the tool, manufactures several different interchangeable models of rotary tools and accessories. They also manufacture a workstation that holds the rotary tool at a variety of angles and can transform it into a light-duty, space-saving drill press as well (see Figures 6.10 and 6.11).

Jigsaw

A jigsaw is useful for cutting complex curves in wood up to one inch thick. Thinner gauges of metal may also be cut, but this does require a special blade (see Figure 6.12).

FIGURE 6.11 Dremel manufactures a workstation that holds the rotary tool at a variety of angles, and can act as a third hand or a drill press. *Photograph courtesy of the Dremel brand, Mount Prospect, Illinois.*

Cordless Drill/Driver

One of the most useful tools in your toolbox—a portable drill or driver—can drill, drive, sand,

polish, buff, mix, or even route if you have the right accessories. Dremel manufactures an extremely compact driver that is more than adequate for the light- and medium-duty requirements of model making. When choosing a driver, look for a compact design and slim nose. This will allow you to access tight spaces and awkward angles more easily than is possible with conventional drivers. Bosch manufactures small drivers as well as a driver with a head that adjusts to several different angles.

Flashlight

A flashlight is useful for peering into the dark recesses of your model, testing the effects of lighting, or finding that tiny piece you dropped on the floor. Although most of these tools come with their own special batteries and chargers, it is a good idea to keep extra batteries at the ready for tools, such as flashlights, that may not be rechargeable.

Palm Sander

This power tool is made for sanding, smoothing, or adding texture to large areas of wood, metal, glass, plaster, and plastic. A palm sander is often called a detail sander. In woodworking, it is used for sanding corners or small spaces. It is ideal for model making.

FIGURE 6.12 Jigsaws are extremely useful for creating larger, curved cuts, but lack the accuracy of a table saw.

Soldering Iron

A soldering iron is used for soldering copper and steel wire, wax welding, and for adding texture to wood.

FIXED-LOCATION POWER TOOLS

Architectural models that utilize materials such as wood, metal, and acrylic should be cut using larger power tools. The following is a list of tools you should eventually have in your shop. Again, many materials can be cut using hand tools, but you will find that the safe use of the power tools mentioned here will increase both the speed and accuracy of your model making skills. Whenever working with any tool, especially those in the following list, always ensure adequate ventilation and wear ear and eye protection. Finally, understand the correct and safe operation of the tools in question before operating them.

- Chop saw or miter saw
- Table saw
- Belt or disc sander
- Band saw
- Scroll saw
- Drill press
- Router with table
- Lathe

Chop Saw or Miter Saw

This is extremely useful for cutting larger pieces of wood to length. It can make **mi-tered,** straight, or **compound mitered** cuts. It accepts a wide variety of blades depending upon the level of accuracy or material that needs to be cut. Along with the table saw, this is one of the most useful tools to have in a shop (see Figure 6.13).

Table Saw

A table saw is the most versatile of all the fixed location power tools discussed here. It is basically an inverted circular saw mounted on a bench or table. This tool is useful for cutting down sheets of wood used for projects such as shipping crates, bases, model cases, and other simple, geometric forms. A good table saw will have a blade with adjustable depths and angles. Also essential is a **rip fence,** a **miter gauge,** and a blade guard. Standard blade sizes range from 7 to 12 inches. For the purposes of this book, a 10-inch blade should be sufficient. In addition to being the most useful, this saw is also one of the most dangerous. Be sure you read and understand all safety precautions that relate to this tool (see Figure 6.14).

Belt or Disc Sander

Belt or disc sanders are ideal for sanding and smoothing surfaces of narrow and wide boards and other sheet goods. A belt sander uses a rotating belt of sandpaper, and is good for long, narrow surfaces. A disc sander uses a rotating disc of a sandpaper-like substance.

Band Saw

A band saw uses a blade that is a flexible, continuous band of toothed steel. Band saws can be used for cutting a variety of materials, such as wood, metal, and Plexiglas. Band saws were originally designed for cutting irregular shapes. The thinner the band (saw blade), the tighter or smaller the radius that can be cut. If intricate cuts or scrollwork are required, a scroll saw should be used instead. When using a band saw, it is important to remember that the blade has width. If you cut directly on your cut line, your piece will end up being

FIGURE 6.13 A miter saw, or chop saw, is one of the first fixed location power tools you should acquire. *Bosch Tools*

smaller than you want it. Always cut to the outside of the piece you want to keep.

Scroll Saw

A **scroll saw** is useful for cutting intricate curves deemed otherwise impossible or impractical with a band saw, coping saw, or jigsaw. In addition to the most intricate curves, it is also capable of creating curves with beveled edges. Unlike the band saw, whose blade is a continuous loop, scroll saws use an extremely thin blade, much like those used with coping saws. The saw blade operates using an up-and-down motion. This motion is commonly referred to as **reciprocation.** This tool is used extensively for cutting the curved surfaces on balsa wood and basswood (see Chapter 11).

When choosing a scroll saw, you definitely get what you pay for. Look for a saw with features such as variable speed; a large, heavy-duty table; and as large a throat depth as possible (working surface between the blade and the machine). Also handy is a tool-less or quick-change blade system, a table bevel capacity of at least 45 degrees, a flexible dust blower, and a built-in dust port or collector. If possible, find one with a built-in light. Also helpful is a scroll saw that has a blade holder that can rotate 90 degrees; this will allow you to perform precise cuts of nearly unlimited length. Finally, and most importantly, choose a scroll saw that can be permanently attached to your work surface. This will

cut down on vibrations. Your hand is only as steady as the surface you are working on.

Drill Press

A drill press is used for drilling precisely spaced, vertical holes to an exact depth. There are commonly two types available—bench top and floor model. For the purposes of this book, a bench top model should be sufficient, although the floor models tend to be more powerful and of generally higher quality. When choosing a drill press, make sure it has variable speeds, an adjust-

able table, and a depth stop. With the right attachments, some drill presses can act as a **spindle sander,** or **mortise machine.** If money or space are tight, it is possible to use a Dremel rotary tool and workstation together to create a drill press. Examples can be found in Chapter 9.

Router with Table

Although not essential for many types of models, a router is an excellent tool for creating professional bases and moldings

FIGURE 6.14 As your shop expands, one of the first purchases should be a table saw. It is essential for making heavy-duty bases and shipping crates. *Bosch Tools*

on larger scale models. A router is a tool that can create a wide range of shapes on the edge of a piece of wood. They are available in two varieties—plunge, and stationary. For the projects in this book, a variable speed, stationary base router will suffice.

A router table is an essential tool to be used in conjunction with a router. A router table is a flat surface with a router attached to the bottom. The router is mounted with its bit sticking up through a hole in the center of the table's surface. With the router integrated in to the table, this allows you to keep both hands on your work during the cut. Entire books, courses, and PBS television shows are dedicated to the use of this versatile tool. The techniques presented later in this book are only a drop in the bucket when it comes to the possibilities of a router. Dremel manufactures a smaller router table and attachment that are nice for fine detail work.

Lathe

A lathe is a machine that shapes a rotating piece of wood, plastic, or metal. There are a wide variety of lathes available, but a center lathe should be adequate for the projects detailed in this book. The CNC lathe, or CNC milling center, is commonly used in conjunction with CAD to create foam contour models.

You have just been given a brief introduction to the types of tools that a model maker finds useful. Your shop or school may or may not have all of the aforementioned tools available. Nevertheless, it is important that, at the very least, you familiarize yourself with the potential uses of them.

Regardless of what equipment you have at your disposal, it cannot be stressed enough that these tools are dangerous if not used properly. Always read the operation manual, get instruction, and know the limitations of each and every tool before you use them. When in doubt, ask.

KEY TERMS

archival

burrs

compound mitered

kerfs

miter gauge

mitered

mortise machine

mother molds

polyvinyl acetate (PVA)

reciprocation

rip fence

scoring

scroll saw

spindle sander

throat sizes

try square

Chapter Review and Practice

1. **What is the difference between a craft knife and a utility knife? How do their uses differ?**

2. **Name the four most common types of adhesives used by model makers. List their properties and some possible uses.**

3. **How would one go about familiarizing himself or herself with either portable or fixed-location power tools prior to using them?**

FUNDAMENTAL TECHNIQUES

PART 2

Fundamental Construction Techniques

OBJECTIVES

- *Transfer your design*
- *Learn the proper use of knives and method of cutting*
- *Check for square*
- *Work with adhesives*
- *Create removable or moveable parts*

This chapter will discuss a few basic processes that all model builders use, regardless of the medium. There are occasions where mounting a plan to your board or transferring measurements and drawing by hand are neither practical nor desirable. In instances such as these, we turn to the transfer method.

TRANSFERRING PLANS TO YOUR MATERIALS

There are several ways to transfer images, contours, shapes, measurements, or entire plans and elevations to the materials with which you will be constructing your models. The method you choose to use will depend on the amount of time and money you have at your disposal, and the medium with which you choose to work.

To simplify things, we will be using the term "board" to describe the materials you will be transferring your plans to. The term "board" could refer to anything—cardboard, foam core, wood, mat board, chipboard, etc.

Transfer Paper

This is similar to how patterns are transferred in sewing.

1. Tape your **transfer paper** (carbon, etc.), colored side down, on your materials.
2. Tape down your plan or design on top of the transfer paper.
3. Using a sharp, hard pencil (4H is recommended), trace the lines you want to see reproduced on your model.
4. Carefully remove the plan and the transfer paper. The lines you traced should now be visible on your board.

Homemade Transfer Paper

This method is less expensive and requires less taping time than the aforementioned technique. By using less paper, you reduce the likelihood of your paper moving, and the errors associated with unintentional movement.

1. On the back of your plan, using a soft pencil, such as B or 2B, cover the lines you want to transfer. Taping your plan to a window, plan side toward the glass, will allow you to easily see the lines you need to cover with graphite.
2. Tape the plan to your board, marked side down.
3. Using a sharp, hard pencil (4H is recommended), trace the lines you want to see reproduced on your model.
4. Carefully remove the plan and the transfer paper. The lines you traced should now be visible on your board.

Reverse Transfer Method

This method involves quite a bit of copying and adhering, but ensures a rapid, professional, and accurate transfer of your designs. This is especially useful when building contour models.

1. Begin by photocopying or printing your original drawing onto a clear sheet of **Mylar** or **acetate.** Some copy machines will alter the size of your image by 1 or 2 percent, so be leery of this. Make sure you either use the same machine for every copy, or better yet, use a machine that copies at a true 100 percent size.
2. Using your transparent copy, turn it over so that you are photocopying a reverse image of your drawing.
3. Using spray adhesive, attach your reverse image copy to the back of your board.
4. You are now free to cut out the image; make sure you build the model with the copy side down. This is only useful in cases where the copy side of the model can be hidden from view. I would not suggest using this method for exposed walls.

Spolvero, or Cartoon Transfer Method

The term **cartoon** does not refer to *The Simpsons*; in our case, it refers to the image already on paper—i.e., your plan. This is a variation on a technique used during the Renaissance for fresco paintings. It was a method commonly employed for transferring the master's original drawing, or cartoon, quickly and safely to a recently plastered wall. We will be using a technique slightly modified from that of Michelangelo and his contemporaries. In his book, *Michelangelo and the Pope's Ceiling*, Ross King describes the process that Michelangelo used to transfer his drawings:

The technique of fresco was as simple in conception as it was difficult in execution. The term fresco, meaning "fresh," comes from the fact that the painter always worked on fresh—that is, wet—plaster. This called for both good preparation and precise timing. A layer of plaster, known as the **intonaco,** was trowelled to a thickness of about a half inch over another coat of dried plaster. Intonaco, a smooth paste made from lime and sand, provided a permeable surface for the pigments, first absorbing them and then sealing them in the masonry as it dried.

The design of the painting was transferred to this patch of wet plaster from the cartoon. Fixed to the wall or vault with small nails, the cartoon served as a template for a particular figure or scene. Its design would be transferred by one of two methods. The first, called *spolvero*, involved perforating the lines of drawing on the cartoon with thousands of little holes through which a charcoal powder would be sprinkled, or "pounced," by striking the cartoon with the pounce-bag and thereby leaving on the plaster an outline that was then reinforced in paint. The second, much quicker method, required the artist to trace over the chalk lines on the cartoon with the point of a stylus, leaving marks on the fresh plaster beneath. Only then would he set to work with his paints and brushes.

A contemporary variation on that process is as follows:

1. Tape your plan to your board.
2. Using a pounce wheel, simply run it over your lines. This in turn will poke holes through your plan and into your board.
3. Remove your plan from thc board; a series of small holes should now be visible. To see better, you may want to trace over the holes. Do not use this method if you will be unable to disguise the holes after making them.

Traditional Cartoon Transfer Method

Because pounce wheels were not readily available in the Renaissance, other means were used to puncture the cartoon.

1. Tape your plan to your board.
2. Using a sharp, pointed, instrument (I prefer pins), following your lines, poke holes through your plan wherever you feel it is necessary, and into your board.
3. Remove your plan from the board; a series of small holes should now be visible. To see better, you may want to trace over the holes. Do not use this method if you will be unable to disguise the holes after making them.

Transferring Your Plans

1. Oftentimes the plan will be removed from the board only to reveal the fact that you forgot to trace a line. It is nearly impossible to replace a plan in the exact position it occupied prior to being removed. By simply placing a sheet of tracing paper over your plan and lifting it prior to the removal of the entire plan, you can easily check to see if there are any lines you have forgotten to transfer.
2. Using either store-bought or homemade transfer methods will work well for harder board surfaces such as mat board, chipboard, and harder woods. Due to the soft nature of cardboard and foam core, I would suggest a test run on these materials prior to committing to a technique. If you have a "heavy" hand while drafting, there is a chance you can damage these softer materials.
3. The reverse transfer method is useful for the softer boards, cardboard, foam core, etc., and is my personal choice of transfer techniques when working with balsa or basswood, or working with intricate curves.
4. Using homemade transfer paper tends to be the most accurate and least expensive method. Using store-bought transfer paper can be the fastest method, but most costly. Spolvero, or the cartoon method, is by far the slowest method.

5. After using either store-bought or homemade transfer paper, lightly apply a Skum-X drawing cleaning pad, dry-erase pad eraser, or a kneaded eraser to clean the surface of your board. Using a drafting brush, remove the pad's remnants immediately thereafter. These methods of transferring tend to leave excessive amounts of lead upon the surface of the board. The dry-erase pad ensures that your board will remain smudge free.

KNIVES AND CUTTING

The most fundamental skill in model making is cutting; it should always be done with the utmost care. The following section will introduce the reader to different types of knives and their specific uses (see Figure 7.1). You will also be introduced to some proper cutting techniques. Finally, you will be given an opportunity to practice what you have learned.

- **Craft knife,** usually called an X-Acto knife, and #11 blades or an Alvin zippy no. 1 knife.
- X-Acto, Alvin, and their many competitors manufacture a full line of interchangeable handles and blades. (The #11 blade is an all purpose blade that can be used for both fine and heavy cutting. Change your blades often; the sharper the blade, the cleaner the cut. Your specific

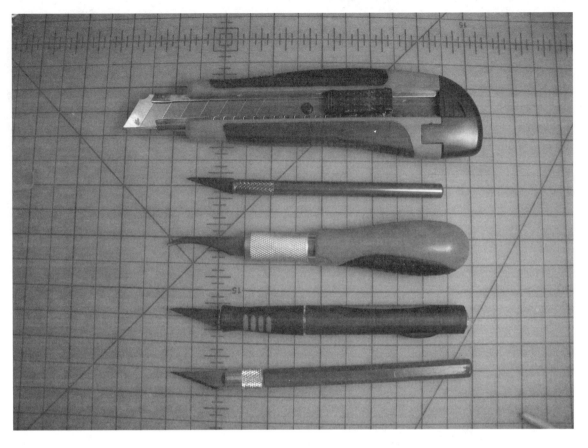

FIGURE 7.1 Primary knives used by most student model makers.

cuts on fine material), this heavy-duty knife is excellent for making long, straight cuts in thicker material, such as foam board, cardboard, balsa, and basswood. Many models offer blade storage inside the knife. Retractable blade **utility knives** are always safer than stationary ones.

Retractable Blade Knife with Snap-Off Segments

This type falls somewhere between the craft and utility knife. It can cut heavier material than the craft knife, and is more precise than a utility knife. Thickness of these blades ranges between 8 and 13 point—the higher the number, the stronger and thicker the blade. A snap-off blade ensures quick access to new blades, and provides a clearly visible inventory of your existing blades.

The retractable blade is a nice safety feature, and the snap-off blade makes it easy to maintain a sharp cutting instrument. As a safety precaution, always use pliers to snap off the blade to avoid the possibility of a flying projectile.

KNIVES AND HAND CUTTING: TRICKS OF THE TRADE

The most important point to remember about cutting is to use a sharp blade. There is abso-

needs—carving, punching, gouging, etc.—will dictate your exact choice of blade.)
- Utility knife (preferably retractable).
- Retractable blade knife with snap-off segments.

The Craft Knife

This will be your primary cutting instrument. The sharper the blade, the cleaner the cut you will be able to make. No amount of skill can substitute for a sharp blade. Change blades often. Some variations of this knife have a rubberized grip, a nice feature during any marathon model making sessions.

Utility Knife (Preferably Retractable)

Although not suitable for detail-oriented work (this should not be used for making precision

lutely no substitute for a sharp knife. Golden rule #1 of the model maker is: the sharper the knife, the cleaner the cut. There are no ifs, ands, or buts. The type of knife you use is up to you. Some professional model makers use scalpels that they sharpen themselves using whetstones; others use disposable surgeon's scalpels. On the other end of the spectrum, I have seen some old-timers create beautiful models using a utility knife. The student model maker generally uses a craft knife with a #11 blade.

Almost as important as a sharp knife is the surface upon which you will be cutting and laying your boards. If the board you are cutting is placed on a rough surface, a roughly cut edge will be the result. Ideally, a sheet of hardboard (sometimes known as masonite) and a second, heavier mat or cardboard stock should be used to protect your work surface. These cutting surfaces will deteriorate over time and should be discarded and replaced periodically. Some companies, such as Alvin, manufacture self-healing vinyl cutting pads that accomplish the same thing. One advantage of the self-healing pads is they ensure a clean cut on both sides of your board. These are expensive, but can last a lifetime. It is never a good idea to leave cutting pads exposed to direct sunlight, or too close to a hot light. They have a tendency to warp, and a warped pad will always cause a wavy cut.

When executing straight cuts, a steel straightedge with a cork backing should be used. This will keep it from sliding when you are applying pressure with your knife. If the straightedge was not manufactured with a strip of cork along the bottom, a strip of masking tape can be applied, but this is still a poor substitute for a cork-backed straightedge. Friction on the underside of your straightedge will not only improve the craftsmanship of your model, but many cut fingers that result from the interface between a slippery work surface and a sharp blade can be avoided. That being said, uneven pressure on a cork-backed straightedge can cause it to flip up, also resulting in a cut finger. Two or three sizes of straightedges, say, 6 and 12, and a T-square, 18 inches or longer, will add to the variety of incision sizes you will be making without unnecessary maneuvering of your straightedge. Inexpensive combination and small machinist squares found at many home improvement stores are excellent additions to any model builder's toolbox.

CUTTING

As a general rule, use several light passes over your material's surface as opposed to cutting through it in a single pass. Attempts to sever material such as mat board or foam core in a single pass will usually result in uneven or wobbly cut lines, beveled edges, choppy exposure of the foam center, accidental cuts to you or your work, or a deviation from the intended line. Always try to keep your blade perpendicular to the board you are cutting; failure to do so will also result in an inaccurate cut.

Mat and bevel cutters are excellent tools for making perpendicular or beveled cuts. These can be purchased with an accompanying straightedge. They are usually found in lengths of 30 inches. Handheld, freehand mat, or bevel cutters are also available at most art or hobby stores. Commercial frame shops have more industrial versions of mat cutters, usually about 48 inches long. These are as delicate as they are expensive, but wonderful to work with if you get the chance. When cutting beveled edges, you must disregard the advice given earlier. To make a clean, beveled edge, the blade must pierce the entire surface of your board on the first try, and your material must be cut in a single pass. Failure to do so will create cuts with jagged edges.

Straight Cutting Step by Step

These general guidelines should be followed whenever cutting paper-based materials such as cardboard, mat board, foam board, chipboard, or balsa wood.

1. Begin by transferring your design to your material. It is also possible to tack a plan or elevation directly on top of your board.
2. Place your steel straightedge along the line to be cut (see Figure 7.2).

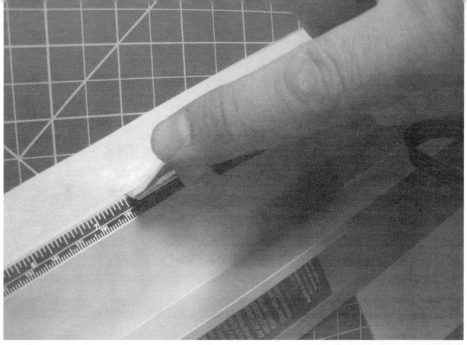

FIGURE 7.2 (Top Left). Place your steel straight-edge along the line to be cut.

FIGURE 7.3 (Top Right). To ensure a clean vertical cut, keep the lateral orientation of the blade perpendicular to your cutting surface.

FIGURE 7.4 (Bottom Right). Make several passes until you have cut through the entire board.

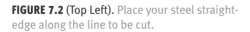

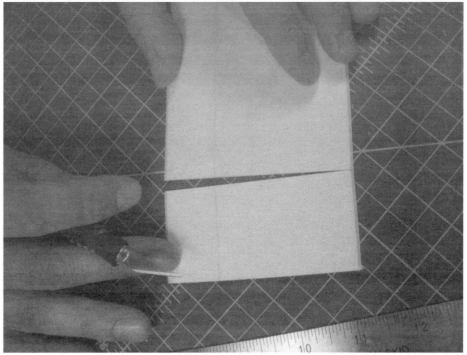

3. Hold the knife so that the angle of the cutting portion of the blade is roughly 45 degrees to the board. To ensure a clean vertical cut, keep the lateral orientation of the blade perpendicular to your cutting surface (see Figure 7.3).
4. Start by doing a single, gentle pass across the board's surface.
5. Repeat this process, making several passes until you have cut through the entire board. Gently pull the two pieces apart. If they do not come apart readily, make a few more passes with your knife until they do (see Figure 7.4).

Note: Make certain the blade stays at roughly a 45-degree angle in the direction you are cutting; this ensures that the maximum amount of new, sharp blade, is cutting through the board. This method offers the least amount of resistance while cutting and ensures the cleanest cuts.

Keep the Ends Clean
Often the ends of the board that you have been cutting tend to be less tidy than the rest of the piece. Before your first pass, use the straightedge to cut a smooth notch at each end. This will keep the ends looking as sharp as the center (see Figure 7.5).

Ninety Degrees Is Key
Make sure you keep your blade at 90 degrees to the board when cutting. Failure to do so will make it extremely difficult to build anything square (see Figure 7.6).

Checking For Square
Failure to use perfect squares where necessary will make it absolutely impossible to create a good model. Always check the pieces you cut out to ensure that they are perfectly square. This can be done by placing your cutout piece between two drafting triangles, or between a drafting triangle and a parallel rule. If your piece is out of square, be certain you trim it before using it in your model, or, if necessary, discard it. Figure 7.7 illustrates this concept as it applies to singular, squared objects, whereas Figures 7.8 and 7.9 illustrate this concept as it applies to walls, cubes, and other three-dimensional squared objects.

Cutting Out Identical Objects
If you want to make several identical objects:

1. Cut out the first shape in its entirety, as neatly and accurately as possible. With some practice, and if care is taken throughout this process, it is possible for this piece to act as both a template and the presentation material.
2. Mark this piece "master." Use this piece—and this piece only—as a template or guide from which to fabricate all your remaining identical parts. The quality and accuracy of your part degrades quickly should you decide to attempt to use

FIGURE 7.5 (Top). Before your first pass, use the straightedge to cut a smooth notch at each end.

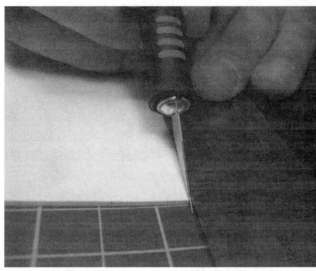

FIGURE 7.6 (Bottom). Make sure you keep your blade at 90 degrees to the board when cutting.

copies of copies as templates. It is entirely possible that you can use this master in your model, so make sure you mark it in an inconspicuous location.

FIGURE 7.7 (Top Left). Checking for square on a single object.

FIGURE 7.8 (Bottom Left). Checking for square, vertically.

FIGURE 7.9 (Bottom Right). Always check the pieces you cut out to ensure that they are perfectly square. This can be done by placing your cutout piece between two drafting triangles.

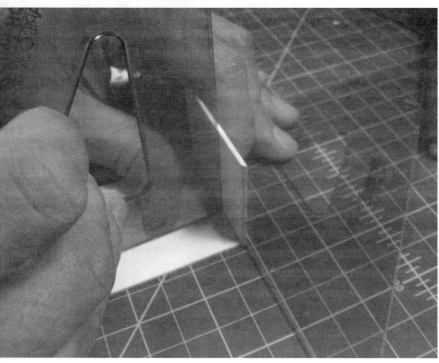

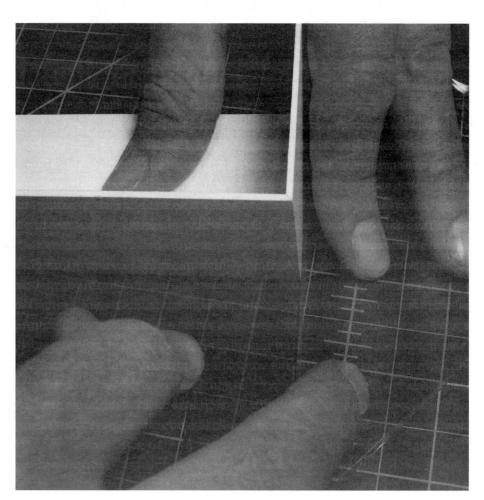

3. Depending on the material, use your knife or sandpaper to ensure that each piece is an identical size.

Creating Openings

Begin by drafting your opening using a sharp 4H pencil, or by using one of the aforementioned transfer methods.

1. Using your craft knife, begin by making one or two strokes along each cutout line.
2. Using the tip of a sharp knife, pierce your board at all four corners (see Figure 7.10). Instead of pulling the knife out immediately, softly draw it toward the center of the cutout line. Make certain you drive the knife through the board as close to perpendicular as possible. Any deviation from a perpendicular angle will affect the quality of your cut as well as your ability to align the cuts. Now, on each side, make a few cuts from the "pin" holes toward the center of your board. Alternate cutting on each side of the board until the cuts meet, and you have cut completely through the board. This technique helps to eliminate overcuts at the corners (see Figure 7.11).
3. Flip the board over; connect the holes using your craft knife. Make several passes. You are now cutting out your intended hole.
4. Alternating sides of the board, continue to make a series of passes with the knife until you have cut completely through the board. Carefully remove the piece using your knife or tweezers (see Figure 7.12).
5. Using your knife for paper-based boards, or a nail file, other small file, or sandpaper on a small, square block for wood, remove any burrs and trim away any excess (see Figure 7.13).
6. Finally, if working with a paper-based board, use a clean burnisher to help disguise any overcuts.

Poor Man's Burnisher

If you do not have a burnisher handy, simply use a scrap of the same material you are cutting. Pull it over the rough edges or overcuts, and many of the tiny burrs will miraculously disappear! (See Figure 7.14.)

Cutting Curves

If the material is thin enough, cut out curves (especially outside curves) with a pair of high-quality scissors. For thicker materials such as museum board and foam board, several manufacturers such as Olfa and FoamWerks have tools specifically for cutting curves. The tool you choose will depend upon the type of material you will be cutting.

If you choose to cut curves freehand, and necessity dictates that you often must do so, use a variation on the technique described earlier. Use a series of passes until you have cut through the surface. The smaller the circle or the tighter the curve, the higher the angle you will need to hold your blade.

1. With thicker material, it is sometimes helpful to puncture your board with pins, and cut from both sides in a manner similar to that mentioned previously.
2. If possible, make a rough cutout of your shape, staying well away from the lines.
3. Cut a series of lines starting at your pattern and radiating toward the rough cuts on the periphery of your pattern.
4. When you are close to your final shape, begin to make a series of passes, cutting along the line and then off.
5. Eventually, your cuts will align in such a manner so as to allow small portions of the roughly cut edges to fall away, thus completing your curves.
6. Sand or gently cut away burrs or rough edges.

Inside versus Outside Curves

You will need a slightly different approach depending on whether you are cutting inside curves (holes) or outside curves (circles). Obviously, you should always aim to be as precise as possible, but outside curves, such as circles, tend to be more forgiving. Whenever you are cutting a curve by hand, the blade has a tendency to want to go straight; therefore, errors tend to occur outside the area you

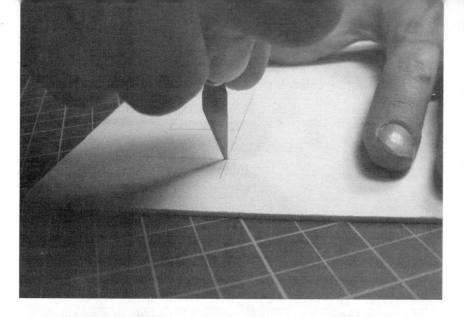

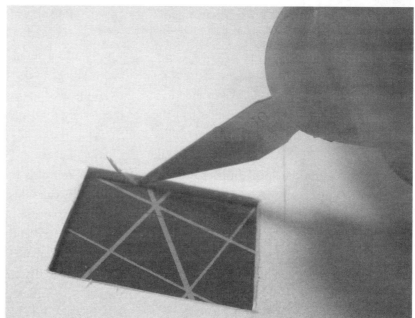

FIGURE 7.10 (Top Left). Using the tip of a sharp knife, pierce your board at all four corners.

FIGURE 7.11 (Top Right). Softly draw the knife blade toward the center of the cutout line.

FIGURE 7.12 (Bottom Left). Carefully remove the piece using your knife or tweezers.

FIGURE 7.13 (Bottom Right). Using your craft knife, carefully remove any burrs from the opening.

FIGURE 7.14 Pull the same type of board over the rough edges or overcuts, and many of the tiny burrs will disappear.

want to keep, and you can "clean up" the edge with some careful trimming or possibly fine sandpaper. Inside corners do not allow that luxury.

WORKING WITH GLUE

When it comes to model making, it is nearly always necessary to connect one board to another. If you are using an adhesive or a material for the first time, test it out before using it on a final model. For 99 percent of all models, you can get by with white or craft glue. In-depth, how-to directions will be discussed in subsequent chapters.

White Glue

Most professional model makers use white glue almost exclusively when working with these materials. I prefer Sobo and Tacky brand white craft glue because I find that they dry at the right speed and deliver a stronger bond than most other craft or white glues on the market. If your glue is too thick, it will dry too fast and will not allow you to reposition your boards, which is often necessary. I had a professor in college who would always say, "the thinner the glue, the stronger the bond." He neglected to mention that the thinner the glue, the longer it takes to dry, too.

When it comes to application, a little dab will do. Run a light bead on one or both sides (depending on the board) and clamp. Too much glue may not dry as quickly nor hold as well as a simple line, or overlapped lines. Excessive amounts of white glue will dry into a thick, brittle, unsightly bead of goop. It will look terrible and not hold.

White glues are useful for joints, and laminating thicker materials together. However, white glues should not be used to apply thin or paper coatings to boards because the lines of glue will warp the paper.

White Glue: A Smooth Application

Often, it is difficult to apply a thin, uniform bead to the edge of a board. In-stead of the smooth bead, it can tend to come out of the tube in globs. An easy way to smooth this out is to place your finger at a 45-degree angle to the edge and then drag it along the edge. The upper portion of the globs will catch on your finger and then be dragged into the next glob. After the two globs meet, they will equalize and settle across the entire surface (see Figures 7.15 and 7.16).

STARTING A SIMPLE STRUCTURE: A FLOOR AND TWO WALLS

In this demonstration, we will be attaching two "walls"—using a foam board base and two pieces of museum board as walls. A white glue will be used for the adhesive.

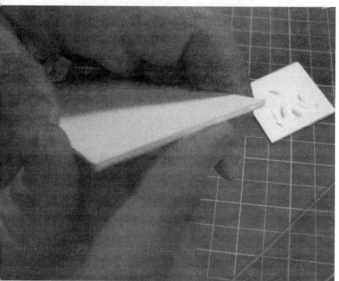

FIGURE 7.15 (Top). Instead of coming out in a smooth bead, glue can tend to come out of the tube in globs.

FIGURE 7.16 (Bottom). To smooth out glue globs, place your finger at a 45-degree angle to the edge and then drag it along the edge.

3. Using the techniques explained earlier, glue the first board (wall) to the rectangular base and check for square (refer to Figure 7.8).

4. Cut out a second piece of museum board, glue it to the *side* of the base, and glue the corners together. Check for square. This will give you two sides (walls) and a base (floor; refer to Figure 7.9). Notice how nicely the beveled edges fit together.

5. If you were starting, say, an interior model, you would then add the third or even the fourth wall.

This is a standard way to begin most architectural models. To make things even easier, start with a thick, solid base, such as foam board or even wood, the *sides* of which you can attach to your walls (see Figure 7.17). The thicker the base, or foundation, the more solid your model will become. When using a thicker, stronger base, it is important that you consider what the thick base will do to your model. If it is an interior model, it will raise the height of the floor, and the height of your walls will need to be increased accordingly. You will also need to consider how that will affect the measurements of any context models you are inserting said model into.

WORKING WITH TAPE

There are numerous adhesive tapes available to the model builder. They can be used as temporary or permanent, structural, or decorative elements of your model.

BONDING BOARD TO BOARD

Pressure and patience are needed here. When working with porous boards, it is best to use a slow-drying adhesive such as white or airplane glue. It is essential that the glue penetrate the surface of the board prior to drying. Failure to do so will create a weak joint. One of the hazards of using the slow-drying cement is it may cause warping of the materials. The only way to know how much adhesive is too much is to practice. Clamp—or rather, place—the entire area of the boards under even pressure as soon as possible. It is always good to have large, clean boards and heavy books on hand for the purpose of evenly distributing pressure across the boards.

Bonding Porous Boards

When working with porous or heavy woods it is best to use a slow-drying adhesive such as white or wood glue. It is essential to permit the glue to penetrate the surface of the board

1. Cut out a perfect square or rectangle.
2. Using museum board, cut out a piece that is exactly the same size as one of your sides; in this case, we chose the shorter side of the rectangle. In this demonstration, we are working with a mitered joint.

prior to drying. Failure to do so will create a weak joint. One of the hazards of using a slow-drying cement is it may cause a warping of the materials. The only way to know how much is too much is to practice. Clamp or otherwise place the boards under even pressure as soon as possible.

Bonding Smooth Boards

If you choose to build something like a contour model using a smoother board—mat board, illustration board, Bainbridge board, or even some types of chipboard—a strong, repositionable, spray adhesive, such as 3M super 77, may be used. This is typically a much faster way to attach board to board.

MOVEABLE OR REMOVABLE PARTS

When it comes to options available for creating models with moveable or removable parts, the sky is the limit, and there are no rules. There are, however, things to think about.

- How will the model be displayed? Will it be assembled or disassembled? Is it possible to view all the sections at once? Who can disassemble it? Is it complicated or simple to take apart and put back together?

FIGURE 7.17 Make your base as thick and strong as possible.

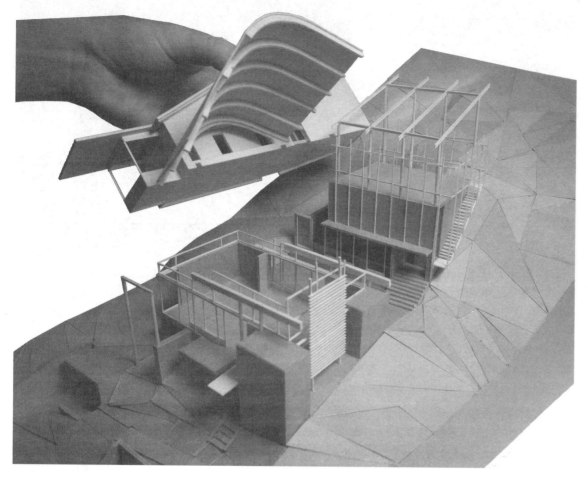

FIGURE 7.18 Models with removable roofs serve many functions. *Model makers and photographers: Josh Brevoort, Lisa Chun, Chad Schneider, and Chad Downard of zero plus architects.*

Notice how the model's focus can completely change depending on its state. Notice also the various methods used to hold it together as well as unify the presentation.

In this chapter, you have been shown the most basic techniques used by model makers. Just like drawing, playing a musical instrument, or learning a new sport, these fundamental skills require practice and repetition in order to master them. Do not be concerned whether you make a perfect cut the first time because very few people do. The more you do it, the easier it will become. The following exercises will aid in the development of these skills.

- If it is displayed disassembled, where will you place the pieces that have been removed?
- If it has removable floors, how will they fit together?
- Are hinges an option?
- Will the parts be interlocking, or will they slide together?

- Will the model require explanations in its various incarnations, or does it stand alone and make sense to the viewer?
- Will it be obvious to the viewer that the model is being displayed in parts?

For a few examples of models with removable parts, see Figures 7.18, 7.19, and 7.20.

KEY TERMS

acetate

cartoon

craft knife

intonaco

Mylar

transfer method

transfer paper

FIGURE 7.19 Basswood model on cork base with wood dowels to represent evergreen trees. Jones Residence, Whidbey Island, Washington. *William Zimmerman Architects.*

FIGURE 7.20 Removable roofs built with wood keys to lock roofs in place when installed. Jones Residence, Whidbey Island, Washington. *William Zimmerman Architects.*

Chapter Review and Practice

(See "Materials Needed by Chapter," p. xix.)

1. *Using a floor plan from a previous project, transfer an 8" × 8" exterior corner portion of it onto a piece of foam board.*

2. *Cut out ten identical strips of museum board that are 6" × 1".*

3. *Cut out ten identical strips of foam board that are 6" × 1".*

4. *Cut out ten identical strips of cardboard that are 6" × 1".*

5. *Cut out a piece of museum board that is 6"* × 12". Create four rectangular openings of various sizes, minimum of 1" × 1" but no larger than 3" × 3".*

6. *Cut out a piece of foam board that is 6" × 12". Create four rectangular openings of various sizes, minimum of 1" × 1" but no larger than 3" × 3".*

7. *Cut out six circles each (six of foam board, six of museum board, and six of cardboard) with a radius of 2".*

8. *Using alternating layers of museum board and foam board, stack vertically and glue together the 6" × 1" strips.*

9. *Using alternating layers of museum board, cardboard, and foam board, stack vertically and glue together the 2" radius circles.*

10. *Using a piece of foam board for the base and four pieces of museum board for the "walls," create a 12" × 12" × 4" open-top box that could theoretically be used as either an interior model or as a starting point for, say, a single-story residential model.*

11. *Cut out the portion of the foam board plan you made in #1 of this chapter. Now, transfer and cut out the two exterior walls, and attach them to the foam board base.*

Bases and Presentation

8

OBJECTIVES

- *Plan for a good match between the model and its base*
- *Ask the right questions to determine which kind of base suits your model's purpose*
- *Learn construction techniques for a variety of bases*

All too often students and professionals alike, in a creative zeal, begin their model without regard to where it will rest or how it will be presented. Before beginning a model, ask: How will it fit in with the other presentation materials? Will it be complementary to the design drawings, or will it stand alone? More often than not, a poor presentation is the result of poor planning as opposed to poor technique. In addition to techniques and materials, this chapter will discuss integrated issues such as topography, the model's context, and its surrounding built environment.

WORKING WITH BASE MATERIALS

When thinking about the base for your model during the early phases of the project, do not skimp in terms of time or materials. A presentation-quality base can be used throughout the design development process. If made well and constructed on wheels or casters, a single base or pedestal can be used and re-used for several models and purposes.

Regardless of whether a base will feature contours or not, most professionals prefer to construct a foundation board of a solid, rigid material such as MDF, melamine board, or, occasionally, 1/4-inch or thicker acrylic. Acrylic bases are especially useful should you want to illuminate your model from below. Bases for study models or smaller models (11" × 17" or smaller) made from lightweight, paper-based materials can be constructed from 1/4-inch or thicker foam core. Be aware—the larger the foam core base, the greater the chance it will warp or deform over time. It is absolutely impossible to construct a quality model on a warped base.

Just like the graphic layout of working drawings, consider how and where you will be placing information such as the model's scale, the north arrow, the title block, and the legend. Placing this information on the underside of a model is generally not an option.

BASES FOR CONTOUR MODELS

Although there are certainly endless methods available to create contoured bases, most projects will use one of the following two methods.

Isolated Structure on a Flat Base

This is common when designing interior models or isolated presentation models (see Figure 8.1). This is obviously the simplest technique because nothing really needs to be done apart from mounting the model on the already sturdy base. This can usually be done using white glue or spray adhesive.

To better integrate your model with the flat base, consider adhering a material such as mat board, chipboard, or foam core to the rigid surface. The massing models are placed on a flat contour plan, their bottoms are numbered, and corresponding numbers are placed on the plan. Consider laminating three or four sheets of foam board and then covering the entire base with a different board.

Laminating a plan of your landscape—or perhaps an aerial photo from Google Earth—to a flat board is an extremely simple way to display your model in its intended context. Allowing your client to see photographs of the existing context will aid them greatly in the visualization process.

Raised Contour Model

A **raised contour model** is an extremely common and relatively simple way of describing the landscape on which your structure sits. Commonly used materials include cardboard,

FIGURE 8.1 Isolated basswood model on a cork base. *Architect/model maker: William Zimmerman.*

cork, foam core, wood, **stereo lithography apparatus (SLA),** or **computer numeric control (CNC)** milled foam. If built well and accompanied with the appropriate amount of entourage (trees, cars, and other scale imparting elements), this is an acceptable method that can be used in conjunction with final presentation models (see Figures 8.2, 8.3, and 8.4).

The material we will be working with in this segment is mat board. Should you choose to use a different material, the techniques and progression will be the same. Be sure to understand the nuances and properties of whatever material you are working with prior to starting this project. The construction of contours uses a lot of materials and can be ex-

FIGURE 8.2 (Top Left). The contours are built with $1/8$" foam core, which represents 1-foot topographical increments. Sides are basswood cut to match the profile of the steep contours. *Architect/model maker: William Zimmerman.*

FIGURE 8.3 (Top Right). Cork is used for the contours; Barge Cement is painted on the cork to represent a river. *Architect/model maker: William Zimmerman.*

FIGURE 8.4 (Bottom Right). There are always creative ways to deal with material that is smaller than you would like. *Sullivan Conard Architects PLLC.*

FIGURE 8.5 Contours were transferred from map and then cut out.

FIGURE 8.6 Number the cutouts on the back. Number the original contour map as well.

tremely time consuming. It is not a step you will want to do twice.

The following techniques pertain only to **contour models** made by hand, and not those manufactured using CNC, SLA, or similar processes.

HOW TO CONSTRUCT RAISED CONTOUR (TOPOGRAPHIC) MODELS

The quickest and easiest way to create **contour models,** or **topographic models,** is to laminate three individual contour plans to three separate boards. Then, cut every third contour line, number them, and stack them together along the corresponding lines.

1. It is essential that you begin with a topographic plan of your site at the scale at which you will be working. I would suggest at least two, if not three, copies of the map. One to cut up, one for reference, and a third for emergencies.

2. Make sure that the thickness of your material corresponds to an appropriate drop in elevation. For example, a 1/8-inch sheet of cardboard can be used to represent an elevation change of 1 foot at 1/8" = 1'-0"

scale, or a change of 2 feet at 1/16-inch scale, four feet at 1/32-inch scale, and so forth.

3. Begin to transfer the topographic lines to your base and boards. (See Chapter 7 for instructions on transferring plans to your building materials.) Each board should have two lines on it—one line is to be cut, the second is a registration line and should be drawn very lightly because it will be used to perfectly align your next layer. Hint: Number your layers in an area that will not be seen after the model is completed. This will be extremely

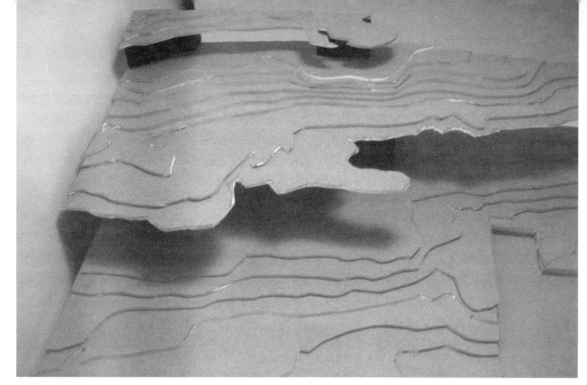

FIGURE 8.7 Sections are laminated together before the entire contour model is assembled.

PLACING A BUILDING IN A CONTOUR MODEL

Cut your contours in the shape of your building such that it will be allowed to rest upon a solid piece of board at the lowest level that meets the model's foundation. If you are not sure as to where or at what elevation your model will be sitting, pin the upper layers of contours together, as opposed to gluing them, so that later you can easily cut out the building's shape without damaging your contour model.

After you are certain as to the placement of your model, it may be used as a template for the areas to be removed. Be sure to check the fit of the model after every cut, and before the layers are permanently laminated together (see Figures 8.8 and 8.9).

helpful during the lamination process (see Figures 8.5 and 8.6).

4. Using the proper adhesive, simply stack your contours in numeric order, one upon the other. Pins are useful for keeping the layers in place while your adhesive dries. If your pins are too long, using your wire cutters, simply cut them before placing them in the model. It is possible to laminate two or three areas of the contour model in separate sections and then assemble them into one cohesive whole after the individual sections dry (see Figure 8.7).

Railroad Contour Model

When executing extremely realistic (and expensive) presentation models for real estate developers or museums, professional model makers will often make what is referred to as a **railroad contour model.** As the name implies, these are often used in the construction of model railroads and their surrounding landscapes. Although the skills required for the construction of this type of contour model lies beyond the scope of this text, and a student model maker completing coursework would not have time to construct such a model, it is important to introduce the terminology.

Inserting Forms into an Existing Contour Model

In the following example, several individuals were charged with constructing a contour massing model. One individual cut out and numbered the contours, a second created the massing models, and a third assembled the parts.

1. The massing models are placed on a flat contour plan, their bottoms are numbered, and corresponding numbers are placed on the plan (see Figure 8.10).
2. Find the lowest contour levels where a form can sit. Using the transfer method,

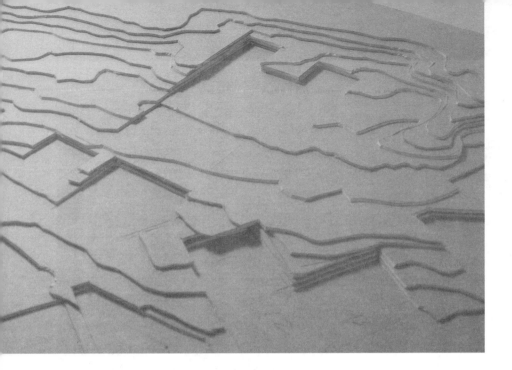

FIGURE 8.8 (Top Left). Be sure to dry fit the model after every cut.

FIGURE 8.9 (Bottom Left). Massing models are dry fit into the contour model.

FIGURE 8.10 (Top Right). Place the models on your plan. Number the plan and the massing models.

mark and number the building's location using a pencil and pin holes (see Figures 8.11 and 8.12).

3. Begin to lay upper layers on the level where your form will rest. Use the form as a template from which to trace outlines on the upper layer (see Figures 8.13 and 8.14). Use pins to poke through and register the corners of the lower layers. It is absolutely essential that everything line up.

4. If you are certain everything is lining up, begin to cut the lower contours out. *Do not cut the level upon which your form will rest!* (See Figure 8.15.)

5. Before gluing or otherwise attaching anything, lay out the contours, and **dry fit**

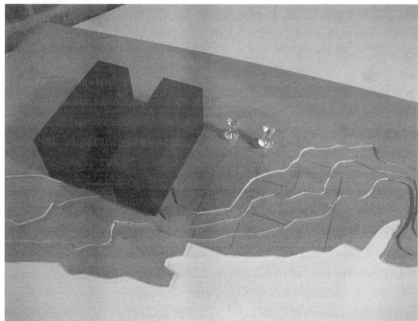

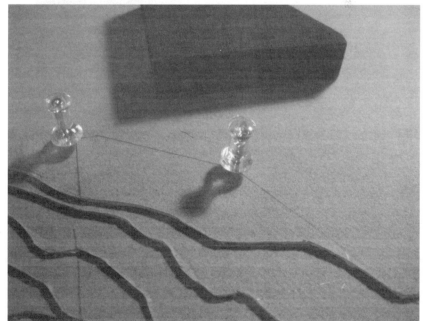

FIGURE 8.11 (Top Left). Find the lowest contour where the form will sit; mark and number.

FIGURE 8.12 (Top Right). Mark the lowest levels and the locations using a pencil and pin holes.

FIGURE 8.13 (Bottom Left). Begin to lay upper layers on the level where your form will rest. Use the form as a template from which to trace outlines on the upper layer.

FIGURE 8.14 (Bottom Right). Use pins to line up each level.

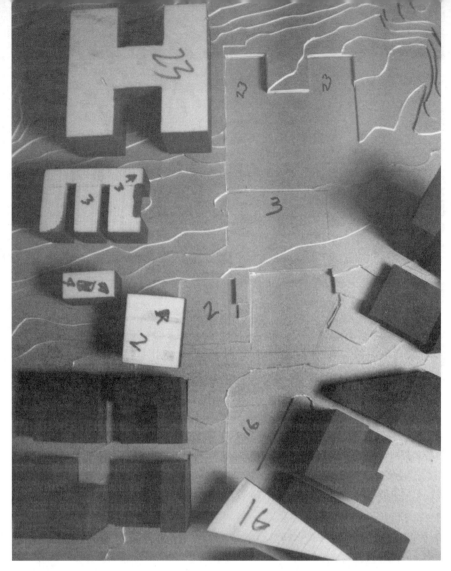

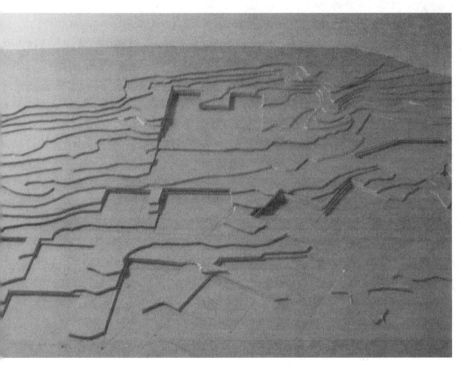

FIGURE 8.15 (Top Left). If you are certain everything is lining up, begin to cut out the lower contours.

FIGURE 8.16 (Top Right). Numbering everything assists in the dry fitting process.

FIGURE 8.17 (Bottom Left). A contour model awaits the insertion of the massing models.

(preassemble and check the fit of the pieces prior to gluing in place) your forms into the model. Notice how numbering everything assists in the dry fitting process (see Figure 8.16). The black forms are already resting in place, whereas the white forms with the numbers written on them are resting, upside down, adjacent to where they will eventually be placed.

6. Figure 8.17 shows a contour model awaiting the accompanying massing models. The finished model can be seen later in this book.

To Save Money, Hollow Out Your Contour Models

As a rule, you will need a single board for every contour or elevation grade. It is possible to save on materials and create a contour model that is more or less hollow, but this can be more trouble than it is worth. Hollow contour models also have a tendency to bow or distort if any significant weight is placed upon them. The lamination of solid sheets, although more expensive, is not only more structurally sound, but also easier to fabricate. Nevertheless, you will inevitably face a situation where timing, finances, or material shortages will force you to create a hollow model. When you do, make sure you have a minimum of a 1- or 2-inch overlap or space for the next layer up to rest on. If you notice the layers beginning to dip or sag, as-

semble some supportive "columns" *from the same materials* as your contour model if you choose to stack your columns, or from a material that has a high compression strength. You can then support or rest any distorting areas on your columns (see Figure 8.18).

Use Google Earth

To leave no doubt in the viewer's mind as to the actual location of the site, you can laminate correct scale printouts from Google Earth directly onto your contours.

FIGURE 8.18 Notice how the building's foundation to the right sits flat upon the sturdy wooden base, and the contour is built up around it.

FIGURE 8.19 A faceted plane site model. *Model maker: Jason Hanner, Weber Thompson Architects.*

FACETED SITE MODELS

An interesting and not often seen approach to the site model is known as a **faceted site model.** Instead of reproducing the contours level by level, separate triangles, or facets, are assembled together to form an undulating site. The hard edges of the facets make for an interesting transition between the amorphous contour of the site and the geometric model that sits upon it.

> The faceted planes site models are relatively simple in concept, but can be really tricky to pull off cleanly. They are basically a matter of triangulation. If you have a set of surveyed points, you can set the height on internal posts or walls. I never had a good way to measure the required angle for each piece, so it was always a process of eyeball, test fit, trim, and test fit again until I got it right. Because of the thickness of the material, things don't always want to go together just right so sometimes you have to end up beveling the edge to get a tight seam (Jason Hanner of Weber Thompson Architects and owner of Box Shop, personal communication August 8, 2008). (See Figure 8.19 and review Figure 7.18.)

BASES

A model's base, just like the foundation of the building it represents, must be strong, solid, and level. Regardless of the size, shape, material, color, or intent of your base, it is, in its most distilled form, the foundation of your model. Like all foundations, build it first, and build it right. Failure to do so will always result in a poorly made model.

The Pedestal Base

Constantine Brancusi was a Romanian sculptor who worked with the concept of integration of his bases and sculptures. In many instances, it is impossible to tell the difference between the two (see Figure 8.20). Consider how the physical properties of your pedestal—its depth, breadth, height, materials, and colors—relate to the form of your model. If you want to emphasize the vertical nature of a skyscraper model, consider placing it upon a tall, thin pedestal. If, instead, you want to highlight the project's integration with the surrounding environment, consider a lower, wider pedestal. A model placed upon a tall pedestal can have the effect of overwhelming or even dominating the viewer, whereas a model placed on a lower base gives the viewer a bird's-eye view and allows them to easily and comfortably survey the model in its entirety.

Be careful when constructing a base or pedestal of wood. The graining pattern can create a scale of its own, which in turn may

FIGURE 8.20 Constantine Brancusi was the first to blur the line between the base and the object on it.

affect the perceived scale of your model. It is essential that your base or pedestal be able to fit through any doors that may lie between your shop and your model's final resting place. This includes car doors.

Think about two- or three-part hinged bases that can open to show the interior as well as the exterior of a model. Although this requires quite a bit of forethought, it can eliminate the problem of placement or storage of extra parts associated with models that have removable roofs or walls. (See Figures 8.21a, b, c, and d, and review Figures 3.8, 3.9, and 3.10.)

The Sides of Your Bases

Pay close attention to the sides of your bases. Notice the beautiful wood used in the example shown in Figure 8.22. The immaculate craftsmanship says something about the designer.

FIGURE 8.21 Two- or three-part hinged bases can open to show the interior as well as the exterior of a model.

ARCHITECTURAL MODEL BUILDING

color plate **1**

Study models for Zimmer Gunsul Frasca Architects LLP.
Photograph: Carrie Kapp.

A basswood model of the South Ute Museum and Cultural
Center in Ignacio, Colorado.
Model: Lois Gaylord.
Architects: Jones and Jones Architects and Landscape Architects, LTD.
Photograph: Carrie Kapp.

color plate **2**

color plate **3**

This model of Chiswick House by Richard Armiger of Network Modelmakers. Collection of the Victoria and Albert Museum, London.
Photograph: Andrew Putler Photography (www.andrewputler.com).

color plate **4**

Juxtaposing different grains and thicknesses of wood creates a myriad of effects.
Architect: Sullivan Conard.

Mixed media model of Giants Stadium.
Model/photograph: Alec Vassiliadis, Sound Models, Inc.
(www.soundmodels.com).
Architect: Hellmuth, Obata and Kassabaum (www.hok.com).

color plate **5**

color plate **7**

Federal Courthouse Model.
Model: Alec Vassiliadis, Sound Models, Inc.
Photograph: Steve Keating, Architect, NBBJ.

color plate **6** Basswood, cork, and dowel model.
Model: William Zimmerman, Architect.

Model of Canary Wharf, London, by Richard Armiger of
Network Modelmakers, London.
Photograph: Andrew Putler Photography (www.andrewputler.com).

St. Bride's Church, London. Architectural sculptor Timothy
Richards creates exact replicas of historic models and casts
limited editions in plaster.
Model: Timothy Richards (www.timothyrichards.com).

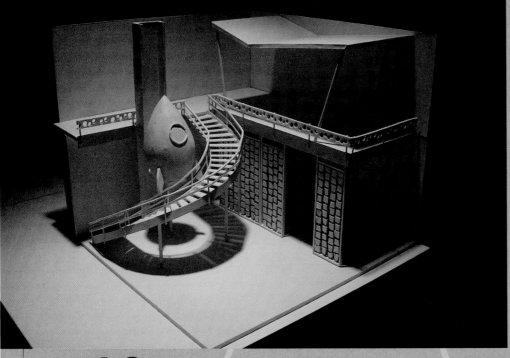

color plate **12**

(opposite page) Basswood model on a gypsum base.
Model: Stuart Silk Architects.
Photograph: Carrie Kapp.

color plate **10**

Student model by Breanna Wucinich.

color plate **11**

Acetate gives the appearance of glass and transparent
space. Thicker, rougher materials and entourage contrast
with the acetate to effectively ground this study model.
Model: Sophie Hong and Aaron Swain of Tiscareno Associates.

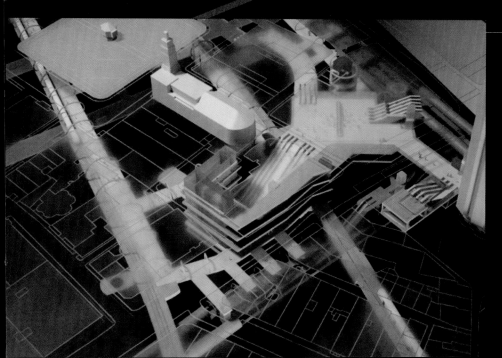

color plate 13

Interior model of the Federal Courthouse Courtroom (Seattle).

Model/photograph: Alec Vassiliadis, Sound Models, Inc.
Architect: NBBJ.

color plate 14

Early proposal for new Crossrail and London
Underground stations at Tottenham Court Road.

Model: Richard Armiger, Network Modelmakers, London.
Photograph: Andrew Putler Photography (www.andrewputler.com).

(opposite page) Layered acrylic and different colored acetate on this transparent model helped the client and hospital staff visualize vertical and horizontal program connections and circulation.
Model: Zimmer Gunsul Frasca Architects LLP.

color plate **15**

Photo from the Seattle Architecture Foundation's 2009 exhibit, "Representations." In the foreground is a conceptual model, a composition of Process Models, by Zimmer Gunsul Frasca Architects LLP. In the background is a 1:1 model for a portion of a caryatid, by the author.

color plate **17**

Interior model of the Fred Hutchinson
Research Center.
Model: Scott Jennings for Zimmer Gunsul Frasca Architects LLP.

color plate **19**

This model of the Frye Art Museum by Olsen Sundberg illustrates the effects and paths of daylight on an interior space.

color plate **18**

The entourage in this model serves to emphasize the public nature of its space.
Model: Scott Jennings.

This model for the Seattle International Film Festival was created using internal lighting, acrylic, and museum board. Cast plaster was used for the base.

Design/photograph: Owen Richards Architects.

Alternatively, study Figure 8.23. The lack of care and craftsmanship says something very different, does it not?

Although it is not practical for students to fabricate a beautiful hardwood base, it is possible for them to pay attention to the sides and corners of their models (see Figures 8.24 and 8.25).

DISPLAY CASES

If your model is to be displayed either publicly or for an extended period of time, and especially if it is made from fragile materials such as mat board or foam board, consider an acrylic display case. Displaying your model in a vitrine (a glass showcase) not only adds to the professional appearance of the model, but also serves to protect the pristine surface you worked so hard to create. I know some architects who use them specifically to keep their clients' children from touching the delicate models that decorate their offices. If at all possible, consider the lighting in the room in which your model and case will be displayed. Excessive reflection can be distracting and make it difficult to see the model in its entirety. Display cases are not recommended for process or study models. If the model is the subject of a meeting or discussion, you should be able to touch it, cut it, and add to it.

WALL-MOUNTED MODELS

Before creating a wall-mounted model, make sure you know what type of wall or surface it will hang on. Models mounted on permanent walls can be heavier than those mounted on temporary partitions.

Landscape and topographical models lend themselves particularly well to wall-mounted presentations. Smaller, interior models of, say, one story can be particularly effective when graphically unified with other wall-mounted presentations such as floor plans and materials boards. Figures 8.26 and 8.27 show a wall-mounted cork model of the excavations in Pompeii, on display in the Archaeological Museum in Naples, Italy. Despite the small scale, the enormous scope of the actual site necessitates a wall-mounted model so that the entire site can be viewed. Contained in the same room is a model of the same site, made nearly 100 years ago. This pedestal-mounted model is an excellent tool for visualizing smaller areas as they relate to the whole because its horizontal alignment more closely mirrors that of our own as we would travel through those existent spaces. By comparison, the wall-mounted model is much more effective at illustrating the overall scope and

FIGURE 8.22 (Top). The immaculate craftsmanship says something positive about the designer. Buck/ Pelton Residence, Seattle, Washington. *Architect/ model maker: William Zimmerman.*

FIGURE 8.23 (Bottom). This type of craftsmanship is fine for a study model, but think twice before submitting something like this to a competition.

scale of the excavation. This is a case where two nearly identical models, presented together yet in different ways, create a wonderful synergy and very clearly communicate the ideas of space in a way that a model and a set of plans could not.

MIRRORS

Mirrors placed at an angle—above, below, or adjacent to your model—will allow the viewer to look at certain parts of the model without drastically changing his or her own viewpoint. In the basement of Antonio Gaudí's Sagrada Famiglia in Barcelona, Spain, is a plaster model of the nave of church, currently under construction. The fragile nature of the plaster 1:10 scale model makes it impossible to actually walk through. A slightly angled mirror placed below the model makes it easy for the viewer to simultaneously view the form of the nave and the vaulting above.

When placed behind a model, in a diorama setting (also at a slight downward tilt), a mirror can give the impression of a larger space, a sky, and a horizon.

LAZY SUSAN

Putting a **lazy Susan** on the sturdy base of a smaller model will allow you to easily rotate the base during discussions. This will give your client easy access to the different areas of the model without having to move around the table. Enabling clients to interact with or turn the model is really quite empowering to them.

FIGURE 8.24 Always start at the bottom and work your way up—a well-built base is the foundation of a well-built model. No pun intended. *William Zimmerman Architects.*

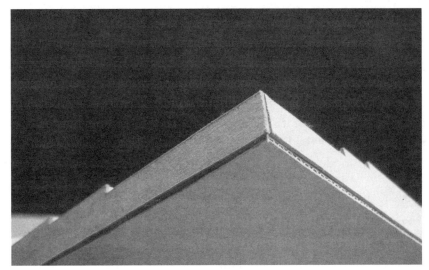

FIGURE 8.25 Well-crafted base for a study model by William Zimmerman Architects.

FIGURE 8.26 (Left). One of two enormous models of Pompeii in the Archaeological Museum in Naples, Italy.

FIGURE 8.27 (Right). The enormous size of these two models necessitates two presentation strategies—one is mounted to the wall; the other sits on a table, below eye level.

KEY TERMS

computer numeric control (CNC)
contour model
dry fit
faceted site model
lazy Susan
railroad contour model
raised contour model
stereo lithography apparatus (SLA)
topographic model

Chapter Review and Practice

(See "Materials Needed by Chapter," pp. xix–xx.)

1. *Create a 12-inch square base by laminating three identical pieces of foam board together. Sheathe the sides using museum board. Make sure this base is strong and level.*

2. *Using illustration board, cut out a 3" × 3" square, a circle with a 2-inch diameter, and a triangle with one side of at least 2 inches. Save these because they will be used as a template for this project and the next. Use a compass to create the circle, not a circle template.*

3. *Create a 10" × 10" contour map with ten different levels:*

   A. *Include footprints for a 3" × 3" square object, a triangular object with one side of at least 2 inches and a 2-inch diameter cylindrical object. The square object must rest on the third level, the triangular object must rest on the sixth level, and the cylinder must rest on the ninth level. (Hint: Mark the center point of each circle, and use the compass to draw each circle, as opposed to transferring them.)*

   B. *Using the transfer method discussed in Chapter 4, transfer your topographic design to ten sheets of 10" × 10" cardboard. Be certain that you include the footprints of each of the geometric objects mentioned in step 3A on each contour level. Remember to number each piece on the back.*

   C. *Using your craft knife, cut out each contour. Save the footprint cutouts of the geometric objects because you will be using them as templates for the end-of-chapter projects in Chapter 9 (Project 1).*

   D. *Dry fit the contour model together; do not glue or otherwise laminate until you have finished the exercises at the end of Chapter 9.*

   E. *After you have finished creating the three geometric objects (cube, cylinder, and triangle), dry fit the layers together, and insert the geometric objects into place.*

   F. *Once you are satisfied with the fit, assemble the entire composition.*

Paper-Based Models

9

OBJECTIVES

- *Acquire basic model making skills and apply them using paper-based materials*
- *Learn the benefits and limitations of these materials*
- *Work on building walls and windows*
- *Learn how to add realism to your model*
- *Make a cylinder*

For the student of architecture and its related fields, the tools, techniques, and materials discussed in this chapter should serve to meet very nearly every need you will have. These are the cheapest, most versatile, and easiest materials that any model maker can choose to work with. Landscape architecture students, of course, will need to focus a bit more on entourage, whereas students of interior design will be required to fabricate furnishings and focus not only on the communication of spaces, but also on the effects of various non-structural materials.

The student can build nearly anything using just a craft knife, a straightedge, glue, and some type of brace or clamping system. As discussed in the previous chapter, contour models also rely heavily upon the use of these materials. In this chapter we will also be discussing the concepts behind the construction of floors, walls, partitions, stairs, windows, and various other openings. Finally, we will introduce you to the creation of curves.

PAPER-BASED BOARD PRODUCTS

The following list offers a brief description of board products typically used for model making. In this chapter, paper-based board products will henceforth be referred to as boards.

Foam Board

Although foam board does fall under the general guise of a paper-based model, its unique qualities and frequent use as a model making medium necessitate an entire chapter on its use. Foam board dulls any type of blade extremely quickly, and looks terrible if it is cut using a dull blade; have plenty of extra blades at hand when working with foam board.

Bristol Board

Bristol board is a lightweight board, about 1/10 of an inch thick, or more. The thickness and its description are dependent upon the amount of layers, or plys, of paper it contains. Although usually used for illustration, it differs from illustration board in that both sides of it are suitable for drawing. It is available with both **hot-pressed** and **cold-pressed** surfaces.

Hot- and Cold-Pressed Boards

Hot- and cold-pressing refers to the processes by which the different types of illustration boards are manufactured. As far as model making is concerned, we will focus on the surface characteristics of each type. Hot-pressed boards have a smoother surface, whereas cold-pressed boards have a rougher surface. Depending on the scale, I often utilize the rough surface of a cold-pressed board to represent interior plaster walls (1/4" = 1'-0") or stucco or concrete masonry unit exterior walls (1/8" = 1'-0").

Cardstock

Cardstock is thinner and more pliable than cardboard, yet several times thicker and stronger than typical drawing or writing paper. Also called pasteboard, paperboard, or cover stock, it is often used for items such as business cards, playing cards, postcards, and invitations. The thin yet durable nature of cardstock makes it ideal for model building. It is particularly useful in study models and for creating or sheathing complex or curved surfaces.

Chipboard

Chipboard is a recycled, matte surfaced type of paperboard. It is grayish in color, and is typically used in study, contour, or massing models. It is utilized in many types of models because its unique color and range of available thicknesses (1/32"–1/8") make it useful for differentiating materials when juxtaposed with other board types. When cutting, try to use a utility knife or other heavy-duty knife for straight cuts, or a professional-quality mat cutter for mitered corners and edges. Chipboard readily accepts pencil, ink, and marker. Use a test strip to see how readily it reacts with different types of paints.

Corrugated Cardboard

Corrugated cardboard is an inexpensive, often free, all-purpose model making material. It is especially useful for study or conceptual models. When cut and fabricated well, it is a completely acceptable choice for contours when used in presentation models. More expensive, archival cardboard is also available.

Gatorfoam

Similar in construction to foam board, **Gatorfoam** is stronger and available in a variety of thicknesses, colors, and sizes up to 5' × 10'. Gatorfoam is an excellent choice for a lightweight base material. Gatorfoam is available from Alcan Composites.

Illustration Board

Illustration board is typically available in sizes of 16 × 20 inches, or 18 × 24 inches. Because of the pristine hot- or cold-pressed, white surface, many professional model makers enjoy using illustration board for their models. Bear in mind, although the front is white, the back is usually a greenish color, so it is not the ideal choice of materials if you want to see both sides. Furthermore, the joints should also be disguised because the core of the board is typically a darker gray. Finally, it has a much harder surface than mat or museum board, and is therefore more difficult to cut. When cutting, try to use a utility or other heavy-duty knife for straight cuts, or a professional-quality mat cutter for mitered corners and edges. Illustration board readily accepts pencil, ink, and marker. Use a test strip to see how readily it will accept certain types of paints.

Mat Board

Mat board is typically used for custom picture framing. Typically, it has a colored face, a white core, and a white back. It is slightly less than 1/16" thick; thus it is easier to cut than illustration board. Either craft or utility knives are acceptable tools to use for cutting.

Museum Board

Museum board is an archival version of mat board. Typically the core of archival mat board will be a bright white, as opposed to the slightly yellowed core found in nonarchival mat board. A color integrated type of museum board is available in some solid colors, although white and black are the most common. Museum board is an excellent choice for presentation models. Because the core and surfaces are the same color, a simple butt joint will still have a professional appearance without the extra hassle of a **mitered** corner or **rabbet edge.**

Textured Museum Board

It is possible to find a wide variety of museum board with pebbled textures that emulate stone, stucco, or brick. It is also possible to find it faced with textiles, such as faux velvet or canvas. Oftentimes these boards will suffice, but they can also act as a base color or texture for later applications of color.

Poster Paper

Poster paper is similar in appearance and performance to cardstock. It typically comes in sizes of 18" × 24", or 24" × 30". In addition to art stores, it can usually be found most large chain drugstores.

Strathmore Board

Strathmore is a brand name for a type of museum board. It is excellent for making models, can be cut easily with a craft knife, and has a core color that is identical to its

face. It is available in either black or white, and ranges in sizes from 1/32" to 1/8" thick, and sizes of 22" × 30" and 30" × 40". It is available with a hot- or cold-pressed surface. This is another fine choice for presentation models.

Strawboard

Strawboard is a rough, yellow-brown board made from straw pulp. Strawboard has very little strength, but can be stiffened when its surface is made more rigid via the application of a semi-stiff veneer such as cardstock. This is generally the case when it is used in book binding. It does not react well (swells up) with moisture or glues, nor can it be folded, bent, or easily cut with a craft knife.

Strawboard is more compressed than it is laminated; therefore, it is less likely to split over time. The archival nature of strawboard is its strength. It is most useful as an archival, structural material, and should generally not be exposed.

Material Selection

Keep a variety of scales in your backpack or glove compartment. One should always have a scale handy when selecting materials for any given project. Purchase materials only after you are certain of its exact dimension. Bear in mind that laminating paper-based boards with materials such as

fabric, wallpaper, or even cardstock will significantly alter the thickness of your materials. The thickness of the walls on the model should be equivalent in scale to the thickness of the walls of the proposed building or object.

WORKING WITH PAPER-BASED BOARDS

Every material the model maker works with has slightly different properties, thus requiring slightly different approaches in cutting, bending, gluing, etc. The following segments should serve as an introduction to, and help to eliminate some common problems associated with, working with paper-based products.

Cutting Out Identical Objects

Although not always practical, or even possible, try clamping several thinner boards one on top of the other and cutting through them simultaneously. This should ensure that they are all cut to identical size.

If you do not have the steadiest of hands, this method may not be practical. Alternatively, you could cut out the first shape in its entirety, as neatly and accurately as possible, and mark this piece as "master." Use this piece and this piece only as a template or guide from which to fabricate all of your remaining identical parts. The quality and accuracy of your part degrades quickly, should you decide to attempt to use copies of copies as templates (see Figure 9.1).

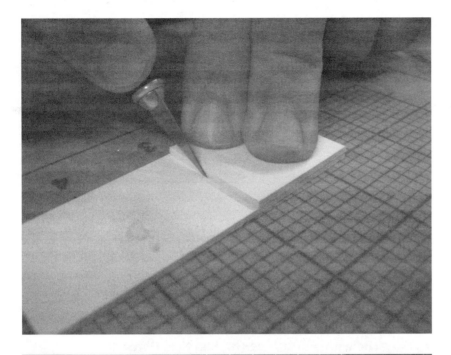

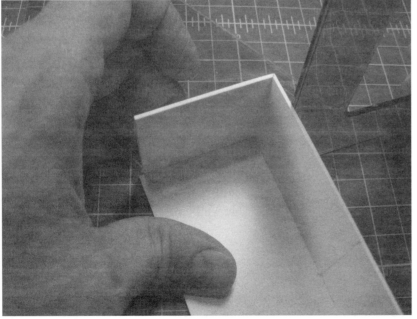

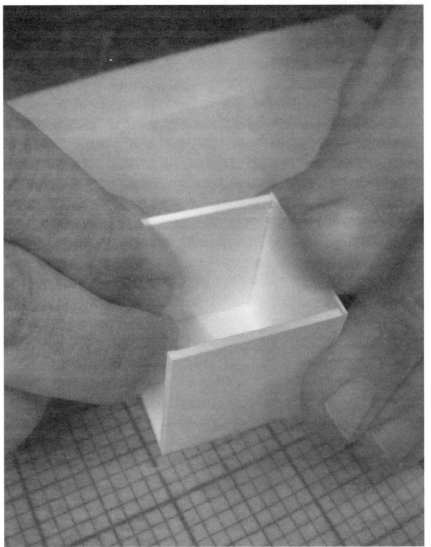

FIGURE 9.1 (Top Left). Cutting identical pieces with a steady hand; you can use your original as a template.

FIGURE 9.2 (Bottom Left). A museum board miter joint is the most attractive, but also the most difficult joint to make.

FIGURE 9.3 (Top Right). Butt joints are used in this cube in process.

Corner Joints

Cutting and assembling corner joints are among the most fundamental and essential skills to have when working with cardboard or mat board models. The two most common types of joints available to you are miter joints and butt joints (see Figures 9.2 and 9.3).

Miter joints are created when each corner is cut a mitered angle, usually 45 degrees, and attached together to create a crisp, clean edge. Miter joints are usually found at 90-degree corners where they disguise the core, and give a professional appearance.

Butt joints are used when joining two surfaces together to form a 90-degree angle. Common uses include attaching walls to floors, or attaching an interior wall to a perpendicular wall, the length of which may or may not extend past the edge of the wall being attached to it.

When using mat board, museum board, illustration board, and the like, outside corners can use a miter joint, but this is generally more trouble than it is worth. A butt joint is generally acceptable even on presentation models, provided the core of the board is the same color as the face.

Flap Joints

A **flap joint** is a quick and simple way of manufacturing a corner. They are especially useful when making study models. A flap joint is exactly what it sounds like. Simply

FIGURE 9.4 (Top). Flap joints are quick to execute and work well for study models.

FIGURE 9.5 (Bottom). Simply slice the outside of the outside corner, bend, and adhere to the floor surface.

score your material and then bend it away from your score mark. This will leave a beautiful inside corner, but an outside corner that is not flush.

When using thinner materials such as paper or cardstock, use a spray mounted or lightly glued flap joint. On presentation models, well hidden tape can be used in conjunction with this type of joint. For example, double-sided tape can be used to attach colored museum board to interior walls, giving a perfect color finish as well as perfect corners (see Figures 9.4 and 9.5). Finally, flap joints are quite handy for pitched roofs.

Measuring Mitered Edge Cuts

Bear in mind, due to the 45-degree angle cuts on the ends, each face of a mitered board will be of a different length, so make sure you take that into account when measuring and cutting your boards.

Timing Is Everything

It is better to cut out the pieces you need and then assemble them as soon afterward as you can. **Thermal expansion** can noticeably change the shape and size (due to the relative temperature of the room) of your materials in as little as 24 hours. It is not uncommon to cut something perfectly one day, only to return the next and be completely befuddled as to why it no longer fits.

Color Counts

Museum board is available in both white and off white. Off-white boards tend to photograph better. They are also easier to keep clean. Most pristine white models do not remain so for long. Dust and even a little grime are much less noticeable on an off-white model. Make sure the core and face are the same color if you are building a presentation model.

CUTTING OUT THE FLOOR PLAN, ATTACHING WALLS

Cutting out the floor plan and attaching walls are the first steps in creating any type of hollow architectural or interior model. An overview of the process was described in the previous chapter. Read the instructions carefully to avoid some common mistakes.

First, transfer your plan to your board surface—you can either draw it on your board, or use one of the methods described earlier. Cut out the floor plan *minus* the width of the material you will be using for the walls. The floor plan can be used as a base upon which you can glue your walls. The walls may need bracing, either during or after the application process. If you choose (and you should) to allow the floor to act as a brace to which you attach the walls laterally, it is a slightly stronger structure, and is a bit easier to keep it square while the glue dries (see Figure 9.6). Remember, when cutting out the walls, measure their length against

FIGURE 9.6 (Top). The basic method of attaching walls to floors. Attach the vertical walls to the side of the thicker foundation for a stronger model.

FIGURE 9.7 (Bottom). Vertical wall brace: Place a single piece of board perpendicular to both the surface of the wall and the surface of the floor.

your model; do not just cut out the size you think they should be—you will most likely be wrong. These techniques will also be used in building a cube later in this chapter.

Internal Bracing and Bracing Walls

Any time you choose to create a model with internal volumes, it will inevitably require some form of bracing to avoid warping. If the interior of the model will not be seen, it is quite easy to brace your walls with some type of internal framework. When building interior models, bracing can be hidden below the floor, disguised inside areas such as closets, and can be accomplished with interior walls. Although foam board construction will be discussed in depth in the next chapter, it is important to know that, due to its rigidity and width, foam board is an excellent mate-

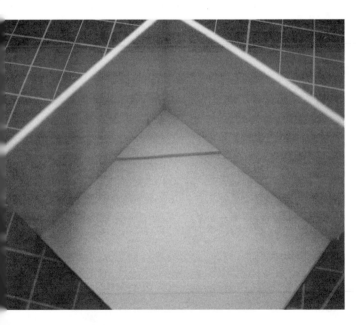

rial to use for internal bracing. A myriad of bracing options are available.

Vertical Wall Brace

Place a piece of board perpendicular to both the surface of the wall and the surface of the floor. You can use glue, tape, or pins to hold the brace in place. Foam board, if it is not warped, makes an excellent brace, especially if the inside corners are hidden. It is better to cut the brace a little shorter than the heights of your walls, as opposed to trying to make it flush and ending up with a brace that is too big and sticks out of your model (see Figure 9.7).

Corner Bracing

This method can be used alone, or in conjunction with a shorter wall brace. Connect a square piece of board on the interior corner of the model. If used in conjunction with wall braces, set it atop two of them, gluing their tops to the brace and the brace to the interior wall (see Figure 9.8).

Diagonal Bracing

This is a modification of the previous two methods. Cut two 45-degree beveled edges on opposing sides of a piece of board. Attach the beveled edges to the inside walls (see Figure 9.9).

Trabeated Bracing

Trabeation refers to post and lintel construction. This method is extremely useful in in-

terior models. Attach a square or triangular piece of board to the top of your walls in a corner. If it constructed in such a manner that it is not a distraction, it is acceptable to leave

FIGURE 9.8 (Top). Corner bracing: This method can be used alone, or in conjunction with a shorter wall brace.

FIGURE 9.9 (Bottom). Diagonal bracing: This is a modification of the previous two methods.

FIGURE 9.10 Trabeated bracing: Attach a square or triangular piece of board to the top of your walls in a corner.

FIGURE 9.11 (Top). A pre-made wooden box was used as the jig against which to brace the object.

FIGURE 9.12 (Bottom). Apply some strips of wood or foam board perpendicular to the grain to keep the cardboard from bending.

the bracing in place. If you want to remove it after the connections between the walls have dried, gently pin the brace in place so that it can be easily removed later (see Figure 9.10).

Corner (Jig) Bracing

This requires a heavier, clean block, a clean, 45-degree jig, and some heavy objects to keep the **jigs** in place. In this case, a jig is basically a template or guide against which you can brace your materials while they dry. Place the block on the inside corners, flush with the edges of your floor. Apply adhesives to the proper edges. Wedge the floor and two corners between the corner jig and the interior block. To keep things from moving, be sure the outside of the corner jig is secure. Pay attention to the amount of glue you use. If too much is used, it will leak out of your joints, and you will ruin not only your model, but possibly your jigs as well. In the case of Figure 9.11, a pre-made wooden box was used as the jig against which to brace the object. If you choose to use a pre-made wooden or acrylic box instead of fabricating one from MDF, make sure it is square. If it isn't square, you will not be able to use it (see Figure 9.11).

Additional Bracing at Joints

A slight bit of glue can be applied to each of the perpendicular surfaces, between which an additional strip of wood or foam board can be inserted for additional strength and stability. This is basically a vertical wall brace used in conjunction with other types of braces.

Bracing Cardboard

Cardboard has a tendency to bend parallel with the grain, or along the lines of corrugation. If you can see a series of loops in the exposed side of your cardboard, it should be extremely easy to bend it along that axis. To keep the cardboard from bending involuntarily, apply some strips of wood or foam board perpendicular to the grain. When using strips of foam board, make sure you glue and apply along the foam edge; it is strongest in this direction (see Figure 9.12).

CREATING A SIMPLE CUBE USING MUSEUM BOARD

The cube at the end of this series of images, Figures 9.13 through 9.21, was created using 1/16" museum board, a craft knife with a number 11 blade, drafting triangles, and Sobo glue.

1. Begin by cutting four identical squares (see Figure 9.13).
2. If you choose to use butt joints, like we have here, cut down two of the squares

and reduce their size by the width of the material you are using (in this case, 1/16 inch). These will be your top and bottom. Notice how the top and bottom are made from a thicker material (1/8 inch) than the sides of the cube. This is for strength and to help you keep track of which piece is which.

3. Apply glue to one side of what will be the thicker, base portion (see Figure 9.14).
4. Using another piece of board, apply even pressure along the glued edge while keeping the surfaces vertical and square (see Figure 9.15).
5. Add the top piece, again applying even pressure and keeping everything square (see Figures 9.16 and 9.17).
6. After four sides have been attached, strengthen the inner seams by adding glue and then even it out using a small tool, such as a toothpick, or, in this case, a thin piece of museum board (see Figure 9.18).
7. Use the existing cube as a guide to ensure that each successive side is cut to the perfect size. Be certain you attach the fifth side prior to cutting the sixth side (see Figure 9.19).
8. Remember, continue to apply pressure, and allow the glue to dry between steps. Notice the difference in thickness of the boards. Whenever possible, apply the glue to the edges of the thicker boards, and glue the thinner boards to them. This

will add strength and stability (see Figure 9.20).
9. Add the sixth side to create a perfect cube (see Figure 9.21).

CREATING WINDOWS

Begin by drafting your opening using a sharp 4H pencil, or by one of the aforementioned transfer methods. Illustrated examples of the first portion of this process, creating an opening, can be found in Chapter 7, Figures 7.10 through 7.14.

1. Using your craft knife, begin by making one or two strokes along each cutout line.
2. Using your knife or a pin, pierce your board in both directions, at all four corners. Make certain you drive the instrument through the board at as perpendicular an angle as possible. Any deviation from perpendicular will affect the quality of your cut as well as your ability to align the cuts. It is essential that your cut does not extend past your intended window opening. This can be facilitated by making certain that the sharp end of the blade is facing toward the area that needs to be cut, as opposed to the corners you are piercing.
3. Now, on each side, make a few cuts from the initial holes toward the center of your board. Alternate cutting away from each initial plunge until the cuts meet, and

you have cut completely around the hole. This technique helps to eliminate overcuts at the corners.
4. Flip the board over; connect the pin holes using your craft knife. Make several passes. You are now cutting out your intended hole.
5. Alternating sides of the board, continue to make a series of passes with the knife until you have cut completely through the board. Carefully remove the extra piece.
6. Using your knife, a nail file, other small file, or sandpaper on a small, square block, remove any burrs.
7. Finally, use a clean burnisher to help disguise any sloppy cuts.

Adding Mullions to Your Windows

There are basically two ways to add mullions to a window: drawing or building. The drawing method is considerably quicker and easier. The building method involves just that—building mullions and gluing them into your window opening.

Drawing Method

1. On a sheet of board that is slightly smaller than the piece from which you will be cutting your windows, draw your mullions and then very lightly lay out the window openings as well. A good way to do this is to lay your

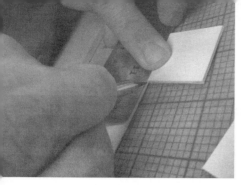

FIGURE 9.13 Begin by cutting four identical squares.

FIGURE 9.14 Apply glue to one side of the thicker, base portion of what will be the cube.

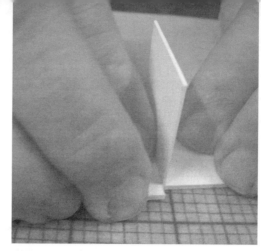

FIGURE 9.15 Apply even pressure along the glued edge while keeping the surfaces vertical and square.

FIGURE 9.16 Add the adjacent piece, applying even pressure and keeping everything square.

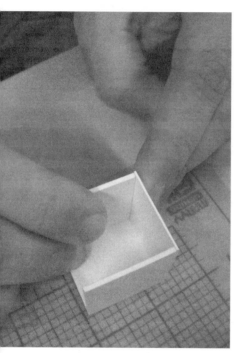

FIGURE 9.17 Add the top piece, applying even pressure and keeping everything square.

FIGURE 9.18 Strengthen the inner seams by adding glue, and even it out using a small tool.

FIGURE 9.19 Use the existing cube as a guide for measurement.

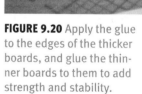

FIGURE 9.20 Apply the glue to the edges of the thicker boards, and glue the thinner boards to them to add strength and stability.

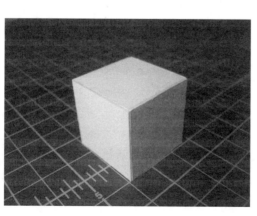

FIGURE 9.21 Add the sixth side to create a perfect cube.

plan on top of the board and then make marks that correspond to the mullions and window openings at the edge of the plan on the board. Remove the plan, and connect the dots. This should leave you with an accurate grid.

2. Lay out and cut out your window openings and frame. This will later be placed over the mullions that you will be drawing in the next step. This can be done either by transferring your drawings, measuring and drawing directly on the board, or by cutting through an extra elevation.

3. Place the openings over the plan; make a series of light marks that correspond to the mullions on the board that has the windows cut out of it (see Figure 9.22).

4. Align the two boards. After you are certain everything will work, use white glue to attach the two boards (see Figure 9.23).

Building Method

1. Cut out your window openings, as previously described.

2. Using 1/16" museum board, begin to cut out the mullion strips as follows.

A. On the edge of your board, mark the width of the mullions. Use a longer piece of board to keep all the mullions the same size.

B. Place the thin piece/strip of board beneath your straightedge. The larger portion of the board should not be covered by the straightedge. A transparent straightedge is being used in the illustration so that you may better visualize this step (see Figure 9.24).

C. Make sure you keep even pressure on the straightedge (see Figure 9.25).

FIGURE 9.22 Place the openings over the plan; make a series of light marks that correspond to the mullions.

FIGURE 9.23 Align the two boards, and attach to create a finished window.

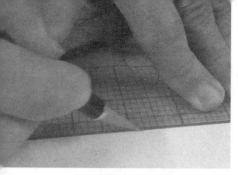

FIGURE 9.24 Place the thin strip of board beneath your straight-edge. The larger portion of the board should not be covered by the straightedge.

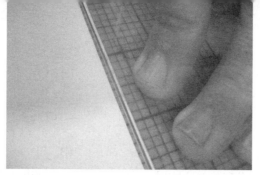

FIGURE 9.25 It is essential that you keep even pressure on the straightedge.

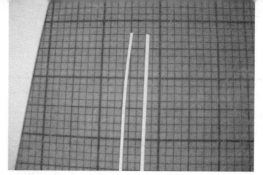

FIGURE 9.26 The strip on the left was cut without keeping pressure on it, whereas the strip on the right had pressure applied to it while it was cut.

FIGURE 9.27 Measure and mark the mullion using the opening as a guide.

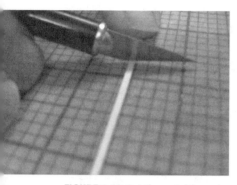

FIGURE 9.28 Cut the outside mullions to size.

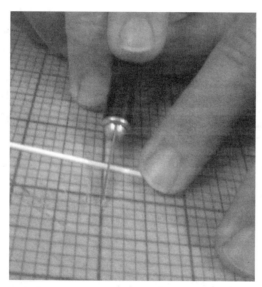

FIGURE 9.29 When cutting the thin strips, use the back of the blade, and push down and forward while cutting to get a cleaner, straighter, more perpendicular edge.

FIGURE 9.30 All four of the outside window's mullions are in.

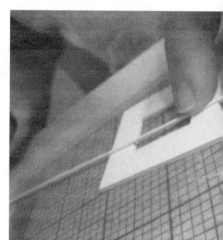

FIGURE 9.31 Measure the inner mullions using the existing window as a guide.

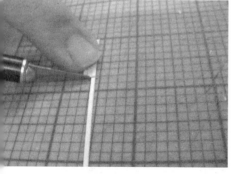

FIGURE 9.32 Using the master as a template, cut the remaining strips to size.

your mullion. If you do not apply even pressure on the thin strip while cutting it, it will warp, twist, and bow. In Figure 9.26, the strip on the left was cut without keeping pressure on it, whereas the strip on the right had pressure applied to it while it was cut. Notice the difference.

3. Measure and mark the mullion, using the opening as a guide (see Figure 9.27).

4. Cut the outside mullions to size. Note: When cutting the thin strips, use the back of the blade, and push down and forward (as seen in Figures 9.28 and 9.29) while cutting. This will give you a cleaner, straighter, more perpendicular edge, and the tiny strip will not fly away while you are cutting it.

5. Using tweezers, begin to insert and glue, one at a time, the outer mullions. Figure 9.30 shows a window with all four outer mullions inserted.

6. After all of the outer mullions are in place, begin to measure the inner mullions, and cut your master (see Figure 9.31).

7. Using your master, cut the remaining strips to size (see Figure 9.32).

8. Place your windows over your plan. Use the plan as a template to find the exact placement of the *horizontal* mullions. Use your tweezers and a small amount of white glue to put them in place. Make sure you insert all the horizontal mullions before installing the vertical pieces (see Figure 9.33).

9. Measure and cut the vertical mullions (see Figure 9.34).

10. Insert the first vertical mullion (see Figure 9.35). Make sure it is perfectly vertical; all the other mullions will be using this as a reference.

11. Measure, cut, and insert the shorter portion of the mullion (see Figures 9.36 and 9.37).

12. Measure and cut the adjacent vertical mullion (see Figure 9.38).

13. At this point, disregard the elevation drawing and use the grid lines and the existing vertical mullions to align any additional vertical mullions (see Figure 9.39).

14. This is an extremely delicate operation; you should probably be using tweezers and very small amounts of glue (see Figure 9.40).

15. Figure 9.41 shows the finished product.

Transferring Cuts

In Figures 9.42a and 9.42b, an elevation was taped directly to the museum board. A craft knife was used to cut along the openings. This left a clean (free of any pencil lead) line on the board. From there, the opening was removed by following the preceding steps.

REPRESENTING GLASS

More often than not, the negative space caused by cutting out a window, door, skylight, or other opening should suffice. In the instances where this is not sufficient, acetate, styrene, Mylar, or acrylic can be combined with your paper-based models. See Chapter 12 for more information on these materials. Pay close attention to the thickness of your glass material in relation to the thickness of your building materials.

Installing Windows

Whenever possible, install your window materials last. The addition of window materials is tedious and time consuming; make certain all touch up, painting, cutting, installation, or other accident-prone procedures are finished first. It is agonizing to install a window into a façade, only to discover later that the entire façade piece is the wrong size. Use the least amount of adhesive possible when gluing windows. The slick nature of some window materials such as acetate or acrylic only exacerbates the viscosity of the glue, causing it to run all over the window. This is distracting and unprofessional. When working on small areas, a toothpick or pin is useful for the application and removal of glue. Better yet, use a transparent double-stick tape.

CREATING CURVED SHAPES

There are two options available to you when it comes to creating curves: **kerfing** and bending with the grain.

FIGURE 9.33 Place your windows over your plan to find the exact placement of the *horizontal* mullions.

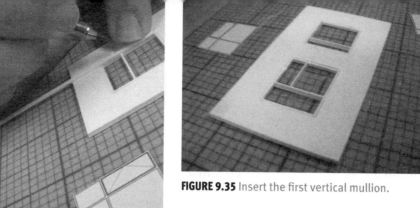

FIGURE 9.34 Measure and cut the vertical mullions.

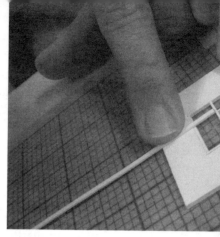

FIGURE 9.35 Insert the first vertical mullion.

FIGURE 9.36 Measure and cut the shorter mullion.

FIGURE 9.37 Insert the shorter mullion; line it up with the one above it.

FIGURE 9.38 Measure and cut the adjacent vertical mullion.

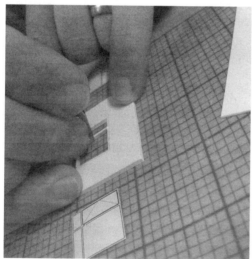

FIGURE 9.39 Use the grid lines on your cutting mat and the existing vertical mullions to align any additional elements.

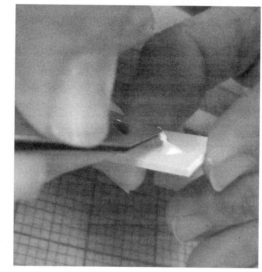

FIGURE 9.40 With all delicate operations, use tweezers and tiny amounts of glue.

FIGURE 9.41 The finished window.

Kerfing

Kerfing is a quick and fairly clean way to create a curve in a board. It is done by creating a series of evenly spaced cuts on your board, on the opposite side of the curve. It is essential that each kerf is evenly spaced, of the same depth, and runs the entire length of the board. Failure to do this will result in an uneven curve.

Foam board is easier to kerf than mat board. While an adhesive dries, it can be held in its curved position by pins or other similar methods. The surface that has the cuts exposed can be disguised or sheathed by spray mounting a heavier paper or cardstock on its surface. See the following chapter on foam board construction for detailed instructions on kerfing.

Bending With the Grain

For this demonstration, I have chosen to work with 1/32-inch museum board. The thinner the museum board, the easier it is to bend. First, cut out a 2" × 2" square from the corner of your stock. Make certain it is square, and make certain you mark the orientation of your square as it relates to the stock from which it was removed. With one finger on each side, gently try to bend the board. It will bend much more easily in one direction than the other. The direction in which it bends most easily is parallel to, or "with the grain" (see Figure 9.43).

Creating a Cylinder Using Museum Board

For this demonstration, we are using an X-Acto knife with a #11 blade, 1/16-inch and 1/32-inch museum board, and Sobo glue.

1. First, find the **grain** of your board. Remember, thinner is better (1/32-inch museum board; review Figure 9.43). Eventually, you will be cutting some long strips, which are perpendicular to the grain. Lightly mark the direction in which you will be cutting your strips.
2. Cut out two identical circles using a thicker board, (1/16-inch museum board in this demo; see Figure 9.44). *They must be identical!* If they are not, you will not be able to make a perfect cylinder.
3. Find the centers of the circles. Divide the two circles into four equal quadrants (see Figure 9.45).
4. Burnish the edges of your circles (see Figure 9.46).
5. Cut a *perfectly squared* center brace the *exact* length of the diameter of your circles (see Figure 9.47).
6. Attach the brace along the axis of your bottom circle. Using a drafting triangle, make certain it is attached perfectly vertical to the circle (see Figure 9.48).

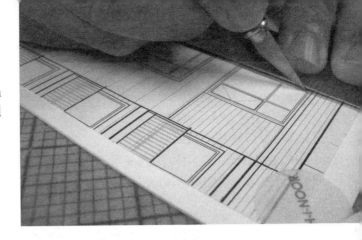

FIGURE 9.42 Place an elevation on your board and cut; this is a quick way to transfer cuts.

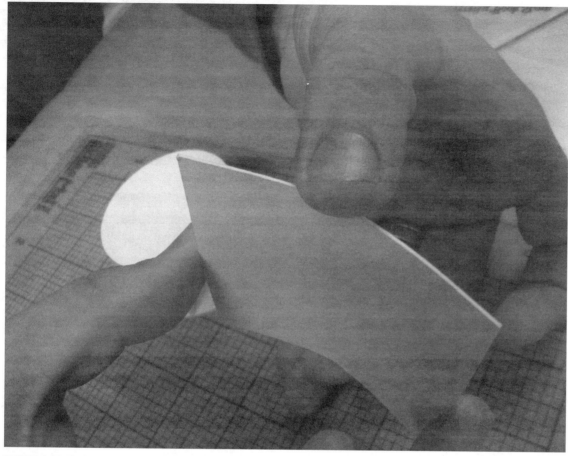

FIGURE 9.43 Finding the grain—the board wants to bend in this direction.

10. Glue the top circle to the braces; once again, use a triangle to make certain that the top and bottom are plum (see Figure 9.51).

11. Cut out a lengthwise piece (perpendicular to the grain) of 1/32-inch museum board, equal to the total height of your cylinder. That is the height of your brace plus the height of two circles. It is more accurate to measure than to do the math.

12. Applying pressure with one hand, pull the strip across a rounded table edge to help create a curve (see Figure 9.52). Depending on how tight the curve needs to be, you may want to repeat this step. Notice how the strip wants to curve (see Figure 9.53). If your strip does not behave in this fashion, chances are you cut the strip in the wrong direction— parallel, as opposed to perpendicular to, the grain.

13. Wrap the curved board around the cylinder. Using a sharp pencil, mark the exact length and then cut the strip to the size of the cylinder. You will be using this strip to sheathe your cylinder (see Figure 9.54).

14. Cut a second strip perpendicular to the grain. Make sure it is the same height, but a couple inches longer than the circumference of your cylinder. You will be using this later as a makeshift **band clamp.**

7. Measure and cut two more braces, the same height as the first one, and one half the length of the first brace, minus one half the width of the material. In this case, we are using 1/16-inch illustration board, so the length of each piece would be the radius of the circle, minus 1/32 inch. Be sure to dry fit each piece first.

8. Glue the two braces along the axis lines, making certain they are square (see Figure 9.49).

9. Add a second brace to one of the existing braces. This will help with attaching the curved surface. The added width will provide more surface area upon which to apply glue (see Figure 9.50).

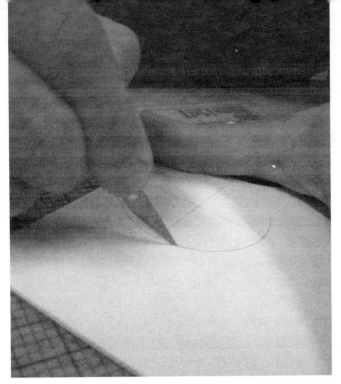

FIGURE 9.44 Cut two identical circles.

FIGURE 9.45 Find the centers of the circles. Divide them into four equal quadrants.

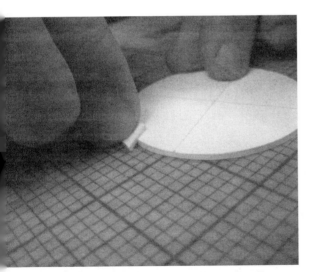

FIGURE 9.46 Burnish the edges using the same type of board.

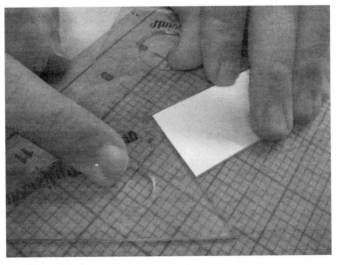

FIGURE 9.47 Cut and square a center brace equal to the diameter of your circles.

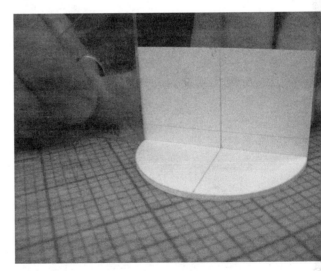

FIGURE 9.48 Attach the brace along the axis of your bottom circle.

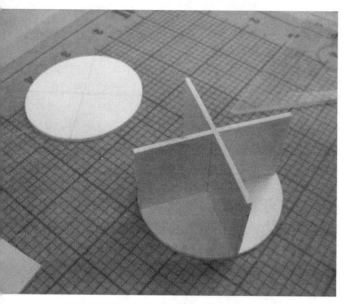

FIGURE 9.49 Glue and square the two braces along the axis lines.

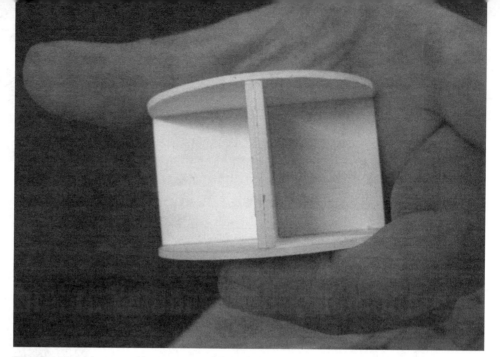

FIGURE 9.50 Add a second brace to one of the existing braces.

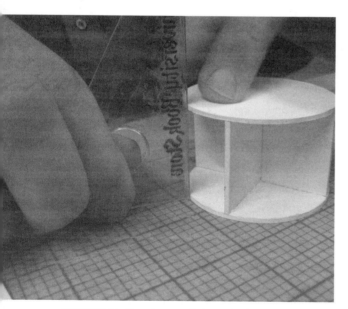

FIGURE 9.51 Glue the top circle to the braces.

15. Add a bead of glue to the edges of the circles and the cylinder braces (see Figure 9.55). Pull your finger along the edge of the circles to help to reduce the surface tension and even out the glue. In Figure 9.56, notice how most of the finger is pressing into the bottom of the cylinder where there is no glue. Only a little bit of your finger needs to touch the glue; the glob will attach itself to the finger until it finds another blob of glue to bond with, again, evening out the glue, and eliminating the blobs.

16. Wrap your curved board around the cylinder. Make certain to place the seam on the area with the double bracing.

17. The longer piece of 1/32-inch board is going to act as a clamp. Wrap it around your cylinder, and hold it until the glue dries. Sobo dries very quickly. The seam of your cylinder should be directly opposite the seam of your "clamp" (see Figure 9.57).

18. Behold, a finished cylinder (see Figure 9.58).

BUILDING STAIRS

There are a few different ways to approach the construction of stairs. At a small scale, or in a study model, simply mounting a plan view of stairs to a ramp will suffice. However,

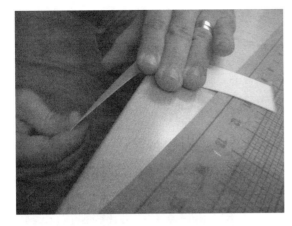

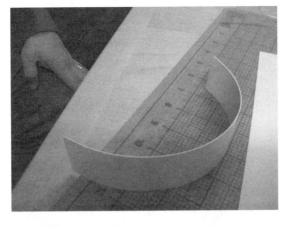

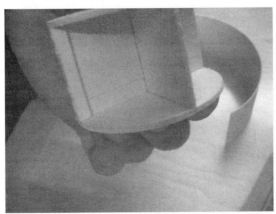

FIGURE 9.52 (Top Left). Pull the strip across a rounded table edge to help create a curve.

FIGURE 9.53 (Top Center). Notice how the strip wants to curve.

FIGURE 9.54 (Top Right). Wrap the curved board around the cylinder, mark the exact length, and then cut it to size.

FIGURE 9.55 (Center Left). Add a bead of glue to the edges of the circles and the cylinder braces.

FIGURE 9.56 (Above Center). Pull your finger along the edge of the circles; this will help to reduce the surface tension and even out the glue.

FIGURE 9.57 (Center Right). Take the longer piece of $1/32$-inch board, wrap it around your cylinder, and hold it until the glue dries.

FIGURE 9.58 (Bottom Left). A finished cylinder.

as the model increases in scale and/or complexity, you will need to observe the following guidelines.

Cantilevered Staircase

1. Begin by drawing a grid of your staircase's rise and run. If you have enough material, be certain to leave a small space between the two sets of stairs; it will be easier to cut them out (see Figure 9.59).
2. Cut out the two staircases, and slice between the two sets.
3. Before proceeding, *be certain that both sides of your stairs are square!*
4. Carefully remove the excess; this is done in a manner similar to cutting an opening—drive the blade down as close to vertically as possible and then pull the blade away from the corner, making several passes until the excess is removed.
5. Draw the cantilevered portion of the stringer, and cut it out (see Figure 9.60).
6. Attach the full-size stringer to the base and check for square.
7. Use the unattached stringer as a template. Align it with the other side of your stairs. Make sure everything is the same size. Finally, trace the bottom of the stringer (see Figure 9.61).
8. Use a small strip of material to attach a **cleat** to the larger stringer. Be certain you attach it *above* the diagonal line you just drew in Step 7 (see Figure 9.62).

9. Draw a line on the floor perpendicular to the stringer. This will be used to line up the other stringer (see Figure 9.63).
10. Attach a wall that is perpendicular to the existing stringer; then attach the hanging stringer to the wall and floor (see Figure 9.64).
11. This step may or may not be necessary. Measure and cut out a strip of board that will cover the underside of the steps (see Figure 9.65).
12. The staircase in this example has open risers; therefore, only the treads are measured, cut out, and attached (see Figure 9.66). For aesthetic purposes, the treads are purposely cut slightly wider than the outside width of the stringers. This will create a pleasing shadow that accentuates the three-dimensionality of the form. Notice the difference in depth between the lower steps, which have a slight overhang, and the upper steps, which were intentionally attached flush against the side (see Figure 9.67).

Closed Stringers, Risers, and a Landing

1. Draw out your parts (see Figure 9.68). Be sure to consider which parts will overlap which.
2. Cut out the parts; attach one stringer, the back wall, and the front riser. Always check for square (see Figure 9.69).

3. Attach the second stringer; double check to ensure that the entire structure is square (see Figure 9.70).
4. In this case, all the parts were premeasured and cut. The risers need to be added first to give the effect of stair nosing and make things fit properly (see Figure 9.71). Notice how they are pressed flush with the sides of the stairway with the drafting triangle while being attached.
5. Add the runners after all the risers are attached. Notice how they are slightly oversized; this increases the shadows (see Figure 9.72).

DRILLING HOLES

There are occasions where you may need to drill small holes into your boards, for example, when you are adding a balustrade to a stairway. For this process, you can use an electric drill, or a smaller hobby or model drill. To create a clean hole on each side of your board, sandwich it between two other sheets. Failure to do so will result in a frayed or torn edge on the side from which the drill exits. When drilling identical holes in identical pieces, using clamps, try to sandwich all the parts together and then drill through the entire stack at once. This should serve to align all the holes. If possible, use a drill press or Dremel drill press to ensure that your holes are perpendicular to the boards. This is extremely difficult to do by hand. More often

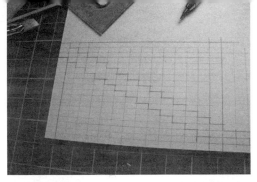

FIGURE 9.59 Begin by drawing a grid of the rise and run of your staircase.

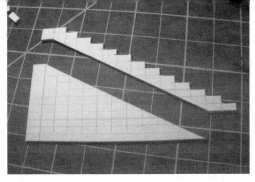

FIGURE 9.60 Draw the cantilevered portion of the stringer, and cut it out.

FIGURE 9.61 Use the unattached stringer as a template.

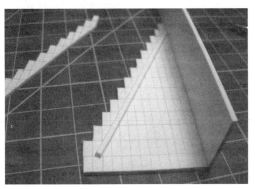

FIGURE 9.62 Use a small strip of material to attach a cleat to the larger stringer.

FIGURE 9.63 Draw a line on the floor that is perpendicular to the stringer; this will be used to line up the other stringer.

FIGURE 9.64 Attach a wall that is perpendicular to the existing stringer; then attach the hanging stringer.

FIGURE 9.65 Measure and cut out a strip of board that will cover the underside of the steps.

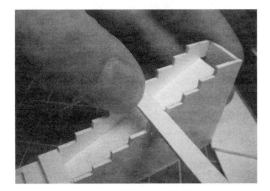

FIGURE 9.66 Measure the treads.

FIGURE 9.67 Notice the difference in terms of depth and shadow—depending upon whether the treads overhang or are flush.

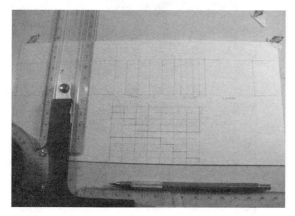

FIGURE 9.68 Draw out your parts. Be sure to consider which parts will overlap which.

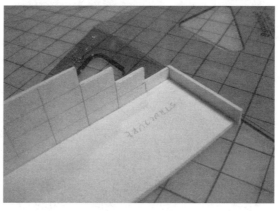

FIGURE 9.69 Cut out the parts; attach one stringer, the back wall, and the front riser.

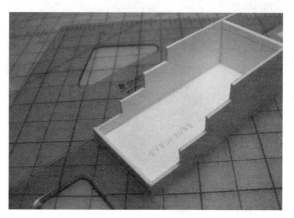

FIGURE 9.70 Attach the second stringer.

FIGURE 9.71 The risers need to be added first.

FIGURE 9.72 Attach the runners or treads.

than not, it makes sense to drill your holes in smaller pieces, such as stair treads, before assembling the requisite parts.

VARIATIONS ON THE PROCESSES, PITCHED ROOFS, AND UNUSUAL ANGLES

A pitched roof can be created by following the bracing principles put forth earlier in this chapter. Simply attach a truss-shaped form, which represents a pitched gable, on either end of a strong slab, and a couple of braces between each one to keep everything square. After the basic framework has been constructed, cut out and add the sloped roofs. A flap joint can be used instead of cutting out each side of the roof individually. A folded piece of cardstock can be used to disguise the flap joint from above, if need be.

Complex roofs will usually need to be created as a study model or otherwise mocked up at scale using cardboard, paper, or cardstock before cutting out the final pieces. More complicated variations of roof construction are illustrated in Chapter 10.

FAUX BUILDING MATERIALS

There are a variety of simulated material finishes such as brick, wood, concrete, and more available in sheet form in a variety of sizes and scales. These can be purchased from companies such as Alvin that cater to architects and engineers. Some of these sheets are self adhesive; others will need to be spray or dry mounted. It is best to apply these sheets, plus a little overlap, to your boards before cutting them. Attempts to save materials by piecing or seaming together often result in a disjointed and unprofessional appearance. Always try to use a single or continuous sheet of simulated material per cutout.

Whenever possible, use a miter joint at the corners when joining two boards together. If necessary, you can use a marker to best match the exposed bevel to that of the newly applied material. This will help to disguise the connection and any shadows that are cast as a result of a gap at the corner.

Depending upon the scale and/or materials you are working with, it is entirely possible to simulate said materials on your own by drawing, embossing, mounting colored paper, or painting. It is also possible to photograph and print a texture you are looking for. As always, practice these techniques prior to using them in a final project.

GRAPHIC TAPES

Graphic tapes are available in a variety of sizes (1/8 inch to 3 inches), colors, and textures. These can be used to great effect, especially when representing windows, mullions, door frames, and more on smaller scaled, international-style skyscrapers and the like. Likewise, they are useful for representing parking lot stripes or similar landscape delineations.

When applying graphic tape, extend the tape slightly past its intended boundary, and gently cut it to size using a sharp craft knife. If two pieces of tape meet to form a corner, allow them to overlap and then slice them diagonally from the inside to the outside corner. Peel up the excess. This will give a smooth, clean angle with no bumps caused by several layers of tape. (See the chapter on layering for more on the uses of graphic tape.)

PRESSURE-SENSITIVE OVERLAYS

Pressure-sensitive overlays are available in a variety of colors and faux textures. More often than not, they are semi-transparent. Experiment by laying these sheets over themselves, precolored or painted boards, graphic tapes, or various other overlays or drawings, to create unique effects of color and texture.

PAINTING

Before deciding to paint paper-based boards, look for a commercially produced mat board, overlays, or colored paper that can be used to create similar effects. If nothing satisfies, look to spray paints, or to an airbrush, should you have access to one. When using other types of paint, such as artist's acrylics or watercolors, you run the risk of warping or otherwise distorting your board, so proceed with caution. If you are certain that your model will require painting, it is a good idea to test any new techniques during the design development and study model phases.

Remember:
- The larger the scale of your model, the more realistic in terms of color, texture, and detail it may need to be. For example, on interior models, depending on the model's purpose, every attempt at realism, especially in terms of color, may have to be made.
- When using spray paints, be sure to use only in a well-ventilated area.
- Color has a tendency to overwhelm a composition and draw attention to itself. Always be aware of this, and feel free to diminish the intensity of any colors that detract from the overall effect you want the model to convey.
- White spray paint can be used to subdue the color of a mat board. It can also be used to unify an entire model.

Painting Bricks

A wax-based colored pencil is excellent for creating mortar or grout lines. I prefer to draw the lines first and then paint over them. The wax creates what is called a **resist,** which does not allow the paint to adhere to it. This is a case where excessive pressure placed upon the pencil is a good thing. Using this technique, you will create a type of embossing, or a lowered area that corresponds to the grout lines.

Experiment with colors and layering of colors. Spraying a lighter uniform layer of red over a smooth misted layer of a darker shade of red will add verisimilitude. Grout lines can also be redrawn over the existing lines, or you can paint first and then draw the lines. Each method will create a different effect.

Painting Concrete and Concrete Block

Use an old toothbrush to lightly splatter two or three shades of black, white, and gray acrylic paint on your board. Do not overdo the splatter, especially the black. Experiment with different consistencies of paint by adding water. Light gray automotive primer can then be sprayed over the splatters to unify the board. As the scale increases, an effective means of adding texture is to adhere 220 grit or higher sandpaper to the board, and then spray it with the automotive primer. Joint lines can then be added with a colored pencil.

Painting Wood

More often than not, it is simpler to use basswood or balsa wood where wood needs to be represented. In the case of complex shapes, start with a light basecoat of flat paint. The next step can be accomplished by using a variety of earth tone markers to emulate wood grain. Add a few highlights using colored pencils; if necessary, plank or joint lines can be drawn in using a fine black pen. Finally, a coat of clear sealant should be added to unify the surface and further emulate the desired finish of the wood.

Painting a Roof Texture (Composite Shingles)

Start with a board that emulates as closely as possible the texture of the roofing material, such as pebble board. This is a case where the roof material should be cut out prior to painting. Failure to do so will result in a white edge that does not match the rest of the material.

Painting Corrugated Metal

The texture is actually more important than the color in this case. I know of some model makers who strip one of the paper faces off of cardboard to get this effect. If done neatly, it can work quite well. This technique takes some practice to master. After you have achieved the corrugation effect, spray the entire roofing structure with the appropriate paint. Bear in mind, should you choose to use a metallic paint, it may have the tendency to overwhelm the rest of your composition.

Painting Glass

This is another case where using paint to represent this material is probably not the best choice. If you must paint, simply using a dark glossy gray should suffice. A glossy black has a tendency to overwhelm.

Painting Grass

At a small scale, green illustration board should suffice. At a larger scale, use a toothbrush to splatter a few shades of green on a green board, and unify by spraying a green over the entire surface. See the section on entourage for additional tips (see Chapter 13).

Painting Water

Use a few shades of blue and blue green watercolors on a white board. After the watercolors have dried, apply a clear gloss spray finish. This will help to emulate the reflective qualities of water.

Painting

Make sure you save a small amount of leftover paint, especially if you custom mixed it. It can be used later for touch up.

The materials, tools, and techniques discussed in this chapter should meet nearly every need you will have when it comes to creating most student grade models. These are the cheapest, most versatile, and easiest materials that any model maker can choose to work with.

You should be able to create a model of nearly anything using just a craft knife, a straightedge, glue, and some type of brace or clamping system. As discussed earlier, contour models also rely heavily upon the use of these materials. At this point, you should have a fundamental understanding of some construction techniques involved in the creation of floors, walls, and other partitions, as well as various openings, and structural components, such as stairs and basic pitched roofs. Finally, you should understand how to create complex angles, curves, and other forms.

KEY TERMS

band clamp
bristol board
butt joint
cardstock
chipboard
cleat
cold-pressed
flap joint
Gatorfoam
grain
hot-pressed
illustration board
jig
kerf or kerfing
mat board
mitered
miter joint
museum board

rabbet edge
resist
strawboard
thermal expansion
trabeation

Chapter Review and Practice

(See "Materials Needed by Chapter," p. xx.)

Project 1

Using the three geometric templates from the exercises in Chapter 8, build the following out of museum board:

1. A 3" × 3" cube.
2. A triangular object with one side of at least 2 inches. Make this object at least 3 inches tall.
3. A cylinder with a 2-inch diameter that is 1$\frac{1}{2}$ inches tall.

Note: The templates represent the *outside* dimensions of the objects. These templates cannot be used as a base upon which you add walls or other types of sheathing. Take into account the thickness of your wall materials, and reduce the size of your templates accordingly to create your bases. These three objects can now be inserted into the contour project you created in Chapter 6.

Project 2

1. Cut out four 6" × 6" squares using $\frac{1}{16}$-inch illustration board.

2. In the center of two of the squares, make a 1$\frac{1}{2}$-inch-wide by 2-inch-tall opening. In one of the openings, cut out and add mullions. In the other, back the hole with another piece of illustration board, and simply draw in the mullions with a pencil.

Project 3

Using illustration board, build two six-step staircases, one at $\frac{1}{2}$" = 1'-0", and the other at $\frac{1}{4}$" = 1'-0".

Note: Build each set according to the examples demonstrated in this chapter. Experiment with overhangs, and the effects of light and shadow that the various techniques produce.

Project 4

1. Attach the four 6" × 6" squares to a foam board base, as if you were starting an architectural model. Make sure you dry fit everything before you decide to glue anything in place.
2. On each interior corner, add a different type of corner brace. Set them at least $\frac{1}{2}$ inch below the top of the model.
3. Using the techniques you have learned in this chapter, add a pitched roof to this structure, such that it can be easily removed so as to show the bracing techniques you used in Step 2.

Foam Board, Foam Core, or Bainbridge Board Models

OBJECTIVES

- *Learn foam board techniques—both freehand and using tools*
- *Learn to cut circles*
- *Learn to perfect edges and assemble joints*
- *Learn advanced uses of foam board to represent real materials*

Due to the thickness and ease of gluing, a foam board model is one of the most popular model types among design students. It is usually one of the first mediums students are exposed to. It is strong, clean, and relatively simple to work with. It is a completely acceptable medium for use in study and presentation models.

One of the drawbacks when building exclusively in foam board is its thickness. Although it is true that foam board is available in a small variety of thicknesses, using foam board as the only medium in a model is generally not the best idea if you are trying to convey actual material, wall, or door thicknesses. Foam board is an excellent structural material onto which other materials may then be applied. See Chapter 12 for more information on mixing materials.

ABOUT FOAM BOARD

Foam board is often referred to by one of its brand names, such as Foam Core or Bainbridge Board. It is a type of display board, the core of which is made from foam, sandwiched between two rigid sheets of paper. It is extremely lightweight and easy to cut. It is one of the preferred mediums for the creation of architectural models. Foam board is available in a variety of thicknesses. One-eighth inch and 1/4 inch are readily available at most art supply stores. Models at or larger than 1/4" = 1'-0" scale are often made from foam board.

Some foam board, such as Bainbridge Board, has something called "memory." **Memory** means that the board retains its crisp edge after it is cut, instead of curving down slightly in the direction of the cut. It also has an extremely smooth, white surface that is more resistant to dents than other foam boards.

Typically available either in black or white, some companies carry up to 28 additional stock colors, and have the ability to custom tint up to 1,000 additional pantone colors. The foam "core" of these boards usually remains white.

The surface of foam board is generally made from clay coated paper. Some of these surfaces, in addition to being colored can be archival, have a self-adhesive surface, come laminated with foil, or can even be ordered in a fireproof version. Bear in mind, these specialty foam boards are not cheap.

A craft knife is adequate for cutting foam board, but the blades must be extremely sharp. Unfortunately, this material will quickly dull your knife. Cuts made with a dull blade will result in an uneven, torn core.

Unless you have the proper tools, foam board is not the best choice for contour or similar structures that require curved cuts. Whenever possible, choose an alternative material for such a use.

Foam board does not accept pencil as readily as say, mat, museum, or illustration board, but will readily accept ink or spray paint if applied carefully.

Foam board is an excellent choice for structures, onto which can be applied a myriad of other materials, such as wood veneer, acrylic, museum board, or paper materials.

FOAM BOARD TOOLS AND TECHNIQUES

There are several companies, such as Alvin, Logan, and FoamWerks that manufacture foam-board-specific tools. It is possible to achieve many of the effects mentioned in this chapter without using theses specialty tools, but the bottom line is that foam-board-specific tools will make your life much, much, easier. If you purchase only one foam board tool, make it a rabbet edge foam board cutter. This chapter will focus on the various techniques available to achieve effects with foam board. The freehand cutting of foam board is exactly the same as other paper-based boards. Bear in mind, it is doubly important that you use a sharp knife when cutting foam board. A dull blade will leave a jagged edge and tiny foam pieces, known as **Klingons**—very, very, unprofessional looking. Also, foam board will dull your knife faster than any other paper-based product. When armed with a #11 blade, a craft knife, and a straightedge, use a series of passes until you cut completely through your board. Because foam board is thicker than other boards, failure to keep your blade perpendicular to your cutting surface will result in an extremely ugly cut.

Using a FoamWerks Channel Rail and Straight Cutter

1. Mark a line where you want to cut.
2. Lightly mark a second line 1/8 of an inch back from where you want to cut.
3. Using drafting tape or drafting dots, tape the edge of channel rail on the second line you just drew. This should place the blade of the straight cutter directly on top of your cut line.
4. Apply pressure to the cutter so that it plunges all the way through the foam board. Then, *using a single pass,* pull the straight cutter across the length of your board. This should give you a straight, square cut, the quality of which is much better than you can do by hand.

Cutting Square Openings

This is done the same way as in the previous chapter. The exception is instead of using your blade to pierce the board at the corners, use a pin. A blade will tend to drift from vertical, oftentimes resulting in unsightly **overcuts,** whereas a pin is a little easier to vertically plunge through the board. Cut from both sides, and keep your blade perpendicular to ensure a good cut.

Foam Board Joints and Corners

When it comes to corners, the options with foam board are the same as with other paper-based boards. You basically have two choices—butt joints (see Figures 10.1 and 10.2) or miter joints (see Figure 10.3).

When using a foam board butt joint, especially at corners, an unsightly exposed edge is likely to be seen. Most clients and instructors will not look favorably upon this and could see it as a lack of craftsmanship. There are two options for disguising the foam core. The first is to use a rabbet edge foam board cutter; the second is to perform the same task freehand. Using either one of these techniques will leave you with a professional looking, finished edge.

FIGURE 10.1 Butt joint with exposed edge.

FIGURE 10.2 Two boxes using different joints—miter joints on the left, and rabbet edge butt joints on the right.

FIGURE 10.3 Miter joint on the left, rabbet edge butt joint on the right.

Freehand Foam Board Butt Joints with a Disguised Edge

This particular method, shown in Figures 10.4 through 10.9, takes quite a bit of practice. First, draw a line where you want to cut out the material. Use either your scale or a piece of foam board to get the exact width. If using foam board, simply butt the board you will be trimming against another piece of foam board. Instead of tracing the foam board (which could move), simply draw a couple tick marks, and connect them later using a straightedge. Make certain the line you have just drawn is perfectly parallel to the edge. Now, place your steel straightedge against the line, and begin to slice through the foam core. Take your time, and use several very light passes. When you begin to feel the paper backing on the underside of

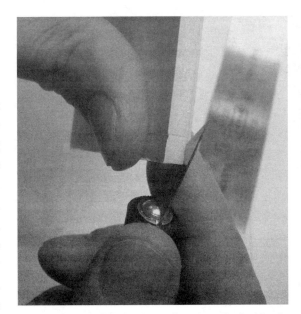

FIGURE 10.5 Carefully begin to slice along the inside of the paper backing.

FIGURE 10.6 Carefully begin to slice along the inside of the paper backing—this time, perpendicular to the first cuts you made.

FIGURE 10.4 It is possible to use a piece of foam board to get the exact width.

the foam, stop cutting. Now, rotate the board 90 degrees, and begin to slice along the inside of the paper backing. Take several passes until your blade intersects with the area you have already cut into (see Figures 10.5 and 10.6). If done correctly, the excess will fall away, leaving you a clean tab at the end of your board (see Figure 10.7). This clean tab will cover the foam edge of the wall perpendicular to it (see Figure 10.8). Should there be any unevenness on the exposed flap, this can be removed using one of two methods. First, you could try slicing along the inside edge of the paper a second time. The other way to accomplish this is by placing the board facedown on a solid work

FIGURE 10.7 If done correctly, the excess will fall away, leaving you a clean tab.

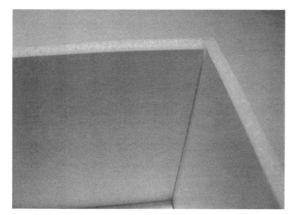

FIGURE 10.8 Clean rabbet corner.

FIGURE 10.9 Remove any unevenness by scraping your blade across the surface.

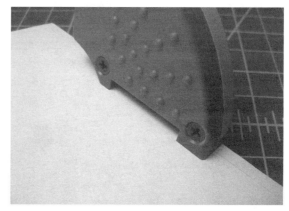

FIGURE 10.10 Alvin Rabbet Foam Board Cutter in use.

surface, and dragging your blade perpendicularly along the length of the edge. The second method described will dull your blades very quickly (see Figure 10.9).

Rabbet Edge Foam Board Cutter

A **rabbet** is an L-shaped groove that is cut into the end of a board. These model building tools were designed for creating a joint so that when joining two pieces of foam board together, the exposed edge will be disguised. As was mentioned earlier, if you purchase only one foam-board-specific tool, this would be the one.

Using a Rabbet Edge Foam Board Cutter

There are a couple different rabbet edge foam board cutters on the market. As long as you keep your blades sharp, they will all deliver a quality cut. We will concern ourselves with

two types: the first is manufactured by Alvin; the second by FoamWerks.

The smaller, Alvin-brand cutter requires two steps.

1. Place the cutter at the end of your foam board; make sure it is perpendicular to the board. The side of the cutter that is in your hands is the side where the foam board strip will be removed. Carefully pull it toward you until you have cut completely through the board (see Figure 10.10).
2. Rotate the cutter 90 degrees, and place it at the end of the board. Make sure the colored portion is adjacent to the strip that you want to keep. Carefully pull it toward you until you have cut through the board completely, and the thin wedge of foam has fallen off (see Figure 10.11).

The larger, FoamWerks rabbet cutter requires only one step, and, using either your left or right hand, can be either pushed or pulled to complete the cut. Lay the board on a flat surface. Keep the handle to the outside of the board and either pull or push the cutter

FIGURE 10.11 Clean rabbet edge.

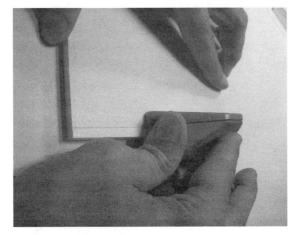

FIGURE 10.12 Using a FoamWerks Rabbet Cutter.

FIGURE 10.13 Removing the wedge.

FIGURE 10.14 (Top). Cutting with a FoamWerks Straight/Bevel Cutter.

FIGURE 10.15 (Bottom). You should now have a perfectly beveled, 45-degree cut.

the length of the board until the wedge falls off (see Figures 10.12 and 10.13).

Cutting a Mitered Edge Foam Board Corner

When cutting a beveled edge, it is essential that you do this in a single pass, as opposed to the recommended numerous passes you should use when cutting 90-degree cuts. Make sure your blade is sharp, and you pass through the paper on both sides. If you try to make numerous passes on a beveled cut, it is nearly impossible to line up your blade, and a wavy exposed edge will result.

There are several commercially produced beveled edge cutters available through companies such as Alvin, Logan, and X-Acto. I have seen professional model makers tape a blade to a beveled piece of wood and slide it along a straight edge, but this is neither safe nor recommended.

Using a Beveled Edge Foam Board Cutter

Many different companies, such as Alvin, Logan, and FoamWerks manufacture beveled edge cutters. FoamWerks manufactures two different foam-board-specific tools that will work to create beveled edges.

The first tool is a bevel cutter; it works in conjunction with a specialized straightedge. Basic use of the FoamWerks straightedge was explained at the beginning of this chapter.

1. Measure the *outside* dimensions of the board you want to cut. Draw a light line where you will be cutting.
2. Lightly draw a second line 1/8 inch to the inside of where you will be cutting (see Figure 10.14).
3. Place the straightedge on the second/inside line.

4. While keeping pressure on the straightedge, start on the outside of the board and gently pull the blade toward you until you have cut completely through the board (see Figure 10.15). You should now have a perfectly beveled 45-degree cut.

Using a V-Groove Cutter to Cut a Beveled Edge

Using a **V-groove cutter** is a method of creating two beveled edges that will eventually be folded together to make a corner. The benefit of this method is, if you choose the correct depth setting for the blades, an extremely clean outside edge. Although it will still need to be glued together, the outside corner will appear seamless. However, if this is not done exactly right, the outside corner could take on a dented appearance.

1. When using this method to make corners, getting a precise measurement is difficult. It is easiest to cut the heights of the walls first.
2. Make certain you have a piece of board slightly longer than the combined lengths of both of your adjacent sides.
3. Draw a line on the back of the board, or on the inside corner, exactly where you will want the outside corner to be. The guide notch of your V-groove cutter will line up with this line.
4. Draw a line parallel to the previous line, exactly 1 1/4 inch from the line that indicates your corner. This is the guide line upon which you will place your straightedge.
5. Using the V-groove cutter on the back of the board, or on the side that will have an inside corner, place your straightedge on the guide line and make certain the notch of the V-groove cutter is on its corresponding line (see Figure 10.16).
6. Starting on the outside of your board, gently pull the blade toward you until you have cut the entire length of the board.
7. You should now have a V-shaped groove in your board (see Figure 10.17).
8. Carefully, begin to fold the two outside walls toward each other until you begin to see a crease appear (see Figure 10.18).
9. Softly, pull the blade of your craft knife along this crease; this should leave a subtle cut in the surface of your board (see Figure 10.19).
10. Gently fold the two sides toward each other until the beveled edges meet. The subtle crease you cut in the previous step will allow the outside corner of the wall surface to form without wrinkling (see Figure 10.20).
11. From the crease, measure and cut the exact lengths that you need.
12. This should give you two correct sides and one tidy corner. Of course, the corner will still require gluing.

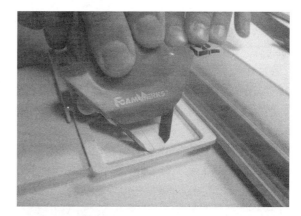

FIGURE 10.16 (Top). Using a FoamWerks V-groove cutter.

FIGURE 10.17 (Center). After cutting, you should have a V-shaped groove in your board.

FIGURE 10.18 (Bottom). Fold the two outside walls toward each other until it creases.

FIGURE 10.19 (Top). Softly, pull the blade of your craft knife along this crease.

FIGURE 10.20 (Bottom). Gently fold the two sides toward each other until the beveled edges meet.

GLUING FOAM BOARD

I prefer to use a white, or hobby glue, such as Sobo or Tacky Glue. Feel free to experiment with different glues and types, but never on a finished piece.

Gluing Foam Edge to a Thin Tab at the Corner (AKA Gluing a Foam Edge to a Rabbet Cut Edge)

It is essential that this edge be clean and professional looking. Excessive glue against the paper edge will cause it to warp. To alleviate this problem, run a small bead of glue along the exposed foam edge. After the bead is applied, rub the glue into the foam, being careful not to get it on any sides that will be exposed (see Figure 10.21). This piece will be glued to the thin tab on the rabbeted piece.

Working quickly, add a thin bead of glue to the exposed edge of the rabbet cut foam board (see Figure 10.22). Carefully rub the glue into the foam like you did in the previous step.

Square up and butt the glued board against a second piece of foam board, gently clamp, and allow it to dry. Be sure to use a pin or something similar to clean off any excess glue that may have leaked out of the joint. Pay special attention to upper and lower edges of the paper tab because these have a tendency to rise up, and may require a little extra attention.

FOAMWERKS TAPE

FoamWerks manufactures a tape specifically for foam board. Although difficult to see, it still does not appear as professional as a well-glued joint. However, it is by far the best product available for disguising an exposed foam edge. It is especially useful for exposed top interior models.

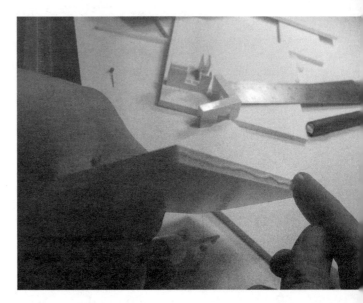

FIGURE 10.21 (Top). Carefully rub the glue into the exposed foam edge.

FIGURE 10.22 (Bottom). Carefully rub the glue into the exposed edge of the rabbet cut foam board.

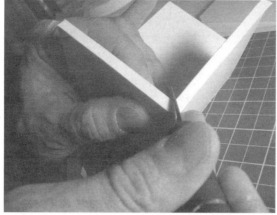

FIGURE 10.23 (Top Left). Apply the foam tape to the exposed foam edge you want to hide.

FIGURE 10.24 (Bottom Left). Pull a sharp blade along the edge of the board, trimming the excess tape. Leave some extra tape where you will have a corner.

FIGURE 10.25 (Top Right). Slice the overlapping pieces of tape at a 45-degree angle, and pull up the excess.

FIGURE 10.26 (Bottom Right). A perfect corner.

Trimming Rabbet Edges

When the joint has dried, place the model facedown. Make sure the portion that needs trimming is on your cutting surface. Using a light touch, score and trim the exposed edge until it comes off on its own accord. If possible, and/or practical, try to assemble the entire model and allow it to dry before trimming (see Figure 10.27).

Disguising Exposed Foam Edges

1. Cut your board to length.
2. Apply the FoamWerks tape to the exposed foam edge you want to hide. Be sure to leave a little excess tape wherever two corners will meet (see Figure 10.23).
3. Place the board, tape side down, on your cutting surface.
4. Pull a sharp blade along the edge of the board, trimming the excess tape. Leave some extra tape where you will have a corner (see Figure 10.24).
5. After the corners have been assembled, slice the overlapping pieces of tape at a 45-degree angle (see Figure 10.25), and pull up the excess. This should leave a perfect corner with no unsightly lumps of tape (see Figure 10.26).

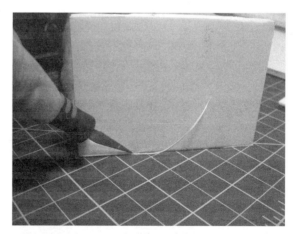

FIGURE 10.27 Score and trim the exposed edge until it comes off on its own accord.

Gluing Mitered Foam Board Corners

I prefer to apply a small bead of glue to each of the exposed foam, mitered edges. On one of the edges, rub the glue into the foam, and leave the thin bead alone on the other. Now, brace the two edges together, and let them dry. Impregnating one of the edges and merely applying a bead on the other ensures a good bond and helps to close the outside corners. This is similar to the process used to glue rabbet edges together. The key is not to use too much glue because it will squirt out the sides of the joint and cause the paper surface to warp.

FOAM BOARD L CLIPS AND T CLIPS

These are extremely useful products that will hold your foam board corners in position while you wait for the glue to dry. Like the rabbet edge cutter, these are worth their weight in gold. L clips are used at 90-degree corners, and T clips are used at 90-degree wall intersections. You can choose to double them up, placing one on the top of your board and another on the bottom. If you choose this method, be sure to use additional clips on the bottoms of the other boards because this will keep everything level (see Figures 10.28 and 10.29). Another method is to glue foam board walls directly to a perfectly squared horizontal (floor) surface, and use the T or L clips to keep the tops square. Figure 10.30 shows two clamps being used along the flap edge. Notice

FIGURE 10.28 (Top Left). Using FoamWerks L clips.

FIGURE 10.29 (Top Right). Gently place the clips over the corners.

FIGURE 10.30 (Bottom Right). Using the L clips in conjunction with hobby clamps and an additional piece of foam board will ensure that the entire edge is bonded tightly.

how an additional piece of foam board is between the clamp and the model's surface. The reason for this is twofold. It helps to equalize pressure along the flap edge and ensures a smooth glue job, and it keeps the clamps from denting the surface of the foam board model.

CUTTING CURVES IN FOAM BOARD: FREEHAND

Although possible, it is especially difficult to cut curves in foam board. The techniques are the same as those already mentioned throughout this book. First, using a 4H pencil, *lightly* draw your curve on the foam board. With your craft knife, use a series of passes until you have cut completely through the board. The tighter the radius of your curves and the deeper into the board your knife plunges, the more you will need to keep your blade vertical. Failure to do so will result in a jagged edge. After you have gotten to the point that you have cut through most of the board, but not 100 percent of it, follow the directions from Step 6 in the following section.

Using a FoamWerks Foamboard Freestyle Cutter

Although not perfect, the FoamWerks Foamboard Freestyle Cutter is definitely the best tool for cutting curves in foam board. Placing an additional piece of foam board beneath the one you are cutting will yield better results than a vinyl cutting mat. Refer to Figures 10.31 through 10.34, and practice a few times to improve this skill.

1. Lightly draw the line you want to follow on the foam board.
2. Place the board you want to cut on top of another piece of flat foam board, preferably larger than the board you are cutting.
3. Before you start cutting, place a small piece of scrap foam board next to where you plan to start your cut. This will give

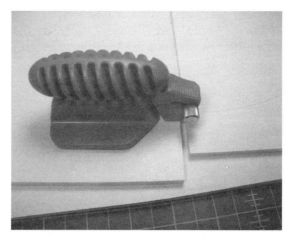

FIGURE 10.31 (Top Left). Before you start cutting, place a small piece of scrap foam board next to where you plan to start your cut.

FIGURE 10.32 (Top Right). A perfect curved cut.

FIGURE 10.33 (Bottom Right). Using the lightest touch possible, drag/slice your craft knife along the indentation of your intended pattern.

the back of the tool something to rest flat upon while it enters the board. Failure to do this will most likely result in a jagged point of entry (see Figure 10.31).

4. Pushing down and forward on the cutter, slowly follow the line you have drawn. You must keep pressure on the tool at all times. If you fail to do so, the cutter will rise up, and you will not cut through the entire board. Figure 10.32 illustrates a perfect cut.
5. After you have finished your cut, the two pieces of board should separate on

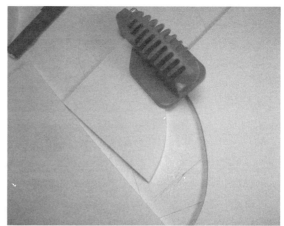

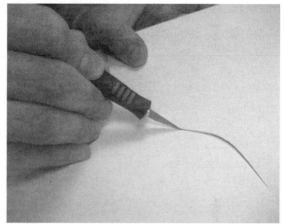

their own. If you did not apply sufficient pressure to the tool, and there are a few areas where you were not able to cut through completely, do not worry; go to the next step.

6. If you did not cut completely through the board, carefully turn the board over; you should still be able to see lines, or inden-

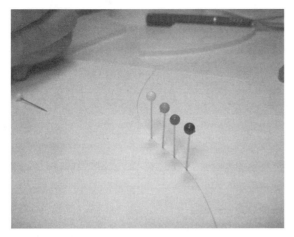

FIGURE 10.34A Drive pins into the foam board along the cut line.

FIGURE 10.34B A series of holes are left on the other side, which you can follow with your craft knife.

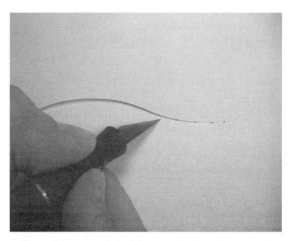

FIGURE 10.34C Carefully follow the holes with your blade to make a nice cut.

tations of your intended pattern. Slowly, gently, twist the two boards so that they begin to separate. Do not twist them so much that the paper face begins to tear.

7. Using the lightest touch possible, drag/slice your craft knife along the indentation of your intended pattern. Start with the rear of the knife, and slowly pull it along its length. This will cut the paper gently, and more importantly, cleanly (see Figure 10.33).

8. If, for some reason, you are unable to see the cut line you need to follow, flip the board over; begin to drive pins into the foam board. This will leave a series of holes on the other side that you can follow with your craft knife. Go back to Step 6 and repeat (see Figures 10.34a, 10.34b, and 10.34c).

Cutting Curves, Go With the Flow

Regardless of what type of tool you are using to cut curves, it is nearly impossible to cut exactly on the lines you have drawn. Fixed blades have a natural turning radius, and, especially with foam board, will tend to bind up or make jagged cuts if you try to over-correct when your blade begins to drift away from your desired line. The best thing to do is to try to gradually return to the line you wish to follow. Chances are, unless you are cutting a perfect circle, the curves are fairly naturalistic, and it is probably more important to have a clean edge than to follow exactly the lines you may have drawn. If you must cut something perfectly, you may want to consider changing materials to something else such as hardboard and use a scroll saw for your cutting.

CUTTING CIRCLES

The human eye is remarkably perceptive when it comes to recognizing inconsistencies in things such as the human face, cylinders, and circles. Trying to cut a perfect foam board circle by hand is an exercise in futility. Olfa and FoamWerks both manufacture circle cutters. The Olfa cutter can easily cut a perfect foam board circle (see Figure 10.35), but the FoamWerks circle cutters can cut both perfect circles and perfect holes. FoamWerks manufactures a foam board hole drill that acts much the same as a carpenter's hole saw, with the same limitations; although it will cut an absolutely perfect circle and hole, it can only do so in four sizes—0.75, 0.5, 0.28, and 0.18 inches. FoamWerks also manufactures a foam board

FIGURE 10.35 The Olfa cutter can easily cut a perfect foam board circle.

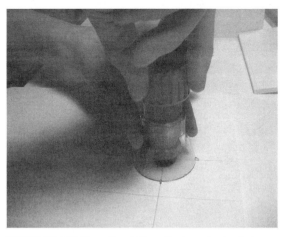

FIGURE 10.36A Place the drill on the board; slowly turn the handle on top until the blade has cut completely through the board.

FIGURE 10.36B A perfect hole and a perfect circle.

circle cutter that will cut both perfect circles and holes anywhere from 1 to 6 inches.

Using a Foam Board Drill

1. If you want to cut a circle into a board, draw your circle or series of circles first. If possible, find the center of the circles, and use a template. Divide the circle into four equal quadrants; align the four notches on the outside of the drill with the four lines you have drawn.

2. Place the drill on the board; slowly turn the handle on top until the blade is nearly touching the board. Take this opportunity to make sure the circular blade is properly aligned with the circle you have drawn.

3. Continue to turn the knob until you have cut completely through the board (see Figure 10.36a).

4. Carefully remove the drill by pulling it straight out.

5. Push the little blue knob on the top of the cutter to eject the circle (Figure 10.36b).

6. If the edges are a bit jagged, use a burnisher to clean them up.

Using a Foam Board Circle Cutter

1. As in the previous Step 1, if you want to cut a circle into a board, draw your circle or series of circles first. It is imperative that you find the center of your intended circle before you begin cutting.

2. If you intend to cut a circle of less than a 2-inch diameter, lay two strips of foam board below the board you want to cut, at approximately the same width apart as the transparent dome (see Figure 10.37).

FIGURE 10.37 A FoamWerks circle cutter.

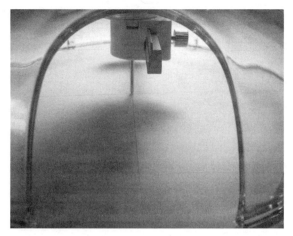

FIGURE 10.38 Lower the cutter so that the centering pin is directly on the center of your circle.

FIGURE 10.39 A perfect circle, and a perfect hole.

Elevating the smaller circles while cutting will allow the blade to cut through the board much more cleanly than if it had a piece of foam or mat board below it. If the circle is between 2 and 6 inches in diameter, make certain you have a piece of foam board below it before cutting.

3. The handle on the top of the dome goes in two directions; one direction raises the blade, and the other direction lowers it. Make sure the blade is raised before positioning the cutter on your board.

4. Adjust the scaled cutting beam to the correct diameter of the circle you wish to cut. This can be done by turning the adjustment knob and sliding the beam until it reads the proper dimension. This is found on the underside of the cutter, attached to the blade.

5. Lower the cutter onto your board such that the centering pin is directly on the center of your circle (see Figure 10.38).

6. Apply pressure to the dome while turning the knob clockwise. Continue to cut until you are certain the blade has completely cut through the board (review Figure 10.37).

7. You should now have a perfect circle and a perfect hole (see Figure 10.39).

8. Be safe—turn the knob counterclockwise until the blade is raised as far up as possible.

9. Burnish any rough edges.

CREATING CURVED WALL SURFACES USING FOAM BOARD

Note: For the purposes of this section, the term *wall* will stand for any curved surface.

Bear in mind, these techniques are not exclusive to vertical surfaces.

Unlike thinner museum board, foam board is too rigid and thick to bend naturally. It is, therefore, necessary to more or less impose a grain upon the board by slicing it vertically. This process is known as kerfing. This process can be done with a craft knife and a straightedge, or with the aid of a V-groove cutter. More often than not, viewing the vertical slices is not desirable. This is easily remedied; simply spray mount a piece of cardstock or other appropriately colored paper to the cut surface. Regardless of whichever method you choose to use, make certain that you always adhere to the following guidelines:

1. Keep the depth of your cuts and the spacing between them consistent. Failure to do so will result in a curved surface that has dents in it.

2. The tighter the curve, the closer the spacing of the kerfs or cuts. The tighter the curve, the greater the likelihood that you will get a curved surface with dents in it.

3. Never, ever, cut all the way through your board. If you do, it will require quite a bit of cosmetic work or starting over.

4. Curved walls work best when glued to the side of a perpendicular surface, as opposed to on top of one. If possible, use pins to keep things in place while the glue dries.

5. One way to ensure fairly clean tops and bottoms is to leave the height of the board slightly oversize, kerf the board, and then trim it to size.

Freehand Kerfing, Exposed Cuts on an Outside Curve

1. Cut your curved base to the exact interior dimensions you want.
2. Make a series of evenly spaced cuts, making sure they are all more or less cut to the same depth.
3. These cuts must correlate with area of the outside curve you want to create. If, like the example, your curve undulates, it will be necessary to cut on both sides of your wall (see Figure 10.40).

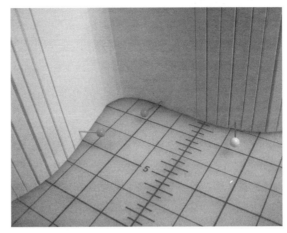

FIGURE 10.41 Use pins to hold your wall in place while the glue dries.

4. Dry fit your curved surface to ensure a proper fit.
5. Trim the piece at the top and bottom to the desired wall height. It is a good idea to trim any facing paper or cardstock (that you will be using to disguise the cuts) at the same time.
6. Use pins to hold your wall in place while the glue dries (see Figure 10.41).
7. Use repositionable spray adhesive to apply the paper covering.

Freehand Kerfing: Creating an Outside Curve with No Visible Cuts

It is possible to create an outside curve while maintaining the integrity of the foam board surface. However, this is not a process to follow should you want to see both sides of your wall because the opposite side will be, at the very least, not of presentation quality.

1. Make sure the height of your board is greater than that of your intended wall. In other steps it is recommended that you kerf first, and trim second. In this step it is not a recommendation—it is a necessity.
2. Cut out the curved pattern/floor to which you will be adhering your wall.
3. On the back side of the wall or the inside of the curve, tear off the surface of the foam board, exposing the foam (see Figure 10.42).
4. Proceed to kerf the foam side of the wall. After you have finished kerfing,

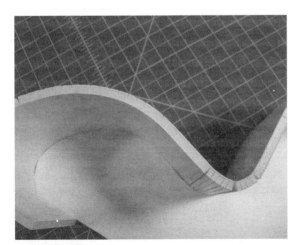

FIGURE 10.40 These kerfs must correlate with area of the outside curve you want to create. In this case, they are necessary on both sides.

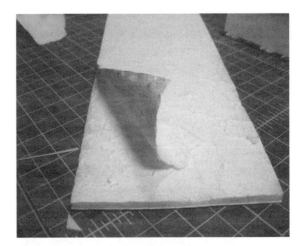

FIGURE 10.42 On what will be the inside of the curve, tear off the surface of the foam board, exposing the foam.

trim the wall to the correct height (see Figure 10.43).

5. Using glue and temporary pins, attach the wall to the floor (see Figure 10.44).

6. When the glue has dried, remove the pins, and you should have a finished wall.

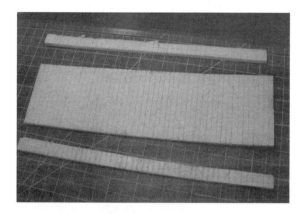

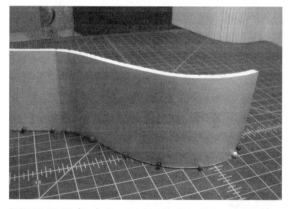

FIGURE 10.43 (Top). Proceed to kerf the foam side of the wall; then trim the wall to the correct height.

FIGURE 10.44 (Bottom). Use pins to hold your wall in place while the glue dries. Here, they are stuck laterally into the floor surface.

FIGURE 10.45 Adjustable depth blade cutters ensure consistency in your cuts.

Using a Straight Cutter to Create Perfect Kerfing

The biggest problems you will encounter when kerfing freehand are accidentally cutting completely through your board or creating inconsistent depths of cuts. If the depths are inconsistent, some areas may give more than others, creating an unsightly dent in the curved wall surface. This can be eliminated if you choose to use a straight cutter with an adjustable depth setting for the blade. Place the channel rail on each of the equally spaced lines you have drawn, and draw the straight cutter across the board until you have the requisite number of cuts. FoamWerks has two different adjustable depth straight cutters available. Figure 10.45 shows the depth gauge.

Using a V-Groove Cutter to Create an Outside or Undulating Curve with No Visible Cuts

1. Be certain your wall is oversize, both in terms of length and width.

2. Cut out the curved pattern/floor to which you will be adhering your wall.

3. On the back side (inside curve) of the wall, draw a series of vertical lines 1/2 inch apart from each other.

4. Set the depth on the V-groove cutter to approximately 1/8 inch. If it is any deeper than this on 1/4-inch foam board, the outside curve will show a series of vertical lines.

5. Place the channel rail on the lines you have drawn.

FIGURE 10.46 Cut a series of V-grooves on the back of your wall.

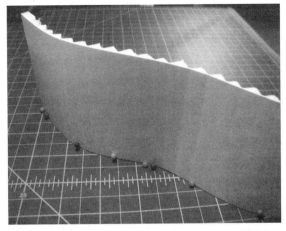

FIGURE 10.47 Using pins and glue, attach the wall to the floor.

a flat, horizontal surface to two vertical surfaces. Note: The following process requires a bit of practice to perfect. Do not try this process for the first time on something like a presentation model.

1. Create a rabbet edge corner; make sure it is perfectly square. These are your vertical surfaces, or your wall.
2. Following the outside dimensions of your wall, cut a piece of foam board to those exact dimensions.
3. Rabbet cut any edges that will intersect with your walls (see Figure 10.48).
4. Apply glue to the surfaces you intend to join.
5. Figure 10.49 illustrates how the pieces will fit together.
6. After the pieces have dried, clean up and trim any poorly crafted edges.

6. Cut a series of V-grooves on the back of your wall. Make sure the foam board channel rail is supported at either end by foam board. Failure to do so will result in a sloppy entry or exit point (see Figure 10.46).
7. Trim the top and bottom of your wall to the correct height.
8. Dry fit the wall; trim to the correct length.
9. Using pins and glue, attach the wall to the floor (see Figure 10.47).

JOINING THREE OR MORE SURFACES

Should you need to create an object with three or more corners (stairs, flat roofs, boxes, etc.) without revealing any of the foam core, simply observe the following instructions. For demonstration purposes, we will attach

FIGURE 10.48 (Left). Rabbet cut any edges that will intersect with your walls.

FIGURE 10.49 (Top Right). A tidy top to your box.

FIGURE 10.50 (Bottom Right). Two boxes with finished corners. Notice the difference in craftsmanship between them.

7. Figure 10.50 illustrates two boxes with finished corners. Notice the difference in craftsmanship between them.

Concrete Block and Brick

An interesting texture can be obtained by removing the paper face from foam board, scoring the joint lines, and spray painting it an appropriate color. Make sure you test the paint on a scrap first; some paint can react adversely with the exposed foam. This is only feasible at larger scales.

1. Begin by drawing your brick pattern on the face of the foam board.

2. Make a cut along each side of the mortar lines. Allow the blade to cut about 25 percent through the foam board. Allow the tip of the blade to drift toward the center of the mortar lines. This should give you a rough V-groove. In this case, a rough texture will add to the lifelikeness of the brick.
3. After you have cut tiny V-grooves into all the grout lines, begin to remove the paper facing. Use tweezers to remove any mortar lines that did not come up when you removed the paper facing.
4. Lightly spray paint an appropriate brick color onto the wall. Hold your can of paint at about a 45-degree angle above your wall. This will keep the paint from getting into the mortar lines. Figure 10.51 illustrates a painted brick surface. The penny is included for purposes of scale.

Foam board models are one of the most popular model types among design students. The tips and techniques demonstrated in this chapter should be of assistance to you when working with foam board. It is a completely acceptable medium for use in study models, and, if it is well crafted, in presentation models as well.

Remember, one of the drawbacks of building exclusively in foam board is its thickness. Be careful if you are using foam board as the only medium in a model, especially if you are trying to convey actual material, wall, or door thicknesses. For students who lack a fully stocked shop, foam board is very nearly always an excellent choice for a structural material onto which other materials may then be applied. See Chapter 12 for more information on mixing materials. Remember, to make a clean, professional-looking cut, keep your blades sharp and change your blades often.

KEY TERMS

Klingons
memory
overcuts
rabbet

Chapter Review and Practice

(See "Materials Needed by Chapter," p. xxi.)

1. *Build three 6" × 6" foam board cubes. Cut out two 2" × 2" holes in the center of two of the sides. For one of the cubes you may use a rabbet edge foam board cutter. For the second cube, you must freehand the rabbet edge; for the third, use mitered edge corners.*
2. *Using foam board, create an undulating wall, 6 inches tall and 12 inches long. Using spray mount and cardstock, disguise the kerfed edge. Disguise all exposed surfaces. Read #3 in this section before starting this particular exercise.*
3. *Create an undulating wall identical to the one you created in #2. Remove the paper backing from one side of the foam before forming the wall. Disguise all exposed surfaces.*

Balsa and Basswood Construction Techniques 11

OBJECTIVES

- *Understand the properties of wood that make it a good material for models*
- *See how wood fits into the array of materials a model maker has to choose from*
- *Develop your personal preference for materials*
- *Understand how to choose the best materials to communicate the model's purpose*

Both balsa and basswood are beautiful materials for model making. Because of their strength, they make excellent materials for use in models that highlight a building's skeletal structure. The warm quality of wood makes it a good choice for presentation models, regardless of whether the building in question will be constructed of wood. This chapter will introduce you to a variety of techniques that are useful for working with theses types of wood. Some of these techniques are modifications of the basics you've already learned. You will also learn some new techniques.

Make sure you have the following tools available when working with balsa and basswood: craft knife, razor saw, miter box, mini clamps, white glue, razor plane, engineer's or try square, sandpaper, and balsa wood stripper.

BALSA WOOD

Balsa is a porous wood that has the highest strength-to-weight ratio of any wood on earth. It is extremely soft, bends well with the grain, and is easily cut using a craft knife. It has a tendency to splinter when it is cut or sanded into complex curves. Even after sanding, balsa may still have a rough appearance.

It can warp with the grain when stained, but accepts semi-transparent markers. It can be painted, but usually requires more than one coat. It can be glued extremely easily.

Balsa wood can usually be purchased in 4-inch by 48-inch planks, which are typically available in thicknesses from 1/16 inch to 1/2 inch. Balsa wood sticks are typically available in lengths of up to 36 inches long and can be anywhere from 1/16 to 7/8 of an inch square. Recently, a few companies have begun manufacturing balsa wood **dowels**, as well as laser cut wheels or circles.

Balsa wood has three grades or types of grains—A, B, and C. Although fairly inconsequential to the architectural model builder, the grading system is of great import to the model airplane builder. Always think about the scale of the grain as it relates to the scale and material descriptions of your model.

A Grain

A grain has the longest, thinnest grains, and bends (and distorts!) the easiest when compared to other grades. This is a good choice for curved surfaces. It should not be used as a structural material, or a **cantilevered** surface.

B Grain

B grain is the type found in most hobby shops. It is a general purpose and economic balsa wood. It has a grain width between that of A and C. This should work for 90 percent of student models.

C Grain

C grain is the strongest and stiffest of the balsas across the grain. It is an excellent choice as far as balsas go if you intend to paint or stain your model. C grain is also good for cantilevered and structural models.

BASSWOOD

Basswood is harder and has a tighter grain than balsa wood, yet is still an extremely soft wood. It is easier to carve than balsa wood, yet harder to cut. Thin basswood can be cut with a craft knife; whereas if you choose to cut this wood by hand, a razor saw and miter box are recommended. Complex curves are best cut by hand with a coping saw. Cross cut curves can be easily sanded using a small file or sandpaper. Unlike balsa wood, the surface of basswood can be sanded smooth. Basswood is cut easily using the power tools listed in the following section.

Basswood accepts paint easily, but can blotch unevenly when stained unless treated beforehand with a wood conditioner. Polyurethane finishes look particularly sharp when applied to basswood. It can be glued easily.

Basswood can usually be purchased in 4-inch by 48-inch planks, which are typically available in thicknesses from 1/8 inch to 1/2 inch. Because it is less porous than balsa wood, it accepts detail more readily. This is why it is possible to find basswood precut into ornamental strips, moldings, and scale siding.

POWER TOOLS

If you are extremely fortunate, you will have access to the following specialty tools for use with balsa or basswood.

Micro Table Saw

This is similar to a standard 8- or 10-inch table saw. Look for a 4-inch version with about 10,000 RPM. Make sure it has a blade with an adjustable height and angle, as well as an adjustable rip fence.

Micro Miter Saw

Similar to a larger chop saw, this should perform the same functions, only on a reduced scale.

Scroll Saw

This is an essential tool if you will be making numerous curved cuts. Do not skimp when it comes to this piece of equipment. Cheaper models tend to vibrate excessively, which leads to poor quality cuts. Look for a model with an adjustable bench that allows for beveled cuts if necessary.

Band Saw

Depending on the width of the blade and accessories, a band saw can accomplish many of the same tasks as the three previously mentioned tools.

COLORING OR STAINING WOOD

Should you choose to apply stain to your wood, do so prior to using any type of glue. Any gluing prior to the use of stain will create a resist in the wood, and a lighter, sealed area will be the result. Make certain all exposed edges are stained prior to gluing as well. Finally, make sure you stain every surface—failure to do so will cause the wood to warp.

ADHESIVES

When working with balsa and basswood, you will definitely need to use a variety of glues.

Although most of these glues have been discussed in earlier chapters, their uses specific to wood are described as follows. The following glues are listed by brand name for your convenience.

When working with a polyvinyl acetate **(PVA)**, commonly referred to as a "wood glue," be sure to heed the following instructions:

1. Apply a light bead of glue using an S-shaped motion to both pieces of wood. Spread the glue evenly across the surface of your wood.
2. Wait a few moments; allow the glue to become tacky.
3. Clamp the pieces together, or place them under pressure, and allow them to dry.

You may have to experiment with the process because it will differ slightly depending on the type of wood used, the size or type of joint or bond you want to create, and the brand of glue you decide to use.

Gluing Wood

It is essential that you work on more than one part at a time—this will allow the different parts of your project to dry thoroughly before you proceed to the next step. Handling a project before it has time to dry is a disaster waiting to happen.

ALTECO ST50 Super Glue

This glue is extremely useful for quick fixes, tacking, and repairs. It literally dries in a matter of seconds. Not recommended for everyday use.

Elmer's Wood Glue

This is different from standard Elmer's glue, as its use is specific for wood. It is a yellow glue, as opposed to the standard white glue.

Gorilla Glue

This is about twice the cost of most types of glue discussed in this chapter. In this case, you really do get what you pay for. While the glue dries, it has a tendency to foam a bit. The foaming action actually assists the glue in penetrating the surface of the wood, and, as a result, creates a much stronger bond. This glue also takes twice as long as most other glues to dry.

Jet Glue

Jet Glue is available in several varieties, but you should concern yourself primarily with Slow Jet, a slow-drying instant glue that allows you a few seconds for repositioning. Due to its thickness, this glue is particularly well suited for filling gaps.

Sobo Glue

Sobo Glue dries quicker than Gorilla Glue, yet stronger than Tacky Glue. It is a great all-around model glue that will work with balsa and basswood 99 percent of the time.

Tacky Glue

This craft glue is surprisingly useful for building delicate objects such as scale furniture. It dries much faster than most white glues, yet slow enough that parts can be repositioned if necessary. Although adequate for most student grade applications, I would not suggest using Tacky Glue where strength is critical.

Titebond 3, Ultimate Wood Glue

At the time this book was written, this glue was extremely new to the market. This glue is strong and waterproof. Unlike Gorilla Glue, this does not foam while drying (important when neatness is a factor).

User-Friendly Odorless (UFO) Super Glue

This Super Glue will allow you a little bit of time to set up or reposition a piece before it dries. It is thicker than most Super Glues, so it is extremely useful for butt joints and other end grain applications. This is a great glue, and odorless, too.

WORKING WITH BALSA WOOD AND BASSWOOD

The techniques for cutting balsa wood are basically the same as those used for cutting paper-based products.

There are several grades of these woods available; generally the higher the grade, the cleaner the cut you will be able to make. For the cleanest cuts, look into the possibility of using the more expensive wood. The higher-grade balsa is available in stores that cater to the model railroad or radio-controlled aircraft hobbyist. Harder balsa has a tendency to splinter slightly at the edges when cut, whereas softer balsa tends to distort at the edges if your knife is not extremely sharp.

Cutting with a craft knife or razor blade is simple, especially if you are cutting parallel with the grain. Make certain you have a *new* #11 blade and a straightedge. As with mat board, several passes will ensure a clean cut.

MARKING BALSA OR BASSWOOD

Just like in previous chapters, mark your wood using a hard, sharp pencil. Bear in mind, it is rather difficult to erase pencil from a rough-grained surface, such as balsa or even basswood. If you use an eraser on the area you intend to draw on before you actually draw on it, it will more or less smooth out or unify the surface of the wood. Any pencil lines drawn on a wood surface prepared in this manner will erase much more easily than they would if they were drawn on unprepared wood.

CUTTING BALSA WOOD AND BASSWOOD

Both of these woods will be cut easiest with the grain, and require a bit more effort when

FIGURE 11.1 (Top). Check for square.

FIGURE 11.2 (Bottom). Check the edges of your wood to see if they are square, or cut at an acute or obtuse angle.

cutting perpendicular to the grain. That being said, balsa and basswood that is 1/4-inch or thinner can be easily cut using a craft knife with a #11 blade. Of the two types, balsa wood is by far the easiest to cut. Because it is harder, it is easier to make precise or detailed cuts in basswood. Practice a little with both types so you can make an informed decision as to which type of wood will best serve your purpose. Many of the demonstrations in this chapter use a surgeon's scalpel. Cutting balsa and basswood is similar, but not identical to, cutting the other materials in this book. Read the captions and study the illustrations carefully to notice the subtle changes in technique.

1. Mark your cut line, and place a straightedge on the line to check for square. As shown in Figures 11.1 and 11.2, check the edges of your wood to see if they are square or cut an acute or obtuse angle. This is much more critical than when working with paper-based boards.
2. On the edges of the wood, cut a small notch. These will help your blade to start and finish cleanly. Failure to do this can

often result in a slightly wavy edge at the ends of your cuts (see Figure 11.3a).
3. Use a series of passes until you cut through the wood. Be sure to keep your

blade as perpendicular as possible to the cutting surface (see Figure 11.3b).

4. After you have finished the cut, check for square (see Figure 11.3c).
5. Use a sanding block to smooth out any rough edges (see Figure 11.3d).

Cutting Thicker Pieces of Balsa and Basswood by Hand

When cutting thicker pieces, it is prudent to use a miter box and razor saw. These tools are fairly self-explanatory and simple to use. That being said, mastering the razor saw will require a few practice attempts. Simply mark your wood, and place it in the miter box. Make certain your mark is lined up with the correct slots in the box; a typical miter box is designed to cut at angles of 45 and 90 degrees. There are two versions of this particular setup—one has a built-in clamp for holding your material, and the other does not. It

is important to remember that the blade of the razor saw has a width. Make sure you place the edge of the blade to the outside of your mark, not on it. If you cut exactly on the mark, the result will be a piece of wood slightly smaller than the piece you desire.

Use a sanding block to remove any splinters or burrs.

Mitered Cuts

When cutting perpendicular to the grain, or angled sections, use light pressure with a fine-

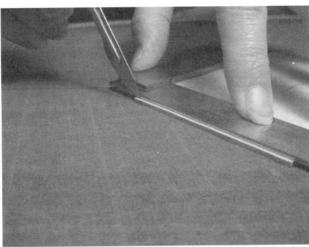
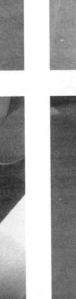
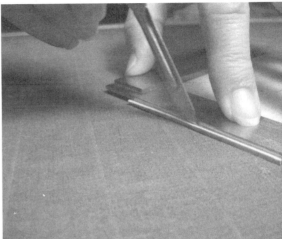

FIGURE 11.3A (Top Left). On the edges of the wood, cut a small notch. These notches will help your blade start and finish cleanly.

FIGURE 11.3B (Top Right). Use a series of passes until you cut through the wood.

FIGURE 11.3C (Bottom Left). After you have finished the cut, check for square. Notice the gap here; this piece is not square and must either be trimmed down, sanded square, or discarded.

FIGURE 11.3D (Bottom Right). Use a sanding block to smooth out any rough edges.

toothed razor saw in a miter to ensure a clean cut. Some light sanding is usually required after cutting.

If you will require an abundance of strips and do not want to spend the money on precut individual strips, use a balsa stripper.

Cutting Identical Pieces from Balsa and Basswood

1. Cut and sand one piece so that it is perfect; this will be your master. Mark it with an "M."
2. Using your master as a template, trace its shape onto the other pieces.
3. Cut out all your pieces.

4. Gather all pieces of the same shape and place them together so as to make their common edges align.
5. Use a sanding block with 180-220 grit sandpaper on a sanding, and lightly sand all the aligned edges square.
6. If you have numerous pieces, as well as access to a table saw, you may want to make two masters from a stronger material such as medium-density fiberboard (MDF). Sandwich the balsa strips between the MDF and then sand by hand. This will ensure that you do not accidentally shave down and alter the size of your master—a very real danger should your master be made of balsa wood.

Keep It Clean, Keep It Professional Looking

Unfortunately, every piece of balsa or basswood you purchase will have either a laser printed barcode on it or a sticker, the residue of which never seems to come off. Never, ever use a piece with a barcode on it where it can be seen. I have seen countless student models that were otherwise beautiful, ruined by the inclusion of an exposed barcode or two.

Cutting Dowels

Depending on the width of your dowel, you can choose to either cut it by hand

FIGURE 11.4 Using the miter box to cut a dowel.

(1/8 inch or smaller) or use the miter box and razor saw. Using the miter box is quite convenient because it has grooves that will seat the dowel while it is being cut (see Figure 11.4).

Cutting Dowels by Hand

1. Mark your dowel the correct length.
2. Place the dowel on a flat, level surface.
3. Place your blade on the dowel, as close to the tip as possible (see Figure 11.5a).
4. While keeping the blade perpendicular to the cutting surface, roll the dowel back and forth. Each time you roll the blade forward, slightly increase the amount of pressure you put on the blade. The blade will continue to cut deeper into the dowel until it "snaps" in two (see Figures 11.5b and 11.5c).
5. This will leave a slightly raised center to the dowel (see Figure 11.5d) and you can simply sand it flat (see Figure 11.5e).

DRILLING HOLES

When drilling holes in balsa or basswood, you may use a small, handheld hobby drill, or, for holes larger than 1/16 inch, use an electric drill press or a drill press attachment for your Dremel rotary tool (see Figure 11.6).

Regardless of what type of tool you choose to use to drill holes, make sure that:

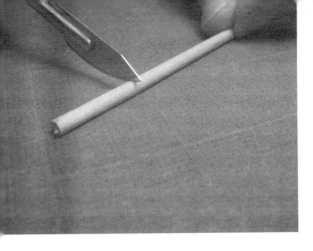

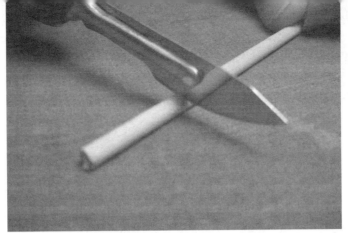

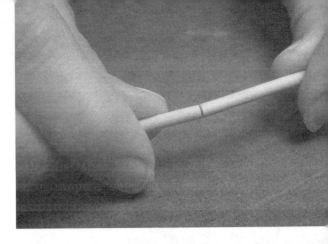

FIGURE 11.5A (Top Left). Place your blade on the dowel.

FIGURE 11.5B (Top Center). While keeping the blade perpendicular to the cutting surface, roll the dowel back and forth.

FIGURE 11.5C (Top Right). The blade will cut deeper into the dowel until it "snaps" in two.

FIGURE 11.5D (Bottom Left). This will leave a slightly raised center to the dowel.

FIGURE 11.5E (Bottom Right). Sand the raised center of the dowel flat.

- Your wood is held down securely.
- There is an additional piece below the piece you are drilling into. Failure to rest your wood on another piece will result in a sloppy "exit wound" on the back side of your board.

If you are drilling holes freehand, be careful to ensure that you drill perpendicular to the board.

CUTTING OPENINGS IN BALSA AND BASSWOOD

In this section, we will be discussing the cutting of openings, generally for windows or doors, in balsa or basswood. In this demonstration, we will be cutting basswood with a scalpel.

1. Using a hard lead pencil, mark your opening.

2. Using a straightedge, the first cuts you make must be perpendicular to the grain of the wood. Wood cut parallel with the grain has a tendency to split and go beyond your intended boundaries. By making your perpendicular cuts first, you will be cutting through the parallel grains, which will act as a stop when cutting parallel to the grain (see Figure 11.7a).

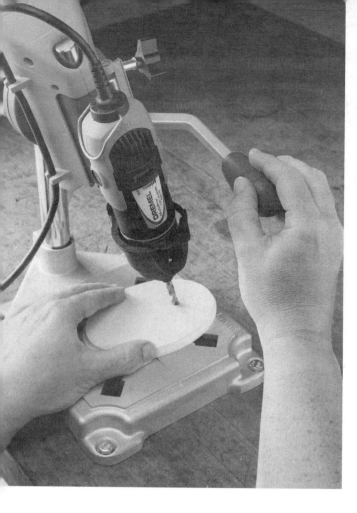

FIGURE 11.6 Drill press attachment for a Dremel rotary tool.

provided that you can keep your blade perpendicular to the cutting surface (see Figure 11.7b).

5. After you have cut through a few spots in the wood, turn it over and begin cutting from the other side. This will ensure a clean cut on both sides (see Figure 11.7c).

6. Using the same techniques, repeat this process, this time cutting parallel to the grain.

7. Carefully remove the extra piece (see Figure 11.7d).

8. Check for bad edges, especially at the corners. Using your blade and cutting toward the corners, carefully shave away any extra, inconsistencies, or curved areas (see Figure 11.7e).

9. Use some finesse at the corners, cut toward a corner, rotate 90 degrees, and cut toward where the last cut ended. This technique will give you a clean inside corner (see Figure 11.7f).

10. Using a small sanding block or nail file, sand the inside edges and corners (see Figure 11.7g). A smooth, square, finished opening is the final result (see Figure 11.7h).

CREATING WINDOWS

There are several techniques for creating windows. The two most common ways of rep-

3. Just like you did when cutting openings in the other materials discussed in this book, start your cuts from the corners, plung-ing straight down. Then cut toward the middle.

4. Make several passes until you begin to cut through the wood. After you begin to have a groove cut into the wood, cutting freehand is completely acceptable,

resenting windows involve either leaving a negative space open behind a window you have cut, or placing an additional piece of wood behind the opening. Both can involve the addition of mullions. The steps are similar, but not identical to, the creation of windows using museum board.

Adding Mullions, Smaller Scale

The window in this demonstration is approximately 1-inch square.

1. To get the most accurate **mullion**, place your balsa strip in the center of the window; make certain it is square. Mark it using your blade, remove it from the window, and cut it to size (see Figure 11.8a).

2. When cutting smaller strips to length, use a slicing motion, as opposed to merely pushing down. Pushing straight down can distort the wood, result in crooked cuts, and even cause the smaller piece to fly away once it has been severed (see Figures 11.8b and 11.8c).

3. Check the fit before gluing (see Figure 11.8d).

4. Apply a small amount of glue to either end of your center mullion. Use tweezers to position the mullion (see Figure 11.8e).

5. Using the same techniques, measure, cut, and apply the vertical window trim to the outside of the opening you cut. Make sure

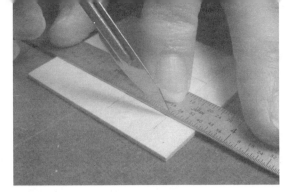

FIGURE 11.7A Make your perpendicular cuts first.

FIGURE 11.7B Start your cuts from the corners, plunging straight down. Then cut by pulling toward the middle.

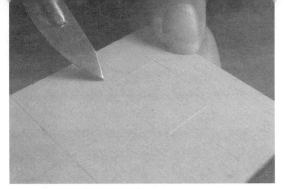

FIGURE 11.7C Turn it over and begin cutting from the other side to ensure clean cuts.

FIGURE 11.7D Carefully remove the extra piece.

FIGURE 11.7E Carefully shave away any extra, inconsistent, or curved areas.

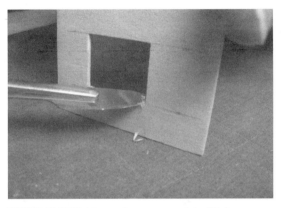

FIGURE 11.7F Cut toward a corner, rotate 90 degrees, and cut toward where the last cut ended.

the ends of your mullions are cut square; use the knife blade as a gauge (see Figure 11.8f). These should be the same length as the opening (see Figure 11.8g). Notice how the blade is used as a stop to ensure that the trim stays flush with the existing opening (see Figures 11.8h and 11.8i).

6. Keep your holding hand where it was in Figure 11.8i. Move the blade to the other side of the trim, and cut it to size. Do

FIGURE 11.7G Sand the inside edges and corners.

FIGURE 11.7H A smooth, square, finished opening.

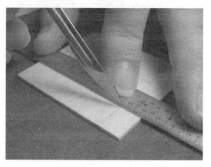

FIGURE 11.8A Place your balsa strip in the center of the window; mark its length using your blade.

FIGURE 11.8B When cutting smaller strips to length, do so using a slicing motion.

FIGURE 11.8C A slicing motion ensures a smooth, vertical cut.

FIGURE 11.8D Dry fit before gluing.

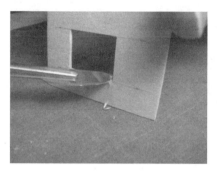

FIGURE 11.8E Apply a small amount of glue, and use tweezers to position the mullion.

FIGURE 11.8F Use the knife blade as a gauge to square your mullions.

FIGURE 11.8G Use the openings as a guide when cutting trim.

FIGURE 11.8H The knife is used to keep the outside trim flush with the opening.

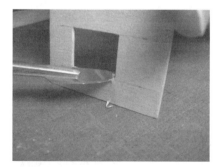

FIGURE 11.8I The blade is used as a stop, thus ensuring the trim is flush with the top of the window.

FIGURE 11.8J Move the blade to the other side of the trim, and cut it to size. Do not allow the trim to move during this process.

not allow the trim to move during this process (see Figure 11.8j).

7. Measure, cut, and install the horizontal trim. Be certain the length is absolutely correct before applying glue and installing. The horizontal trim should be the same length as the distance from the outside of each piece of vertical trim. It is OK to make the piece of lower trim a tiny bit larger, but bear in mind, you will need to

FIGURE 11.9A (Top Left). After the vertical trim is in place, measure the horizontal portions of the trim.

FIGURE 11.9B (Top Right). Dry fit the horizontal portions of the trim.

FIGURE 11.9C (Bottom Left). Notice how it is still a bit large; it was trimmed to size so that it eventually fit (not shown).

FIGURE 11.9D (Bottom Right). Cutting an oversized window sill.

be consistent throughout your model. I find that making everything flush leaves one less detail to worry about (see Figures 11.9a, 11.9b, 11.9c, and 11.9d).

8. Apply glue to the back of the sill, apply even pressure, and make sure you keep it flush with the existing opening.

9. At this point, you are free to decide whether you want to leave the window open, or place an additional piece of basswood behind it.

Making Windows, Larger Scale

The larger the scale, the more detail you may need to show. In Figure 11.10, notice the difference between the various windows. The windows on the left contain individually crafted elements, whereas the windows on the right merely use larger openings placed behind smaller openings. Notice how the tiny construction gaps actually add to the realistic effect. For the purposes of this book, we will call the buildup of detail **layering.** The more layering, the more shadows and highlights your model will have, and the more realistic your model is going to appear. For more information on layering, refer to Chapter 12.

Creating Molding

The strip of molding shown in Figure 11.11 was created by simply gluing two strips of different widths together. It is a good idea to make this type of molding in long lengths so you can just cut off what you need when you need it, instead of cutting several strips to length, and then putting them together. Portions of this strip will be used around the door in the next example.

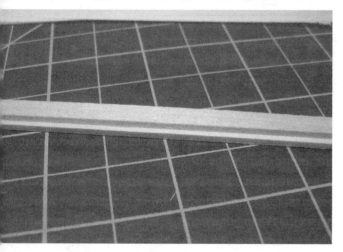

FIGURE 11.10 (Top). Notice the difference in depth, light, and shadows between the two windows. *Architect: Stuart Silk Architects. Photographer: Carrie Kapp.*

FIGURE 11.11 (Bottom). This door trim was made by simply gluing two different size strips together. It will eventually surround a door.

the basswood with a craft knife. The mullions were created using the same technique that was illustrated earlier in this chapter. If you look at an actual panel door, you will see how it is created from several pieces of wood. You will also notice how the grain of the wood in an actual door does not always run in the same direction. Now take a look at the example; the alternating grain in the model door achieves a similar effect.

STAIRS

Stairs can be constructed using the same techniques as described in Chapter 7. Generally, it is also possible to find wood of the exact dimensions as the stair's riser. If this is the case, simply cut the wood to the correct width, and layer the pieces together in a manner similar to the way contour models are constructed. How you choose to build stairs depends on their scale and their location on the model (see Figure 11.12).

ATTACHING WALLS TO FLOORS

Moving toward the exterior, attaching walls to floors is done in precisely the same way

CREATING DOORS

The door in Figure 11.12 was created by miter cutting three pieces of the previously mentioned molding to create a frame. They were then glued to a larger piece. Three thin strips were placed to the inside of the frame. A small, square piece of wood was added for the bottom of the door. The panels in the lower door were created by simply scoring

as if you were working with foam board or mat board. Start with the floor, and add a wall to the outside edge of the floor for stability. Check for square, and add the adjacent wall

FIGURE 11.12 Basswood door made from several different strips of wood. Notice how the grain of the wood alternates.

(see Figure 11.13, lower left). Depending upon what type of model you are making, you may want to begin to add some of the interior walls. Bear in mind that interior walls will need to be glued directly to the floor and an existing wall—you cannot butt them up against the floor slab for stability.

Continue to add exterior walls until you have the requisite amount of walls. (Often this number is four. See Figure 11.13, center.) After the exterior walls are complete, you can begin to add additional layers or larger components to the various façades. In the top model in Figure 11.13, a vestibule and the roof are added. For more detailed models, components such as windows and doors should be added before the walls are glued in place. *Be sure that you dry fit the entire basic structure before you begin to add components or cut openings!* There is nothing worse than putting windows and walls on a façade only to discover that the façade is too small. If you do not intend to have a removable roof, those should be attached last. Figure 11.13 illustrates three consecutive steps in the building process.

FIGURE 11.13 Three consecutive steps in the building process. *Model maker: Lois Gaylord.*

Making Stationary Roofs

Your approach to constructing will be completely dependent on the type of roof you want to construct. In the case of a gable roof, the approach will be fairly straightforward and will not depart much from earlier exercises where you constructed rudimentary roof structures.

Just like in Figure 11.13, simply attach the roof slabs to the existing structure of the building.

MAKING A TRUSS

If you plan on creating a removable roof, or even a partially removable roof, or, if you want to illustrate the structural qualities of a building, you may need to build a truss or two. The simple procedure previously illustrated may not be adequate.

1. Start with a correct scale elevation drawing of your truss. Tape it down to a piece of foam board.

2. Find wood strips that are as close as possible, in terms of both width and depth, to the lumber that the truss calls for.

3. Cut the strips of "lumber" to length, and lay them on top of the elevation drawing. Use drafting dots and/or pins to hold the wood in the correct position (see Figures 11.14a and 11.14b).

4. Using an extremely thin piece of wood (1/16 inch), cut out the brackets using a craft knife. In the case of the illustrated example, 1/16-inch oak veneer was used to illustrate the contrast of materials (see Figure 11.15).

5. Using a small amount of glue, attach the brackets to the truss members.

6. After the glue has dried, turn the truss over and squeeze a tiny bit of glue into the gaps between the truss members. Immediately wipe off the excess. Note: Do not use any of the expanding glues mentioned at the beginning of this chapter on this particular project.

7. Figure 11.16 shows a finished truss. If you will be attaching multiple trusses to your model, be certain they are all the same size and shape. Also make sure they are installed perfectly vertical, and allow plenty of time for them to dry before fastening additional roof components.

MAKING PYRAMIDAL ROOFS

If you want to construct a pyramidal roof, the construction is even more complicated.

1. Start with a square base. Make sure it will rest perfectly upon the walls of your structure. It cannot be larger or smaller than the walls it will rest upon (see Figure 11.17a).

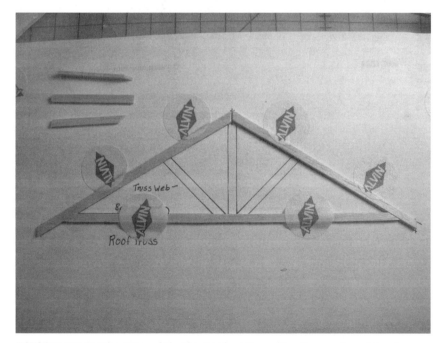

FIGURE 11.14A Cut the strips of "lumber" to length, and lay them on top of the elevation drawing.

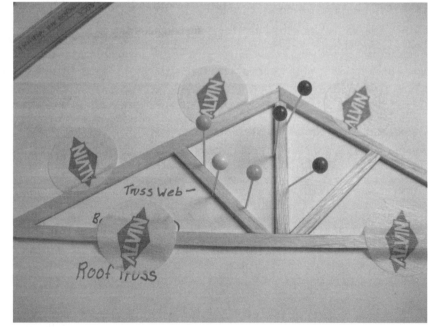

FIGURE 11.14B Use drafting dots and/or pins to hold the wood in the correct position while the glue dries.

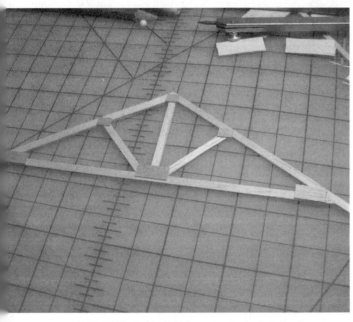

FIGURE 11.15 (Top). Using an extremely thin piece of wood (1/16 inch), cut out the brackets using a craft knife. In this example, 1/16-inch oak veneer was used to illustrate the contrast of materials.

FIGURE 11.16 (Bottom). A finished truss.

2. Determine the angle of the roof plane; each will have the same angle.

3. Assemble two "truss" pieces, leaving the length oversize.

4. Measure the truss against the diagonal span of the square base you created in Step 1. (Cut the truss so that it will sit flush upon the square base; see Figure 11.17b.) The angle at which you cut the base of the truss will be determined by juxtaposing the truss against a straight line equal to the length of the diagonal span. Be certain that each side of the truss is of equal length, and that their angles are equivalent as well. Only then can you be certain you are cutting the base of the truss at the correct angle (see Figure 11.17c).

5. Attach the truss to the square base. To be certain that the truss is perfectly centered and vertical, obey the following steps:

   A. Place a piece of wood, of the same size as the wood used to make the square, in the center of the square. This will be used to rest triangles on.

   B. Using hobby clamps and two small drafting triangles, place a clamp on the hypotenuse (the side of a right triangle opposite the right angle) of the triangle. Rest the base of the triangle on both the board in the center of the square, and the square itself (see Figures 11.18a and 11.18b).

6. Glue the truss to the two corners that are diagonal to each other. Sandwich the truss between the two triangles. If both triangles are resting level upon the wood in the center, the truss should be perfectly vertical and centered.

7. Using the existing structure as a guide, cut and attach the remaining two truss members.

8. Cut four slightly oversized triangular pieces to sheathe the roof. Using a sanding block, begin to bevel the edges so that when they attach to the pyramidal truss they fit flush. It is possible to cut out the triangles with a beveled edge using a scroll saw. Failing that, this can be achieved by hand by using a sanding block (see Figure 11.19).

ADDING A DORMER WINDOW TO A PITCHED ROOF

If your roof is absolutely perfect and follows your plan exactly, measuring and constructing a dormer roof is quite simple. The lengths and angles can be determined by studying the elevation.

However, if there is a chance that some of your angles or measurements may be somewhat less than accurate, the following method is a relatively foolproof way of constructing a dormer. It is easiest if you begin constructing your dormer prior to attaching your roof to its structure.

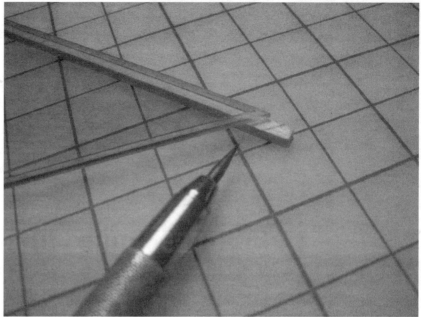

FIGURE 11.17A (Top Left). If you want to construct a pyramidal roof, start with a square base.

FIGURE 11.17B (Top Right). Cut the truss so that it will sit flush upon the square base.

FIGURE 11.17C (Bottom Left). The angle at which you cut the base of the truss, measured against the width of the base.

For this demonstration, we have continued to work with the pitched roof that was made in the previous demonstration. This demonstration will illustrate some common problems, as well as solutions to them.

1. On the main roof, draw a vertical line that will correspond to the peak of the dormer's gable. Draw a horizontal line on the gable that will support the new dormer, and that will correspond to the base of the dormer.
2. Using cardstock, cut out the front of the dormer, and leave extra cardstock on the sides. Lightly score the card so that it will bend easily at the corners (see Figure 11.20).

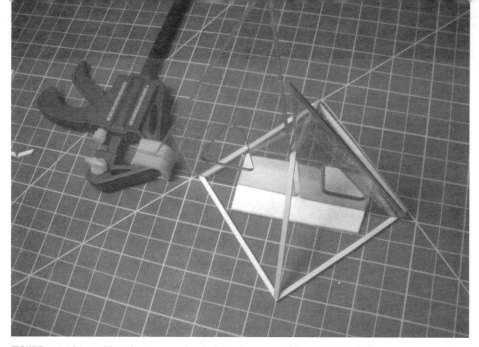

FIGURE 11.18A Installing the truss using hobby clamps and two small drafting triangles.

FIGURE 11.18B Installing the truss: Rest the base of the triangle on both the board in the center of the square, and the square itself.

3. Using your main line or an immovable straightedge on a perfectly level surface, rest the edge of the main roof flush against the straightedge.

4. Use two triangles to make sure your cardstock dormer is both square at the inside corners as well as perfectly vertical (see Figure 11.21a).

5. Lay a larger triangle on the surface of the main roof. Place the 90-degree portion directly on the lower corner of the roof (see Figures 11.21b and 11.21c).

6. Push the cardstock dormer flush against the larger triangle described in Step 5.

7. Draw a line on the side of the dormer, using the large triangle from Step 5 as a guide. This will give you the exact angle of the sides of the dormer. This same angle can be extended and used for the bottom of the dormer's face.

8. Trim the cardstock dormer, and tape it in place to the side of the main roof. Be certain that the center of the dormer is lined up with the vertical center line you drew in Step 1 (see Figures 11.22a, 11.22b, and 11.22c).

9. Place another piece of cardstock on the dormer, put the corner of the cardstock directly on the vertical center line. This

FIGURE 11.19 Cut four slightly oversized triangular pieces to sheathe the roof. Using a sanding block, begin to bevel the edges.

piece will be used to determine the exact angles of the dormer's roof (see Figure 11.23a).

10. Mark the cardstock at all the important points—at the roof's peak, at the front of the dormer, and where the dormer's roof meets its lateral walls. Be certain to draw a straight line between the center line from Step 1 and the peak of the dormer's roof (see Figures 11.23b and 11.23c). Notice the gap on the left side of the template in Figures 11.23a and 11.23b; this asymmetry is common in this process. Steps 17–20 will explain how to resize templates.

FIGURE 11.20 Using cardstock, cut out the front of the dormer; leave extra cardstock on the sides.

FIGURE 11.21A Using your main line, or an immovable straightedge on a perfectly level surface, rest the edge of the main roof flush against the straightedge.

FIGURE 11.21B Use two triangles to make sure your cardstock dormer is both square at the inside corners as well as perfectly vertical.

FIGURE 11.21C Lay a larger triangle on the surface of the main roof. Place the 90-degree portion directly on the lower corner of the roof.

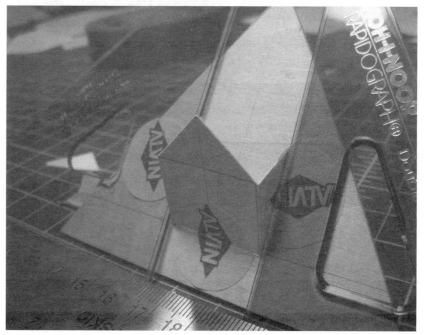

FIGURE 11.22A (Above). A line is drawn on the dormer template that corresponds to the angle of the roof.

FIGURE 11.22B (Top Right). Test the angle of the dormer template cuts, and line up the center line of the dormer with the registration line on the roof.

FIGURE 11.22C (Bottom Right). Using drafting dots, tack the dormer template in place.

FIGURE 11.23A (Top Left).
Place another piece of cardstock on the dormer; this will be used to determine the exact angles of the dormer's roof.

FIGURE 11.23B (Top Right).
Mark the cardstock at all the important points, at the roof's peak, at the front of the dormer, and where the dormer's roof meets its lateral walls.

FIGURE 11.23C (Bottom Left).
Be certain to draw a straight line between the center line from Step 1 and the peak of the dormer's roof.

11. Add a little extra to the front of the dormer's roof. This will be the overhang. Make sure the lines are parallel (see Figures 11.24a and 11.24b).

12. Trim the piece of cardstock according to the lines you have drawn thus far.

13. Trace the piece of cardstock onto another piece of larger card. Cut out most of the shape, but not along the ridge. Score the card along what would be the ridge of the dormer, and fold it in on itself (see Figure 11.25a). Use the existing cutout shape to trace a duplicate on the other side (see Figure 11.25b). Cut out the duplicate piece. Do not sever the card where it was scored.

14. You should be able to place this piece of card on the roof of the dormer (see Figure 11.26a).

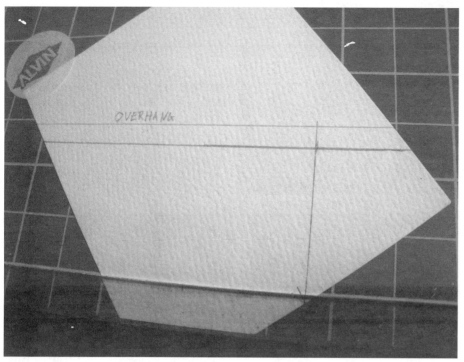

OVERHANG

FIGURE 11.24A Add a little extra to the front of the dormer's roof. This will be the overhang.

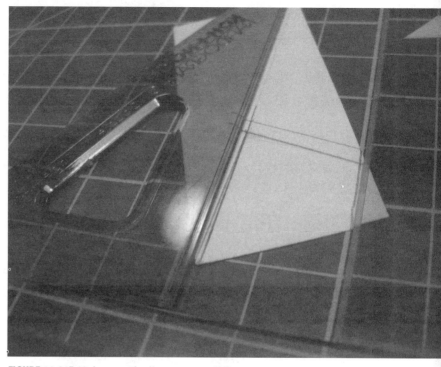

FIGURE 11.24B Make sure the lines are parallel.

15. After it is placed on the roof, it should be obvious what needs to be trimmed off. Draw a line that is parallel to the peak of the roof where you think it should be trimmed. Instead of cutting immediately, place the roof in place again. If the line you just drew looks correct, feel free to cut off the excess (see Figure 11.26b).

16. Place the recently trimmed piece back on the dormer. If it looks correct, move on to the next step. In the figure, it is

obvious that the roof requires a bit more overhang. Before proceeding further, a second, better fitting (wider) card template was made (see Figure 11.26c).

17. If your template requires only a small adjustment, as in Figures 11.23b and 11.23c, use the following technique:

18. Place a drafting dot on the short end of the paper template (see Figure 11.27a).

19. Fold the dot over onto itself (see Figure 11.27b). A second dot was added to the other side for strength. This may or may

not be necessary, depending upon the size.

20. Trim off the excess to create a full template (see Figure 11.27c). Dry fit this piece to make sure the template is correct before proceeding to the next step. There are many variations on this process. Two pieces of cardstock can be taped together if the size of your template necessitates it. In this case, with only a miniscule extension needed, tape was sufficient. In the case of the example

FIGURE 11.25A (Top Left). Trace the piece of cardstock, cut out most of the shape, score the card along what would be the ridge, and fold it in upon itself.

FIGURE 11.25B (Top Right). Use the existing cutout shape to trace a duplicate on the other side.

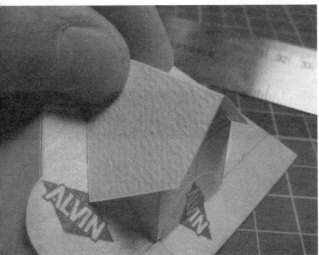

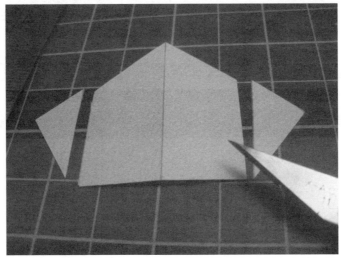

FIGURE 11.26A Place this piece of card on the roof of the dormer.

FIGURE 11.26B After it is placed on the roof, it should be obvious what needs to be trimmed off.

FIGURE 11.26C Place the recently trimmed piece back on the dormer. If it looks correct, move on to the next step.

shown in Figure 11.26c, the existing roof template was traced onto another piece of cardstock and was widened slightly before it was cut out.

21. Transfer these measurements to the wood, and cut out the appropriate pieces. Be sure to bevel the base of the front of the dormer (see Figure 11.28a).

22. Attach the lateral walls to the face of the dormer. Be certain you check and recheck for square (see Figure 11.28b).

23. Before attaching the dormer's walls to the roof, be certain that:
    A. The dormer is going to fit perfectly.
    B. Any additional components such as windows have already been added.

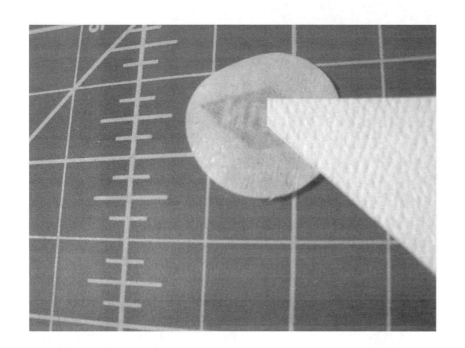

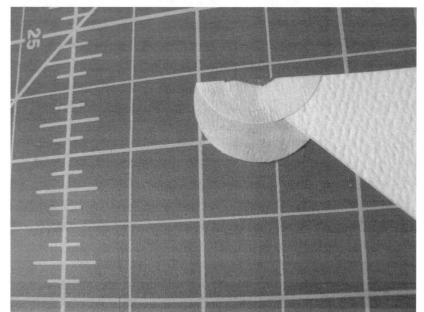

FIGURE 11.27A (Top Left). Place a drafting dot over the short end.

FIGURE 11.27B (Top Right). Fold the dot onto itself.

FIGURE 11.27C (Bottom Right). Trim away the excess to extend the template.

FIGURE 11.28A (Top Left). Transfer these measurements to the wood, and cut out the appropriate pieces.

FIGURE 11.28B (Top Right). Attach the lateral walls to the face of the dormer. Be certain you check and recheck for square.

FIGURE 11.28C (Bottom Left). Attach the fabricated dormer walls to the main roof.

FIGURE 11.28D (Bottom Right). Cut out and bevel the roof portions of the dormer. Dry fit before gluing in place.

24. Attach the fabricated dormer walls to the main roof (see Figure 11.28c). Notice the addition of the window in the figure.
25. Cut out and bevel the roof portions of the dormer. Dry fit before gluing in place (see Figure 11.28d).
26. A finished dormer is shown in Figure 11.29.
27. Attach the cardstock pieces together, and place them on other roofs that may have the same pitch. If the card dormer happens to fit, simply transfer the dimensions. This is much easier than repeating the previously described process for each dormer you may need (see Figures 11.30a and 11.30b). Place a piece of wood, of the same size as the wood used to make the square, in the center of the square. This will be used to rest triangles on.

Ensuring a Tight Fit When Using Odd Roof Angles

According to professional model maker Lois Gaylord (whose hands grace several pages in this chapter), there are a few different strategies for ensuring that your roof planes fit together tightly:

Be sure to sharpen your blade, or use a new blade. If possible, cut the piece long, bevel the edge, then trim to length. This gives you the opportunity to try more than once to get a good bevel without having to cut a new piece. Make small cuts. It's better to trim off a little at a time. This helps avoid the problem of the wood splitting along the grain. Make a sanding block and carefully sand to a sharp edge.

If all else fails, you can fill in gaps with slivers of wood. Be sure to use very little glue and then sand after it is in place. If the glue is still damp when you sand, the dust can help fill and hide the joint. If the glue

FIGURE 11.29 A finished dormer.

is too wet, the piece sometimes will pull out (Lois Gaylord, personal communication, January 15, 2009).

CURVING WOOD AND PUTTING IT ALL TOGETHER

In this section, we will illustrate the step-by-step construction of a model skate ramp. The purpose of the model is to explain visually how a full-size version of it would be built. All of its components will be visible; parts of it illustrate what the finished product will look like, whereas other areas illustrate the connections and locations of specific parts. A myriad of basswood construction techniques will be explained and illustrated while we construct this model.

A typical "mini ramp" is constructed using 4' × 8' sheets of plywood in varying thicknesses, two-by-fours, and aluminum fence posts for the coping.

1. Using a compass, draw a radius onto a thicker piece of basswood; in this case, 3/16-inch basswood (see Figure 11.31a).
2. Repeat this step on the other side.
3. In this case, a Dremel Scroll Saw is used to cut out the radius (see Figure 11.31b). Although difficult, it is possible to cut a curve like this by hand. Experiment with thicknesses and basswood versus balsa wood if you do not have access to a scroll saw. Because of the detail required, a band saw is not recommended for this cut.
4. A Dremel Moto-Tool was used to sand and smooth the curved portion.
5. The original radius was used as a template (see Figure 11.31c). The second

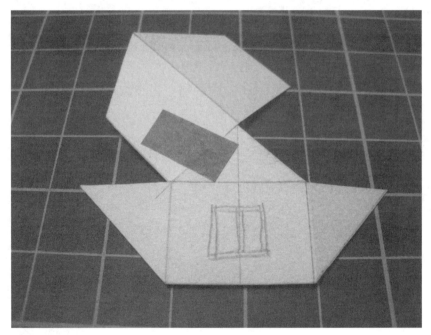

FIGURE 11.30A Do not discard your cardstock template pieces. Instead, attach them together and test them on other roofs that may have the same pitch.

FIGURE 11.30B If the card dormer happens to fit, simply transfer the dimensions.

FIGURE 11.31A Using a compass, draw a radius onto a thicker piece of basswood.

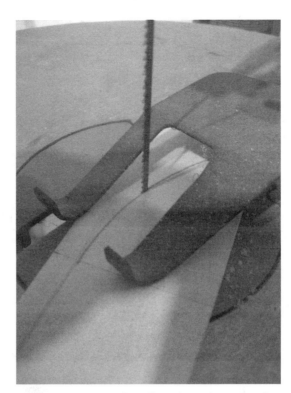

FIGURE 11.31B A Dremel Scroll Saw is used to cut out the radius.

FIGURE 11.31C The original radius was used as a template.

FIGURE 11.31D Identical notches were traced on the radius. These will support the coping later.

FIGURE 11.31E The radii were placed in a hobby clamp for support. A small file was used to smooth out the notches.

set of radii was cut out, again using the Dremel Scroll Saw.

6. Identical notches were placed in the radius; these will support the coping later (see Figure 11.31d). The radii were placed in a hobby clamp for support; a small file was used to smooth out the notches (see Figure 11.31e).

7. Instead of pressure and a triangle, a corner clamp is used to square up and hold the joist to the radius while the glue dries (see Figure 11.32a).

8. A hobby clamp was used to apply pressure to the two pieces while the glue dried (see Figure 11.32b).

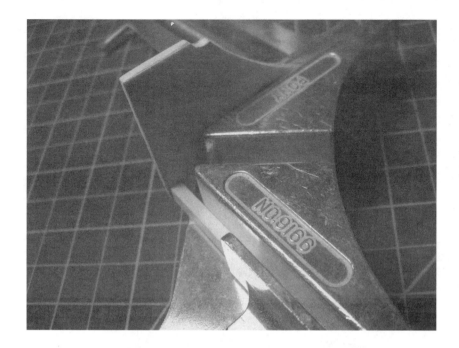

FIGURE 11.32A (Top Left). A corner clamp is used to square up and hold the joist to the radius while the glue dries.

FIGURE 11.32B (Top Right). A hobby clamp applies pressure to the two pieces while the glue dries.

FIGURE 11.32C (Bottom Left). Horizontal joists are added to the top and bottom of the radius of all four forms. A hobby clamp is used to hold the back of the ramp together as it dries.

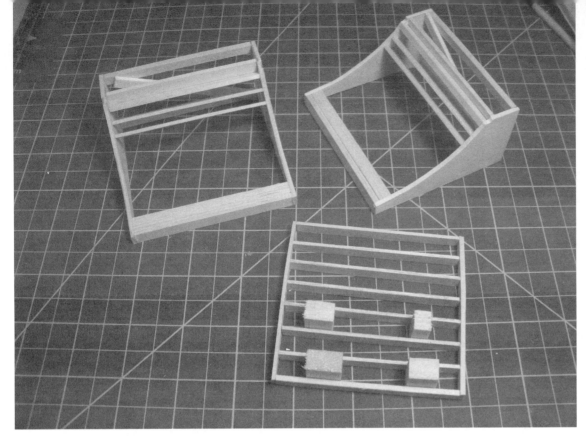

FIGURE 11.33 Scraps of equal width are used as spacers.

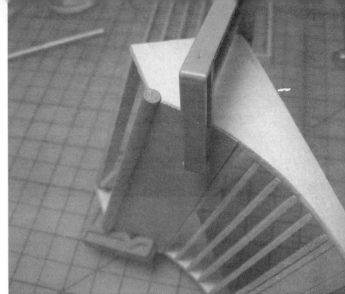

FIGURE 11.34 The ramp is sheathed with 1/16-inch oak plywood.

FIGURE 11.35 A thin bead of glue is applied to each joist that will come in contact with the sheathing.

9. Horizontal joists are added to the top and bottom of the radius of all four forms. Like a building, these will need to be kept square. Four sides will need to be assembled before sheathing can commence. A hobby clamp is used to hold the back of the ramp together as it dries (see Figure 11.32c).

10. The flat bottom base is assembled. Two pieces of equally sized wood are inserted between the joists to ensure even and parallel spacing. Joists are added to the radius. They are also spaced evenly using the previously described technique (see Figure 11.33).

11. The ramp is sheathed with 1/16-inch oak plywood (see Figure 11.34). Basswood could have been used, but the oak was chosen for its contrasting color.

12. A thin bead of glue is applied to each joist that will come in contact with the sheathing. Make sure that you are bending the wood with the grain. The grain of the wood should be running parallel

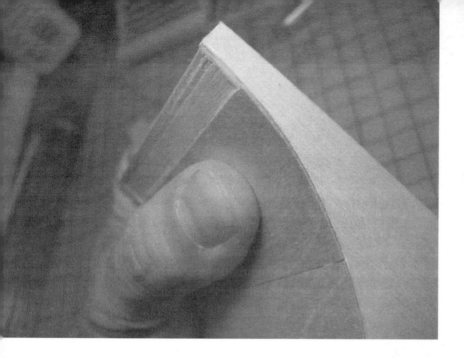

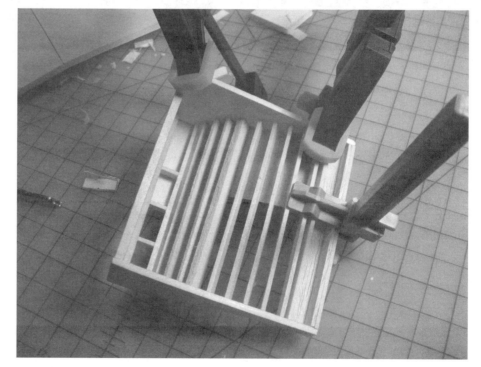

FIGURE 11.36A (Top Left). The bent wood can be held in place by using direct pressure.

FIGURE 11.36B (Top Right). The bent wood can be held in place by using hobby clamps.

FIGURE 11.36C (Bottom). A variety of clamping solutions are available to you. Notice the spacing of the joists.

FIGURE 11.37 The finished model intentionally exposes the underlying structure so as to illustrate the construction of a full-size ramp.

Partial sheathing is added to the other quarter pipe so that both the structure and construction techniques utilized in a full-size mini ramp can be made visible.

16. The entire ramp is then attached to a hollow hardwood base (see Figure 11.37).

17. A light can also be inserted into the hollow base. The light is helpful in exposing and illustrating the underlying structure of the ramp through the thin plywood. Place a piece of wood, of the same size as the wood used to make the square, in the center of the square. This will be used to rest triangles on.

Note: The base was created using a table saw and a chop saw to miter the corners. A **countersink** bit was used at the corners, and drywall screws were used to screw the corners together (see Figure 11.38). The surface of most wooden skate ramps are made using the same process; thus the model's base further illustrates the process necessary to create a full-size version of the model.

LAYERING WITH WOOD

In the example shown in Figures 11.39 through 11.43, I chose to slightly alter a variety of basswood products and construct a model of

to the joists you will be gluing it to (see Figure 11.35).

13. It is possible to bend and attach a larger sheet of thin plywood or basswood. The pieces in this demonstration are purposely made small so as to mimic the behavior and construction techniques that would occur if this ramp were being built full size.

14. The bent wood can be held in place by using either direct pressure or hobby clamps. In this case, the glue that was used was quick drying Tacky Glue (see Figures 11.36a, 11.36b, and 11.36c). Figure 11.36b shows a completely sheathed quarter pipe and the underlying structure of another.

15. All three pieces, both quarter pipes and the flat bottom, are then glued together.

FIGURE 11.38 (Top Left). A countersink bit was used on the base's corners, and drywall screws were used to screw them together.

FIGURE 11.39A (Bottom Left). The basic forms were shaped using a band saw.

FIGURE 11.39B (Bottom Right). The forms were then cut to size using a micro miter saw.

Seattle's Smith Tower. When it comes to layering, it is important to know the final dimensions of your intended model, the thicknesses of the materials you will be using, and be certain that the underlying, or structural, materials you begin with are of the correct size. In short, always make certain your underlying structure is smaller than the final model needs to be.

1. The basic forms were cut from larger pieces of scrap wood using a scroll saw, a table saw, and a micro miter saw (see Figures 11.39a and 11.39b).
2. A darker, oak veneer was chosen for the windows. These were cut to size and glued to the surface of the basic forms.

FIGURE 11.40 (Top Left). Whenever possible, the strips are scored and wrapped around corners.

FIGURE 11.41 (Top Right). Basswood L corners were purchased from a hobby shop for use on the corners.

3. For the lighter horizontal and vertical elements, 1/32-inch by 1/8-inch basswood strips were cut and glued into place. To keep things consistent and level, whenever possible, the strips were scored and wrapped around corners, as opposed to cut and applied individually (see Figure 11.40).

4. One-thirty-second-inch by 1/8-inch basswood L corners were purchased from a hobby shop for use on the corners (see Figure 11.41).

5. A basswood top was cut to size, glued, and clamped into place (see Figure 11.42).

6. The vertical tower and triangular top were created separately using the same techniques as described earlier in this chapter.

7. The various pieces of the building have been assembled, and the entire building has been placed in its context model (see Figure 11.43).

8. The entire model was created using mat board for the contours, closed-cell foam for the massing models of the surrounding buildings, and a mixture of different woods for the Smith Tower, Seattle, Washington.

Both balsa and basswood are beautiful materials for model making. They are an

FIGURE 11.42 A basswood top was clamped into place.

FIGURE 11.43 Finished context model.

excellent choice for use in models that high-light a building's skeletal structure. The warm quality of wood makes it a good choice for presentation models, regardless of whether the building in question will be constructed of wood or not. In this chapter, you have been introduced to a variety of approaches and problem-solving techniques; refer back to them while working on Chapter Review and Practice.

KEY TERMS

balsa wood
basswood
cantilever
countersink
layering
polyvinyl acetate (PVA)

Chapter Review and Practice

(See "Materials Needed by Chapter," pp. xxi–xxii.)

1. *Create two 4" × 4" cubes, one from ⅛-inch basswood and the other from ⅛-inch balsa wood.*

2. *Cut out two 6" × 6" pieces of basswood. Create one 2" × 3" window in each one. Leave one of the windows open, and place an additional piece of wood behind the mullions of the other.*

3. *Build a truss similar to the one shown in Figures 11.14 through 11.16.*

4. *Add two roofs to the cubes you created in #1. The first should be gabled; the second should be pyramidal.*

5. *Add a dormer to the gabled roof, as demonstrated in Figures 11.20 through 11.29.*

ADVANCED TECHNIQUES

PART 3

Advanced Materials and Construction Techniques 12

This first part of this chapter is an introduction to a few more materials that the professional model maker and designer may encounter or use. Depending on your school, not all of the tools used for these mediums may be available to the student model maker. Therefore, a few low-budget techniques and/or solutions will be covered as well. The mediums introduced here—foam, acrylic, and acetate—will rarely if ever be the sole material used to create a model. It is for this reason that after the reader has been given an introduction to the use of these materials, the chapter will conclude with a series of illustrations that employ and explain the use of more than one type of material.

MODELING FOAMS

Foam polystyrene or polyurethane foam are referred to as **modeling foams.** These are grain-free, high-density foams that can be glued, cut, carved, or sanded. These are available from a variety of online sources. Insulation foam, which is available at most home improvement stores, can also be used. If you will be creating massing models, study models, or models that you will neither open nor need to peer into, starting with a foam base and building a solid as opposed to a hollow model is an extremely efficient way to go; especially as a material upon which to layer and build other materials. If your toolbox contains only a craft knife, a straightedge, and glue, fear not. A basic structure can be fabricated using the foam board techniques discussed in earlier chapters.

If, however, your office or school has access to a hot wire cutter, either handheld or stationary, there are a myriad of cutting and shaping possibilities available to you. Should you have access to this tool, modeling foams offer an excellent foundation for building solid models and/or forms.

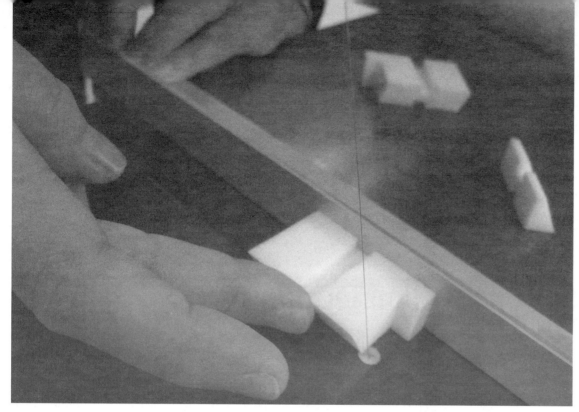

FIGURE 12.1 Foam blocks being cut with a hot wire cutter in the ZGF model shop. *Architects/model makers: Zimmer Gunsul Frasca Architects LLP.*

Working with Foam

Hot wire cutters are the best tools available for cutting foam. They leave a cleaner edge than if you choose to use a table saw or file. They are available in either handheld or bench-top models. Handheld models are available starting at about twenty dollars, whereas the bench-top models can be purchased starting at about one hundred seventy-five dollars. Figure 12.1 shows foam being cut with a bench-top version. A wire can be adjusted to nearly any angle relative to the foam. It is then heated up, at which point it slices through the foam like a hot knife through butter. If you want to shape foam into a conical, curved, or otherwise amorphous shape, start by roughing out the shape using the hot wire tools. After the basic shape is formed, it can be sanded smooth to whatever shape you desire. Figure 12.2 is an early study model for the Fifth + Columbia building by ZGF. Notice the tiny foam context models; the building's impact on the adjacent historical site was of paramount concern to the architects.

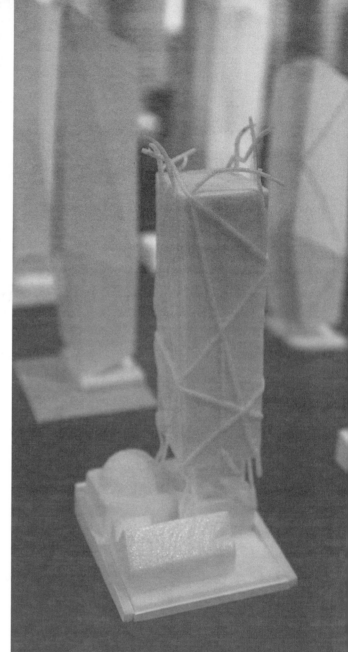

FIGURE 12.2 Foam models can be an end unto themselves. *Architects/model makers: Zimmer Gunsul Frasca Architects LLP.*

Although a little expensive, laser and foam cutters can save a firm hundreds or even thousands of hours in labor each year. Many of the examples you will see later in this chapter are built from components cut on these machines.

ACRYLIC

Acrylic, also commonly referred to as plexi, or Plexiglas, is an excellent choice for windows or other transparent components. It easily accepts straight cuts and paint. Its shape can be manipulated and formed when exposed to heat. It can be scored, polished, and fabricated. Acrylic is available in sheets, round rods, half-round rods, square rods, spiral rods, tubes, discs, cubes, and even balls, all of various sizes. **Acetate,** mentioned at the end of this section, is a thin, acrylic-based, transparent sheet commonly used for drawing and overhead projection.

Cutting Acrylic

Acrylic can be cut one of two ways; either by using a power saw with the appropriate blade, or by scoring/scribing with a plastic cutter or linoleum knife and snapping off the excess with a pair of pliers. Curved cuts can be made using a scroll or band saw. Acrylic can also be shaped using many wood tools; it can be planed or even shaped using a table router. Extremely thin strips of acrylic can usually be purchased or special ordered at hobby shops. Thin sheets can be scored and cut using a standard #11 blade.

Scribing/Scoring Acrylic by Hand

Do not try to scribe and break acrylic that is thicker than 1/4 inch.

1. Using a straightedge, pull your plastic cutter along the edge; this is called **scoring.** The thicker the acrylic, the more passes you may have to make. If the acrylic is covered by a protective sheet, it is best to leave it in place while cutting. The protective sheet keeps it from scratching.
2. Place the acrylic, scored side up. Place the scribe either directly on a round dowel, or along the edge of a table. It is also possible to place a pen under the score line on each side of the sheet. Apply pressure to both sides. The piece should break cleanly.
3. If you need to score and cut a piece of acrylic less than 1 inch wide, use a pair of pliers to snap the smaller piece.
4. Very tiny pieces can be cut from very thin pieces using a craft knife.

Drilling Acrylic

If you choose to drill holes into a sheet of acrylic, for best results, it is recommended that you use a drill press and special acrylic bit. Be sure to clamp your sheet to a piece of wood. Drill all the way through the acrylic and into the wood. Slowly back out your bit; this will leave a clean entrance and exit point. Unlike when cutting acrylic, it is best to remove the protective coating before drilling; otherwise, the coating gets stuck in the hole. The inside of the holes can be polished using steel wool.

Cleaning Up Acrylic Edges

After you have successfully cut your acrylic sheet to size, it will most likely have burrs on its edges. If you used a power saw, the edges will most likely show signs of being burned.

Removing Burrs

Place a steel straightedge at a 45-degree angle on the corner of the acrylic. Simply pull the steel along the edge of the acrylic, and the burr should come right off.

Removing Burns

What was once an impossible task has been made simple. Apply a dab of Novus Heavy Duty Scratch Remover to a clean rag and buff. The burned surface will literally disappear before your eyes.

Acrylic Windows

There are several strategies for representing windows using acrylic. The following strategies are not mutually exclusive; feel free to mix and match them.

Layering Using Mixed Mediums

Mullions and various other vertical and horizontal divisions can be applied to the face of an acrylic sheet. Place the acrylic over your elevation, cut your materials—balsa, basswood, museum board, paper, graphic tape, etc.—and apply them using an appropriate adhesive. If the pieces are large, double-stick tape will work perfectly; if they are smaller pieces, spray adhesive should suffice. Use of a white glue is not recommended because it can get messy. Super Glue works very well.

Scoring the Surface

Simply pull your plastic cutter along your straightedge. It will leave a mark sufficient to describe numerous window textures.

FIGURE 12.3 Spray-painted acrylic window components. *Alec Vassiliadis, Sound Models.*

Painting

You can paint acrylic sheets using water-based acrylic paint. Spray paint also works quite well. Do not paint on the front of the acrylic; use the back side to create a better effect. Never use a pure black paint; dark grays are much more effective. Figure 12.3 shows two different window components. They were both spray painted on the back first, one with a dark gray and the other with a light gray. The front was then masked off to cover the window portions, and the frames and mullions were then spray painted off-white.

Forming Acrylic

If acrylic is heated to a temperature of roughly 350 degrees Fahrenheit, it can be formed into nearly any shape. When it cools, it will keep the shape it has been formed into. A heat gun can be used to bring the acrylic up to temperature so that it can be bent or otherwise manipulated. The specifics of forming acrylic will not be covered in this book, but it is important for you to realize that it is a possibility. This could be applied creatively to add domed windows, skylights, and other unique acrylic features.

Cementing Acrylic

When attaching two pieces of acrylic together, the act is referred to as **cementing**, not gluing. First and foremost, it is essential that you realize that the fumes from acrylic cement are extremely toxic. Use only in a well-ventilated area.

For the purposes of model building, most cementing will be done at 90 degree angles. The chemical process involved in cementing acrylics is basically that of welding, as opposed to attaching, two or more pieces together. When the cement is added to a piece of acrylic, it more or less softens it for a short period of time. It then hardens, and the two pieces of acrylic will become one. The following is a step-by-step example of the process of cementing acrylic.

1. Small pieces of thin acrylic are scored and snapped using a #11 blade (see Figure 12.4a).
2. Apply the cement to the acrylic piece (see Figure 12.4b).
3. Spread out the cement into an even bead; too much will look sloppy (see Figure 12.4c).
4. Small pieces of acrylic must be applied using tweezers. Notice how in Figure 12.4d the large piece of acrylic is scored, and additional elements are attached to it. This contrast will help to add depth to the finished model.
5. In Figure 12.4e tiny pieces of wood act as spacers, a jig, and a brace for the tweezers.
6. Thin sheets can be scored and cut using a standard #11 blade (see Figure 12.4a).

The finished acrylic component can be seen later in this chapter.

Applying Acrylic to Other Materials

Notice that the word *cement* was not used here. In model making, whenever possible, use the quickest, cleanest, strongest processes you can. If the acrylic is to be layered horizontally, or used as sheathing, double-stick tape often works quite well. If, for example, you want to create an awning or something that extends from a surface to complete the window, think about using a mechanical method of attachment, such as brackets. Super Glue and various two-part epoxies are usually quite efficient when it comes to attaching different materials. Be aware of the discoloration that may take place, and be sure to design a way to disguise it. Examples of this process will be shown in a later set of illustrations.

Acrylic Multistory Buildings

Placing thin strips of wood or colored paper between layers of acrylic is a common way of showing multistory buildings. The translucent quality of the acrylic diffuses the color of whatever is sandwiched between it. Transparent double-stick tape is adequate for assembling acrylic in this manner.

Representing Glass with Acetate

If you lack the funds, tools, experience, or materials necessary to begin a project using acrylic, acetate is oftentimes a good choice, especially when you want to represent glass. Acetate is much easier to curve and bend than acrylic. The process for creating quick and inexpensive windows is as follows:

1. Cut out your openings.
2. Lay the acetate over your elevation drawing. Use drafting dots or tape to keep it in place.
3. For the mullions, use Chartpak graphic tape. It is available in widths of 1/16-inch intervals. Choose the correct color—in this case, white is used.
4. Apply the tape to the acetate, directly over the mullions represented on the elevation.
5. Carefully trim away the excess tape (see Figure 12.5a).
6. Apply transparent double-stick tape to the front of the acetate where it will not be seen through the building's openings (see Figure 12.5b).
7. Apply the acetate to the back side of the façade (see Figure 12.5c). It does not take much.
8. Figure 12.5d shows the finished model with acetate windows. Note: The corners were achieved by simply scoring and bending the acetate. This ensured that the horizontal bands lined up perfectly. This process can also be used on bay, bow, or garden windows, as well as skylights.

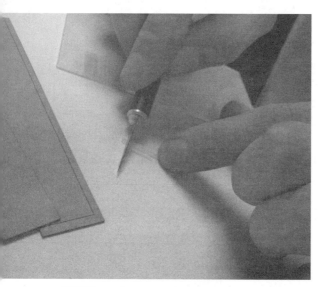

FIGURE 12.4A Score and snap the acrylic pieces to size.

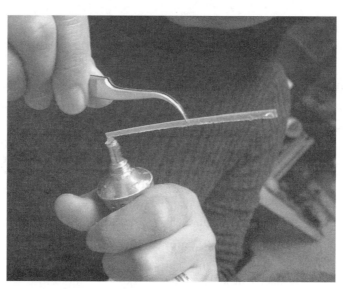

FIGURE 12.4B Apply the cement.

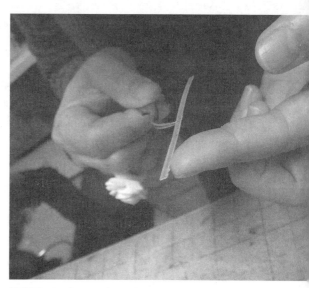

FIGURE 12.4C Spread out the cement.

FIGURE 12.4D Use tweezers to attach smaller pieces.

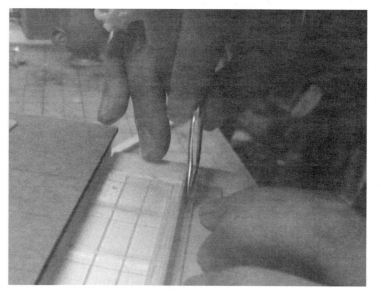

FIGURE 12.4E Tiny spacers of wood can help to steady your hand.

FIGURE 12.5A (Top Left). Carefully trim away the excess tape.

FIGURE 12.5B (Center Left). Apply double-stick tape to the hidden portion of the acetate.

FIGURE 12.5C (Bottom Left). Apply the acetate to the back side of the façade or window opening.

FIGURE 12.5D (Bottom Right). A finished model with acetate windows. *Model maker/architect: Roger H. Newell, AIA, Roger Newell Architects.*

MIXING MATERIALS AND LAYERING COMPONENTS

There are many reasons for mixing materials in a model. You may need a specific effect or color, or your model may contain complex shapes, each of which may need to be fabricated from a different material. Architectural models are, after all, an abstraction, sign, or representation of an actual object, not the object itself. As we have learned in this book, botanical detail and verisimilitude are not essential to the effective communication of an idea. This chapter offers suggestions on the mixing of various and contrasting mediums to achieve effects that will allude to architecture.

In addition to juxtaposing mediums and color, **chiaroscuro**—contrasting light and shadow—can be used to great effect in three-dimensional modeling. The greater the distance between receding and advancing planes, the stronger the difference will be between the light and shadow, and the greater depth your model will appear to have. This chapter contains examples of layering and juxtaposed materials; the techniques used to construct these models have all been explained in earlier chapters.

CHOICE OF MATERIALS

Take care when choosing model materials. The materials you choose to use

FIGURE 12.6 Positive and negative forms are distinguished here by using juxtaposing materials.

when fabricating a model can mislead viewers. A legend that has circulated throughout the British model making community says that when the model makers at Arup fabricated the Richard Rogers Partnership model of Lloyd's of London from wood instead of a highly reflective metal, the patrons were left with the impression that they were commissioning a twelve-story wooden building in downtown London (Richard Armiger, personal communication, February 9, 2009).

The study model of the house shown in Figure 12.6 was designed by Castanes Architects, in Seattle, Washington. Museum board was used for the contours, whereas the struc-

FIGURE 12.7 The attached strips of museum board that were added to the multicolored model add depth to the model. *Lauren Jacobs, student model maker.*

ture was represented using museum board, pencil, cardboard, and balsa wood. The choice of materials is explained as follows:

> The design intent of this project is simple; positive and negative forms are arranged along a central axis [the circulation corridor] so that the house can bring in the natural surrounding landscape. For the model to clearly reflect this idea, the positive and negative forms are distinguished by using juxtaposing materials (Amber Murray, Castanes Architects, PS AIA, personal communication, February 20, 2009).

Earlier study models of this design were created using a single material. The monochromatic effect of a pure museum board model did not adequately demonstrate the massing intent and material choices of the architect's design.

The exterior model shown in Figure 12.7 was made by student model maker Lauren Jacobs.

It was constructed using four different colors, solid-core museum board, balsa wood, and drafting paper. The materials used highlight the choice of different building materials to be used in the actual building without committing to anything specific. The texture of the drafting paper windows blends well with the colored museum board and models level of detail. Had acetate or acrylic been chosen for the windows, the contrast would have been too great, and the windows would have become the focus of the model. The attached strips of museum board that were added to the model add depth to the model and suggest, yet do not commit to, an actual material.

Figure 12.8 shows a portion of a museum board model by Jason Hanner of Weber Thompson Architects. By simply drawing and drafting upon and then laying a single sheet of museum board on top of another, the illusion of a sidewalk is shown in a simple and elegant manner. Notice how the shadows created by the raised plane of the sidewalk create depth.

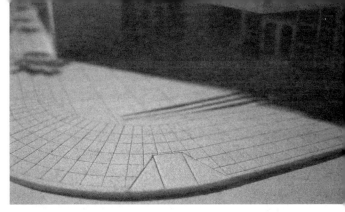

FIGURE 12.8 By simply drawing and drafting upon a single sheet of museum board and then laying it on top of another, the illusion of a sidewalk is shown in a simple, elegant manner. *By Box Shop. Architect: Weber Thompson.*

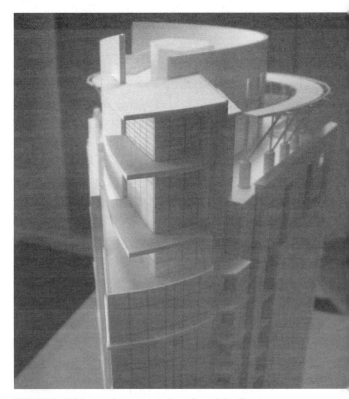

FIGURE 12.9 This purely museum board model relies completely on layering to create an interesting interplay of light and shadows. *By Box Shop. Architect: Weber Thompson.*

FIGURE 12.10 By adding a delicate amount of wood and frosted acrylic to an otherwise white edifice, attention is given to the awnings and mullions.

The purely museum board model shown in Figure 12.9 relies completely upon layering to create an interesting interplay of light and shadows. Hand-drafted pencil lines sufficiently represent the windows. An all-white model, be it foam board, museum board, or even cardstock, is an effective means of highlighting a project's formal and spatial qualities while remaining noncommittal in terms of the design's final materials.

As shown in Figure 12.10, by adding a delicate amount of wood and frosted acrylic to an otherwise white edifice, attention is given to the awnings and mullions. Mullions created from a different material than the main body of the building effectively represent windows. The addition of an acrylic or acetate surface to represent glass would have been redundant, and could even take emphasis away from the awnings. The trees in the lower right corner of the image have the same color and value as the mullions. This adds to the cohesive nature of the model.

When asked why he chooses to work with certain materials, Jason Hanner, owner of Box Shop (model shop) and architect/model maker for Weber Thompson said,

> Material choice: I like Rising (brand name) museum board with basswood highlights where appropriate. I've always liked all-white models because they are really about the form and are a blank canvas for materials and colors. There is something inherently "architectural" about them. Museum board is the ideal medium for this as it is acid free and homogeneous (no different core material) and I find it easy to work with. The basswood can do a lot to make the model feel

warmer (Jason Hanner, personal communication, February 23, 2009).

Figure 12.11 shows another view of the same model. Notice how the horizontal louvers are made from museum board strips. Once again, by changing materials—in this case, sandwiching wood between two layers of museum board—three different architectural materials can be represented. The juxtaposition of the materials gives the model considerably greater depth than it would have had otherwise. Conversely, adding too many materials could have overworked and cluttered the model.

Figure 12.12 shows a study model of a medical office building and parking garage that was built by design team members Sophie Hong and Aaron Swain of Tiscareno Associates, a Seattle-based architecture and urban design firm founded in 2002.

> [The model] was created during design development as a tool with which to examine the skin of the building, and the design of the main building entrance. The larger scale (approximately 3×4 feet) enabled a better understanding of the pieces involved, and pushed the design further by forcing consideration of the materials, colors, and unique conditions created by the various materials (Tiscareno Architects' statement from Seattle Architecture Foundation Model

FIGURE 12.11 By changing materials and sandwiching wood between two layers of museum board, three different materials can be represented. *By Jason Hanner. Architect: Weber Thompson.*

Exhibition 2008 placard, written by Aaron Swain).

In a personal correspondence on February 27, 2009, Sophie Hong added:

Glass was a major feature of this design. We used acetate to keep space transparent. At ground level the materials are heavier to maintain a solid foundation and to blend in with the landscape. The transition from solid to void was used with frosted acetate as the intermediary. We simply layered paper onto acetate or sanded it to achieve this look. The solid steps, ramp, and columns are fully enclosed. Because this model was fairly monotone we decided to add a bit of color through its accessories. The vegetation and people give it a layer of scale and potential life.

A larger scale necessitates an increased juxtaposition of layers and materials. Figure 12.13 is a detail of the model that was shown in Figure 12.12. Notice in these two images how the awning structure is created using chip board, balsa wood, and an acetate awning, whereas the building uses a couple different colors of mat board as well as acetate to represent the windows. In this case, the use of acetate highlights the reflective nature of the proposed building's skin. Cardboard is used to represent the earthen contours.

When asked about their material choices, Sophie Hong of Tiscareno Associates said:

We chose plain modeling materials like chip board, clear acetate, grays, and browns to offer an idea of what the actual building might look like. These started out as design study models and little by little turned into something just a bit more. I wouldn't consider them to be final presentation models, but a working guide to three-dimensional visualization. Papers and woods are easiest to work with because they are pliable, easy to cut and glue as well. It was important to use different shades of color and texture to create layers of material and shadow. It also helped with keeping the model feeling warm.

FIGURE 12.12 Acetate gives the appearance of glass and transparent space, whereas the thicker, rougher materials and entourage contrast with the acetate to effectively ground the model. *Medical office building and parking garage model built by Sophie Hong and Aaron Swain of Tiscareno Associates, a Seattle-based architecture and urban design firm founded in 2002.*

FIGURE 12.13 The awning structure is created using chipboard, balsa wood, and an acetate awning. In this case, the use of acetate highlights the reflective nature of the proposed building's skin. *Model by Sophie Hong and Aaron Swain of Tiscareno Associates.*

The model shown in Figure 12.14, by Robert Combs Architectural Models, built for Sullivan Conard Architects, was created using only two different materials—basswood and cork.

Emma Shultz, of Sullivan Conard Architects said:

> The Pike's Peak Residence is inspired by trips to France and by historic Northwest estates, including the Garrett Home by Charles Platt in the Seattle Highlands and the Bloedel House and Gardens on Bainbridge Island. The model serves to verify the overall massing and landscape relationships developed through two-dimensional drawings (personal communication, February 25, 2009).

Figure 12.15 is an alternative view of the model shown in Figure 12.14. In the two views, notice how the basswood reads not only as wood, but as stone and stucco as well. Notice the differences in the thicknesses of the wood used. The corner quoins read as rusticated stone due to the slightly increased thickness of the wood. Notice also how much the window panes are recessed versus how much

FIGURE 12.14 (Top Left). Wood can represent a myriad of alternative materials. *Photographer/designers: Sullivan Conard Architects. Model maker: Robert Combs Architectural Models.*

FIGURE 12.15 (Top Right). The material thicknesses, as well as the recession and protrusion of certain elements, cast strong shadows, which increase the structure's realism. *Photographer/designers: Sullivan Conard Architects. Model maker: Robert Combs Architectural Models.*

FIGURE 12.16 (Bottom Right). Laser-cut acrylic sheets and wood veneer were attached to each other using only double-stick tape.

FIGURE 12.17 (Top Left). Attention to detail and an accurate representation of the intended construction techniques are factors that contribute to the strength of this model. *Model maker: Lois Gaylord.*

FIGURE 12.18 (Bottom Left). This model was created using internal lighting, acrylic, and museum board. Cast plaster was used for the base. *Designed and photographed by Owen Richards Architects.*

FIGURE 12.19 (Right). Note how the structure and the spatial qualities of this sectional cutaway model of a loft apartment are represented by the successive addition of layers. *Model makers: Eriko Kawamura, Nami Mally, Roark T. Congdon (author), Steven J. Harvey.*

the window frames jut out. The material thicknesses, as well as the recession and protrusion of certain elements, cast strong shadows that increase the structure's realism. By placing irregularly shaped basswood pavers on top of cork, the wood then reads as stone, and the cork reads as earth. A fine-grained basswood was used for the stucco walls. A large-grained pattern may have caused the walls to read as an entirely different material.

Figure 12.16 shows a component of a massing model by ZGF. Although it is extremely small, about 2 × 3 inches, the laser cutter used to cut the pieces creates flawless, detailed cuts. The acrylic sheets were attached to each other using only double-stick tape. The veneer was attached to the acrylic using the same double-stick tape. Although not used in this model, sandwiching colored paper between sheets of acrylic can add an interesting glow to models that utilize stacked acrylic to represent multistory buildings.

Although constructed using only one material, as shown in Figure 12.17, Lois Gaylord used different sizes and shapes of wood to accurately represent this structure. Notice how the sliding screens are represented as being on separate tracks. Attention to detail and an accurate representation of the intended construction techniques are two factors that contribute to the strength of her models.

Figure 12.18 is a model of a Seattle International Film Festival Pavilion that was created using internal lighting, acrylic, and museum board. Cast plaster was used for the base.

Figure 12.19 shows a section model of a loft apartment that was created using only basswood. Take note of how the structure and the spatial qualities are both represented by the successive addition of layers.

Scott Jennings used a rare veneer of hardwood from Afghanistan to sheathe the main body of this structure (see Figure 12.20). The frosted acrylic windows are actually one large block used as the main body or underlying structure of the model. Note the depth achieved by scoring the windows and building up sills and mullions.

Figure 12.21 shows a "pattern" from which a mold will be made; the mold will be used to cast an "architectural sculpture" in plaster. Each column, arch, and window is cast in plastic or urethane from a single mold. Each **cast** is attached/layered to a styrene base. See the color insert for an example of a finished architectural sculpture by Timothy Richards.

Figure 12.22a shows a basswood model placed upon a solid cardboard contoured base. After a spot for the model was created in the base, drywall mud was applied to hide the cardboard, and the model was reinserted once the mud dried. Figure 12.22b is a closeup

of the model. Notice the shadows and depth achieved by using two or three layers of wood for the windows and molding.

LAYERING IN ACTION

The following is a step-by-step illustration of the construction of a model for the University of Washington Molecular Engineering Interdisciplinary Academic Building. The study model was used to explore the relationship of the building to façade, massing, and fenestration to the surrounding campus landscape. First, a context model was created (see Figure 12.23a). A footprint in the basic shape of the study model was left empty. An armature or basic form of the building was then created, slightly undersize, and fitted to the context model. The brown tape on the foam is double-stick tape that will be used later to attach successive layers. The first layer created (the arrangement of doors and windows) is acrylic fenestration. This piece was created in Figures 12.23a through 12.23i.

Using spray mount or double-stick tape, gray paper was applied to represent vertical elements of the building (see Figure 12.23b). Notice that the sheet of acrylic is actually much larger than the windows. Double-stick tape is applied to the acrylic sheet (see Figure 12.23c). Cardboard, which represents a portion of the façade, is cut to size and applied directly to the double-stick tape

FIGURE 12.20 A veneer of rare hardwood from Afghanistan was used to sheathe the main body of this structure. The frosted acrylic windows are actually one large block used as the main body, or underlying structure, of the model. *Model maker: Scott Jennings. Project: Iowa State University Biorenewables Complex, Zimmer Gunsul Frasca Architects LLP.*

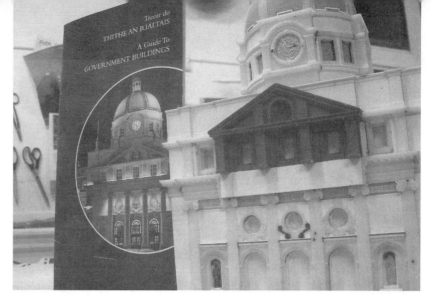

FIGURE 12.21 This is a "pattern" from which a mold will be made; the mold will be used to cast an "architectural sculpture" in plaster. *Model maker: Timothy Richards.*

FIGURE 12.22A This is a basswood model placed upon a solid cardboard contoured base, which was then covered in drywall mud. *Architect: Stuart Silk.*

FIGURE 12.22B Notice the shadows and depth achieved by using two or three layers of wood for the windows and molding. *Architect: Stuart Silk.*

(see Figure 12.23d). The thickness of the cardboard further emphasizes the recessed nature of the windows. In Figure 12.23e, the entire pieces are attached to the foam armature using the double-stick tape that was shown in Figure 12.23a. In Figure 12.23f, construction is begun on some of the smaller massing elements. Notice how the double-stick tape is applied to a sheet of foam. The acrylic windows can be seen to the immediate left of the foam block. Colored construction paper and acrylic windows are applied to the smaller massing element (see Figure 12.23g). The entire mass will then be applied to the larger study model. The successive layers are applied to the foam in order to judge the overall effect of the proposed design (see Figure 12.23h). The final version of the study model is then placed in the context model. Notice the degree of finish in the surrounding buildings. This context model can be reused as the design of the proposed building evolves and a more finished model is produced (see Figure 12.23i).

REPRESENTING MATERIALS

The creation of a model is a balancing act, and you, as the designer, must always make a conscious decision as to how committed you need to be of realistically representing the various facets of your design.

As the scale increases, there may be a need to represent more accurately the materials and finishes in any given design. It is for this reason that you will now be presented with a variety of techniques that may assist you in achieving a more realistic product than is typically found in smaller scale architectural models. This section will be particularly useful when producing interior presentation models.

Remember, if absolute realism is the desired outcome, you would be best served by purchasing dollhouse and railroad model building accessories. These tricks of the trade are listed alphabetically for your convenience. Be careful mixing these *trompe l'oeil* techniques with more abstract, representative finishes. The contrast between the materials may not be what you are looking for. *Always test these processes before using them on a final model!*

In some cases you will be instructed to use the actual material. If this is impractical due to weight, shape, or other reasons, explore the possibility of digitally scanning the material and spray mounting the color print to your model. Consider the texture of your material versus the texture of your scan. It is not advisable to scan a piece of carpet, and print it on a glossy paper. Print it on matte instead. Think also of the scale. For example, when scanning carpet, consider printing it at a reduced scale so that the pile of the carpet better matches the scale of your model. In all of the following cases, consider whether scanning, printing, and spray mounting is an appropriate technique.

The materials or colors that have the most impact on your space should be represented in some way or another. Like an interior designer's materials board, a model is a collage or composition of materials and colors.

If you are mixing mediums, such as colored boards, paints, markers, and more, it is a good idea to save smallish scraps of whatever you come up with. On the back of the scrap, write down exactly what you used to achieve that effect; the color or number of the board, the brand and the name of whatever marker, pencil or paint you used, how much of it you applied, and in what order. Begin to save all of these scraps in a small box so that you can refer to them later. You could, of course, also scan the material, and save the recipe digitally.

Representing Materials in Study Models

After spray mounting your plans to your board, use markers or colored pencils to quickly render it the way you would a plan or elevation. Now build the study model. This little bit of color goes a long way toward visualizing the effects of color on your space. I would not suggest any extremely detailed rendering when using this process. It would be unfortunate to waste a lot of time rendering, only to cut something out wrong.

FIGURE 12.23A Start with a foam armature that fits slightly undersize in the footprint of your context model.

FIGURE 12.23B Acrylic fenestration is the first layer created.

FIGURE 12.23C Double-stick tape is applied to the acrylic sheet.

FIGURE 12.23D Cardboard, which represents a portion of the façade, is cut to size and applied directly to the acrylic sheet with double-stick tape.

FIGURE 12.23E The entire pieces are attached to the foam armature.

FIGURE 12.23F Construction is begun on some of the smaller massing elements.

FIGURE 12.23G Colored construction paper and the acrylic windows are applied to the smaller massing element.

FIGURE 12.23H Successive layers are applied to judge the effect of the proposed fenestration.

FIGURE 12.23I The final version of the study model is then placed in the context model.
Architect and model maker: Zimmer Gunsul Frasca Architects LLP.

Acoustic Tile

On an appropriately colored and textured mat board, use the techniques you have learned in your hand-drafting courses, and simply draft the appropriately scaled ceiling grid by hand. The larger the scale, the heavier your line weights should be.

Brick

There are myriad ways to represent brick—as many as there are kinds and appearances of brick materials. This is an opportunity to combine skills and creativity.

Start by finding an appropriately colored illustration board. If the board is not the exact color you need, the color can be altered slightly by using a series of light applications of spray paint. After the paint has dried, the joint lines can be drawn on by using a white Prismacolor or other wax-based colored pencil. It may also be possible to draw the joint lines on first, allow the wax pencil lines to act as a resist, and apply the spray paint afterward. The results will be completely dependent upon the color of the board you begin with, and the color of paint you choose to apply. For best results, try both methods.

Another method is to start by peeling away and removing the face of the foam board. Next, spray paint the exposed face the correct color. After the paint has dried, drag a sharp object across it. This will pull up the exposed foam to create joint lines. Once your foam board has the face removed, spray paint it the correct color. Drag a sharp object across the surface to remove some paint and create joint lines. A variation on this technique was introduced at the end of Chapter 10.

A third method is to start with a smooth surfaced wood, and spray paint it the appropriate color. If you are working at a larger scale, say 1" = 1' or larger, while it is still wet, smear the paint a little with a rag. This will give the brick a weathered look. Wait for the paint to dry and then lay down a second, smooth coat. Finally, regardless of your scale, add joint lines with white pencil.

Carpet

Carpet also has an array of personalities. One thing to consider is the use of the space and which flooring would be most appropriate and pleasing to the client. There are many methods for representing carpeting.

Carpet can be difficult to work with. If the scale of the model is large and pile of the carpet is low, it is possible to use the actual material in an interior model. Should you choose to do this, you will need to take into account how much the carpet sticks up, and make sure that all the other flooring in the model is flush with it, as well as ensure that your ceilings are all of the correct height.

If the scale of the pile of the actual carpet in question does not match, scan the carpet sample and print it at an appropriate scale on matte paper. Apply it using spray mount. When it comes to spray-mounted flooring, it may be best to apply it to your floor surface first and then add the walls. This way you can have a little extra flooring, and place the walls over them. This will give the model a nice, finished look.

It is also possible to spray mount an appropriately colored fabric to the floor. Be careful using this method; make sure you test this method first because the fabric might shrink in one direction or the other and cause your base to warp.

Ceramic Tile

Whenever possible, you can use the actual material cut to fit your model. Grout lines can be drawn on with an appropriately colored pen. Test the pen first to ensure that it will dry after it is applied to the tile. Read the warning concerning carpet because the same considerations must be given to tile.

Just like carpet, you can scan and print your tile and then spray mount it to the floor. Unlike carpet, however, using a gloss finish on your paper may be appropriate.

Concrete

Start by choosing an appropriately painted or pre-colored mat board. Then use a rounded burnisher to indent the joint lines—they will cast realistic looking shadows. A white pencil can also be used to draw the joint lines.

A dull knife can also be used to scrape joint lines. Begin by spray mounting 400 grit sandpaper to a foam board. To achieve the correct color, sandpaper can be spray painted with automotive primer either before or after mounting, depending on the model. A dull knife can be used to scrape joint lines.

Concrete Block

Concrete block can be simulated using the methods listed in the previous section.

Fabric

Use the actual fabric if the scale of the pattern or thickness of the material is not a distraction.

Silk has an extremely fine weave, and is a suitable substitute for the actual materials, should they prove to be too bulky or cumbersome. Silk accepts dyes easily, should you want to match a color.

Using double-stick tape to apply the silk will keep the surface smooth, unlike using a glue, which would most likely seep through the fine silk.

Glass

Whenever possible, use 1/16-inch acrylic because it is easier to cut and bend than 1/8-inch acrylic. Acrylic can also be purchased slightly tinted, or can be sanded to achieve a frosted appearance. It also accepts self-adhesive colored sheets and spray paint.

Acetate, as long as it is not dented or wrinkled, works quite well, and is an inexpensive alternative to acrylic. For the proper use of acrylic and acetate, refer to the beginning of this chapter.

Marble

Use a small feather and appropriately thinned acrylic paint. Gently drag the feather across the surface to create veins. The surface can be:

- Appropriately colored and textured mat board
- Painted foam board
- Painted hardboard or masonite. It is also possible to find commercially produced paper with a marble pattern printed on it.

You can also scan a piece of marble, or find museum board with a marble pattern already on it.

Metal

There are a multitude of ways to accurately represent metal. Purchase something appropriate. Extremely thin, foil-covered museum board and cardstock are available from most frame shops. Alcan Composites makes sheets of acrylic in thicknesses of 2 to 4 millimeters. These sheets are faced with a variety of metallic coatings, such as blues, reds, blacks, brushed silver, brushed copper, or stainless steel. Samples of plastic laminates with a metallic facing

are an inexpensive option if you are working at a small scale. Laminate is scored and cut just like acrylic.

Another method is to use a metallic spray paint on a hardboard, foam board, or prefabricated wood element. Remember, too much paint can warp your material, especially if you only paint on one side.

Plaster

The cleanest option available to is to use a mat board with a rough finish. A messier option is to use a ready-made orange peel finish (available in aerosol cans from any home improvement store) on foam board or wood. Give the finish plenty of time to dry; then spray paint it the required color.

Porcelain

Simply use a gloss spray enamel to achieve a porcelain-like finish on any smooth surface. Apply the paint in thin coats and on both sides, if possible, to avoid warping. If it does warp, wait for it to dry, and place it under a heavy stack of books for a few hours.

Sheetrock

Use the same techniques as you would with plaster.

Stone

Spray paint a *thin* sheet of cork the appropriate color after you have spray mounted it to a board. Double-stick tape, depending on its strength, can also be used to adhere the thin cork to another surface. You can also try using two different colors of spray paint. Lay down the darker color first, and use a series of light passes to apply the lighter color. The darker color will seep into the lower areas, and this will give the cork a more realistic finish. There are also faux stone finishes available in spray cans.

Another method is to find the appropriate material, scan it, and print it. Review the section on tile for further instructions.

Steel

Review the section on metal earlier in this chapter—the techniques and materials are the same. Often the actual material is available in thin sheets. Thin sheets can be exposed to weather to achieve a natural or weathered patina.

Wall Treatment

Beware of the differences in the scale of your treatment versus the scale of your model. For example, it is not advisable to use full-scale wallpaper on a reduced-scale interior model. It is best to paint your walls the dominant color, and add an appropriate amount of pattern later.

Wood

Wood can be represented by using sheets of basswood or balsa wood, stained or rendered with marker the appropriate color and glued to foam board. One-quarter to one-half-inch fine-grained plywood can also be stained and mounted to a sturdy base. This thicker wood is an excellent base to which you can attach walls.

Wood Siding

This can typically be purchased to scale in a hobby store. Alternatively, use a sanding block at a slight angle along a steel T square, and gently drag lengthwise along balsa or basswood. This should create an adequate relief that simulates siding. An appropriate color can then be applied to the wood.

In conclusion, remember that a larger scale model, especially an interior model, is at once an accurate representation of a three-dimensional space and an abstract, sculptural collage of color and materials.

You have been given an introduction to a few specialty materials that the professional model maker and designer may encounter or use. As you have seen in the illustrations, the materials introduced at the beginning of the chapter—foam, acrylic, and acetate—will rarely be the sole material used to create a model. Rather, they will be used to emphasize various design decisions and material choices.

In addition to the introduction to the use of these materials, you should have studied the series of illustrations that employ and explain the mixing, use, and layering of more than one type of material. Finally, you have been given a few tricks of the trade for producing faux materials at a larger scale. The following questions and exercises should help you develop your skill with these new materials, and assist you in the development of diverse presentation strategies.

KEY TERMS

acetate
acrylic
cast
cementing
chiaroscuro
modeling foam
pattern
scoring

Chapter Review and Practice
(See "Materials Needed by Chapter," p. xxii.)

1. *List ten advantages and ten disadvantages to mixing media as it pertains to architectural model making.*
2. *How is your choice of materials affected by the model's scale?*
3. *When mixing media, what are some strategies you could employ to show a contrast of prospective building materials, yet remain noncommittal to a building's final appearance at the same time? Find five images/examples*

of these strategies, and explain the techniques used. Finally, suggest alternative strategies that could be used to achieve a similar effect.

4. *List five different ways to achieve each of the following effects:*

   A. *Concrete*

   B. *Wood*

   C. *Glass*

   D. *Steel*

   E. *Roofing materials*

5. *List three different ways to represent the following combination of materials:*

   A. *Concrete juxtaposed with wood and steel*

   B. *Wood juxtaposed with glass*

   C. *Steel juxtaposed with concrete and glass*

Project 1

Using 1/8-inch acrylic, score, snap, and cement a 4-inch square box. Practice on a few test scraps first; neatness counts here.

Project 2

Using nonprecious materials such as cardboard, and using a study model as your *only* design tool, create a preliminary and a secondary design that meet the requirements laid out in the parameters of Project 3.

Project 3

Based upon your secondary design in Project 2, and in a similar manner to the model shown in Figures 12.23a through 12.23i, create a solid, presentation-quality model that is approximately 8 × 6 × 10 inches. Feel free to orient these dimensions in any way you see fit. Some of the requirements are:

A. Scale should be between 1/16" = 1'-0" and 1/4" = 1'-0", depending upon your models use (see the following requirement D).

B. Formal requirements: At least 20 percent of the surface area of the form must recede into the building, and 20 percent must extend beyond the approximate dimensions of 8 × 6 × 10 inches listed in Step 3. It must also include something pitched—a roof, an awning, or both.

C. Materials: You are required to apply a series of contrasting materials, in layers, to a solid form. This rough form can be created from modeling foam, or built using foam board. Other materials to be used in this model include acrylic or acetate, balsa or basswood, and museum board—the color and texture are your choice. Include also either chipboard or cardboard. Finally, include at least 8 linear inches of a wood dowel or clear acrylic rod.

D. Use: This structure can be an industrial, commercial, corporate, sculptural, or residential building. The scale you decide to work in will be dependent upon your structure's use.

E. The structure must be inserted into a 12-×-12-inch contour model that has at least six layers. These contour layers can be made of either chipboard or cardboard, which should help to meet some of the material requirements listed in requirement C.

F. Include a title block with your name, and the model's use and scale on your base.

Entourage

13

- *Recognize the important function of entourage in an architectural model*
- *Know when to use entourage*
- *Choose the best scale and objects to place in your model*

Entourage can be defined as any element of your model that is used to indicate scale. For the purposes of this chapter, we will look at some of the more commonly used objects, such as trees, cars, and people. Other elements, such as stairs, windows, doors, railings, boats, and furnishings, could also be considered entourage because they help the viewer to understand the scale of the model.

HUMAN SCALE

One of the easiest ways to impart scale to the viewer is with the addition of human figures. Most of us have an idea of what size we are, and, with the assistance of scale figures, can visualize ourselves in an environment. We would then have a better idea of the real size of the space that is being portrayed in the model. More often than not, correctly scaled human figures can be purchased from a myriad of model shops. Be careful if you are ordering scale elements from a country other than your own. It can be difficult to accurately make the transition between feet and meters.

Think back to the images of finished models that you have seen in this book. How many of them had scale figures in them? How did this affect your perception of the model? Were any of these people a distraction? A few scale figures go a long way. Consider also whether the figures need to be painted; if so, what color? Make sure that human figures—and all other entourage for that matter—complement your model, not clash with it. In Figure 13.1, notice how the human figures, trees, and plantings emphasize the vastness of the plaza that they inhabit.

Ready-Made Figures

Ready-made figures are available in a variety of scales (see Figure 13.1). Be certain you use only figures that match your scale exactly. If you choose to purchase ready-made figures,

FIGURE 13.1 The entourage in this model serves to emphasize the public nature of its space. *Scott Jennings Model Shop.*

make sure that you choose an appropriate level of detail. Figures are available as fully detailed figures in the round, or as simple silhouettes. Consider the purpose of your model. Are your figures sitting or standing? What is the ratio of male to female? Are they adults or children?

Most ready-made figures come on what is called a tree. Make sure you sand off any flashing from the figures before adding them to your models (see Figures 13.2a and 13.2b).

Making Human Figures

Because humans are extremely sensitive to the subtlest of details in other humans, great care

must be taken when attempting to make your own human figures. One simple method is to paste ready-made human images to a piece of cardstock, and merely use the silhouette (see Figure 13.3). This method photographs particularly well. If your model is very large or detailed, it is probably best to purchase figures. If your model is built at an extremely reduced scale, objects such as cut-down pins or match heads, or even grains of rice, can be used to represent people.

It is possible to use a wire armature or skeleton of a human, and add an air drying clay such as Super Sculpey to represent a human figure. If your figures are abstract, it is possible to bend the armature into the position you need—simply dip it in plaster, and wait for it to dry. This will result in a clean-looking yet abstract figure. Bear in mind, the larger the scale of the figure, the more accurate it must be. Unless you are a classically trained sculptor, it is recommended that you stick to ready-made figures in larger scale models. Although extremely accurate, the human figure in Figure 13.4 took nearly three years to create. Nevertheless, it was created by simply adding and sculpting clay to a steel armature. It was later molded and cast in bronze.

VEHICLES

Vehicles, like humans, can be used to give scale. Bear in mind that vehicles may not necessarily be cars or trucks; they may be

FIGURE 13.2 Ready-made figures are available in various scales and levels of detail.

FIGURE 13.3 (Top). These cutout figures were used in a 1:10 scale study model. *Architect and model maker: Zimmer Gunsul Frasca Architects, LLP.*

FIGURE 13.4 (Right). This life-size bronze was made by adding clay to a steel armature. *Commission for the Estate of Jimi Hendrix. Sculptor: Roark T. Congdon (author).*

boats, bicycles, possibly even skateboards. As with human figures, it is safest to simply purchase ready-made vehicles from a model vendor. These shops will have a variety of appropriately scaled vehicles (see Figure 13.5). Depending on the scale and material used on your model, you may want to consider spray painting your model vehicles. Again, vehicles should never be a distraction.

Like people, your choice of vehicles can have a psychological effect on your viewers. In Figure 13.6, notice how the sports car parked in the driveway of an otherwise all-white model grabs your attention immediately, yet shortly thereafter your eye is drawn to the architecture—much in the same way it would behave if you were to park there.

TREES AND LANDSCAPING

Plants and trees are nearly always represented in architectural models. The level of detail you choose for the landscaping depends on the level of detail in your model, as well as the reason for the landscaping.

The BBC broadcasts a do-it-yourself-(DIY) type home improvement program called "Model Gardens." In this program, an exact replica of the client's garden is created by a professional model maker. The client is then given a base that follows the exact dimensions of their yard and a plethora of extremely realistic model making supplies, such as pavers, grass sheets, fencing, any type of tree or shrub they desire, and even odd landscape elements such as grass mounds. Using the model as a design tool, the client and the host/designer then work together to revamp the garden. The show is so popular that "Model Gardens" design kits can be purchased so that viewers can design their own dream garden. For more information on this program, go to www.modelshop.co.uk/pages/m_06.htm.

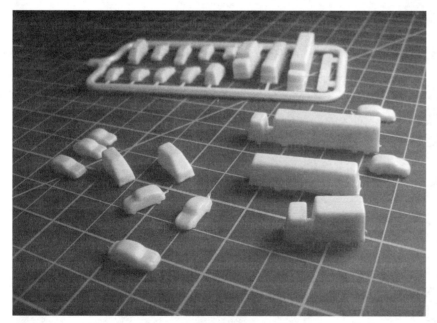

FIGURE 13.5 Vehicles can be purchased in a variety of scales.

FIGURE 13.6 Vehicles can lend prestige to the design. *Model maker/architect: Roger H. Newell, AIA, Roger Newell Architects.*

FIGURE 13.7A Ready-made kits that consist of simple sheets of paper make an effective tree.

FIGURE 13.7B Randomly cut green blobs, pierced with a hole punch, make nice foliage in a study model.

This is a case where verisimilitude is essential because not only is the landscape the focus of the model, but the client/designer/TV viewer most likely lacks the visualization skills necessary to make the program entertaining.

There are as many different ways to represent foliage as there are types of foliage. The following images should provide useful guidance and inspiration for your landscaping needs. Look at the level of detail in the foliage and then compare it to the level of detail in the models.

Two simple ways to create foliage is by rough cutting foam or sponge, and painting it the appropriate color. Shredded burlap glued to a stick makes a pretty effective tree as well. The tree shown in Figure 13.7a is made from a ready-made kit. The shapes of paper can be purchased precut. From there, they can be skewered on a dowel or other type of stick. Figure 13.7b shows a nice trick for representing foliage in a study model. A few different shades of green paper are cut in random shapes and punctured using a standard office hole punch.

The trees shown in Figure 13.8 are wooden balls and beads placed on pins or thin gauge rods. Notice the order to the seemingly random placement of foliage. When it comes to smaller scale models with an abundance of trees, less can still be more. Be careful that the foliage does not take over the model. In this case, it was a

model of the Washington state capitol, and the emphasis was on the massing of the buildings and the layout of the park and city streets.

In Figure 13.9, wooden balls were once again placed on steel rods to represent trees in

FIGURE 13.8 Wooden balls and beads on pins represent trees on this site model. *Model maker: Tomoko Briggs. Architect: Zimmer Gunsul Frasca Architects LLP.*

FIGURE 13.9 The orderly construction of the trees mimics the existent landscaping on the city street. Fifth + Columbia Tower, Seattle, Washington. *Model maker: Scott Jennings. Architect: Zimmer Gunsul Frasca Architects LLP.*

FIGURE 13.10 For this design, various widths and heights of dowels were used to give the effect of a forest. *Architect/model maker: William Zimmerman.*

FIGURE 13.11 Dried plants such as yarrow can be used to represent trees. *Sullivan Conard Architects.*

this context model. The orderly construction of the trees mimics that of the existent landscaping on the city street.

In Figure 13.10, various widths and heights of dowels were used to give the effect of a forest for this design. Regardless of where one views this model, the effect is always that of being in a cabin in the woods. When it comes to trees, regardless of the model's scale, be certain that you include their trunks. This gives the viewer the ability to look through the trees toward the architecture. This particular model is illustrated on numerous occa-

sions in this book. As you reread it, take note of the trees again, and the overall impression of place they convey.

One of the easiest ways to represent small-scale trees is simply to use a dried plant such as yarrow. These can be acquired at floral shops. It is not uncommon to apply a light coat of spray paint to dried plants so as to make them fit in better with the model (see Figure 13.11).

A dull knife can also be used to scrape joint lines. The metallic trees shown in Figure 13.12 were created by placing about ten strands of

FIGURE 13.12 Bundles of copper wires were used to create these trees. *Architect/model maker: William Zimmerman.*

FIGURE 13.13 (Left). The painted driftwood shown here gives the impression of a beach house.
Model maker/architect: Roger H. Newell, AIA, Roger Newell Architects.

FIGURE 13.14 (Bottom Left). Kits for trees can be purchased in hobby shops.

FIGURE 13.15 (Bottom Right). A myriad of different trees can be purchased at model making or railroad supply stores.

copper wire into the chuck of a drill. The opposite ends of the strands were then placed in a vise. The drill was used to twist the strands into a tight bundle. The bundle was then cut to size, and one end was frayed and the ends were cut to various lengths to make the branches. Notice also the contrast among the wooden model, the copper trees, and the cork groundcover. "Topographical increments are 1/8-inch cork. The driveway was represented by masking off the drive and spraying it with varnish to darken the area. The rockery was implied by roughing up the layered edge using a dull knife blade. The trees are twisted copper wire. The sides are 3/8-inch maple plywood with a lacquered finish" (William Zimmerman, personal communication, February 11, 2009).

In Figure 13.13, the painted driftwood gives the impression of a beach house. Plastic tree pieces of various scales can be purchased at model shops. As you can see in Figure 13.14, the pieces come with instructions for making a perfectly realistic tree. Once assembled, the tree is painted a naturalistic color or colors. From there, parts of the tree can be sprayed with an adhesive, and specialized cover such as painted horse hair can be applied to the tree. Finished trees such as this can also be purchased at model shops. Again, watch the level of detail of your foliage. It is extremely easy to go overboard.

If you have more time than money, a myriad of different trees can be purchased at model making or railroad supply stores (see Figure 13.15).

A QUICK GUIDE TO MAKING ABSTRACT TREES

Start with inexpensive—or better yet, free—chopsticks. The tapered nature of low-end chopsticks makes for an easy transition back into trees. Using a heavy-duty knife, randomly carve and score the chopstick until it takes on a more naturalistic appearance. In Figure 13.16a, a utility knife is being used to accomplish this.

Next, cut up random sizes of a furnace filter, and slightly separate the layers (see Figure 13.16b). Then apply a generous coat of white glue to the chopstick (see Figure 13.16c). Don't worry about being messy; the drips of dried glue will make the trunk appear more naturalistic. Now begin to draw or pull the filter over the chopstick. Feel free to add more glue if you think it is coming off or not sticking well enough (see Figure 13.16d).

After the filter has been allowed time to dry onto the stick, randomly trim the tree using scissors (see Figure 13.16e). Make sure that there are no straight edges. Straight edges do not look naturalistic.

Apply a coat or two of spray paint (in this case white) to unify the tree. The paint adds a certain thickness to the foliage, which makes the tree more believable. Notice also the adjacent dried yarrow, which is also painted white. Figure 13.16f shows a finished tree.

WATER

Water can be represented by using rippled glass, mirrors, tinfoil, bluish foil wrapping paper, blue mat board, photocopies of water as seen from above, or even ready-made water cast from thin sheets of urethane. For added effect, consider placing a clear acrylic sheet on top of one of the materials. It will enhance the illusion of depth.

You have been given a brief introduction to entourage and its uses. Furthermore, you have been introduced to a few building techniques. A few excellent online resources for the purchase of entourage are:

4D Modelshop—www.modelshop.co.uk
Hull's Art Supply and Framing—www.hullsnewhaven.com
Model Builders Supply—www.modelbuilderssupply.com

FIGURE 13.16A Use a utility knife to rough up the edges.

FIGURE 13.16B Cut up the furnace filter.

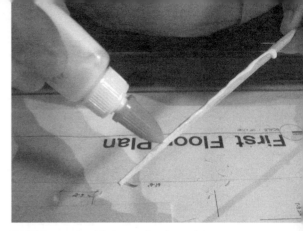

FIGURE 13.16C Add glue to the chopstick.

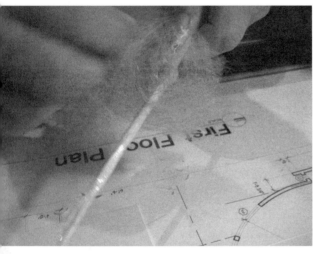

FIGURE 13.16D Pull the filter pieces over the chopstick.

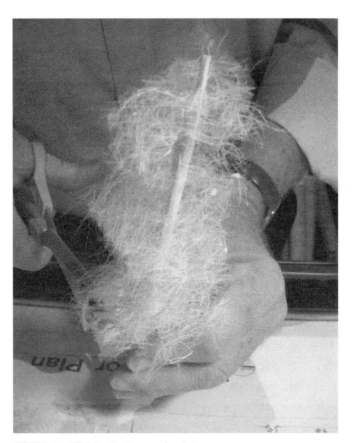

FIGURE 13.16E Trim the tree and paint.

FIGURE 13.16F Behold—a 5-minute tree!

KEY TERM

entourage

Chapter Review and Practice

(See "Materials Needed by Chapter," p. xxii.)

1. ***What are some advantages of inserting human figures into a model?***
2. ***What should one consider when adding trees and landscaping into a model?***
3. ***What are the repercussions for placing an inappropriately scaled object into a model?***

Project 1

Working at 1/2" = 1'-0" scale, create three different versions (levels of detail) of the same landscape design.

Design Requirements

1. This must be a 12' × 16' space.
2. It must include at least one fully matured tree.
3. At least 30 percent of the space must be occupied by some type of planting.
4. It must include one bench large enough for two people to sit on.
5. It must contain some type of pathway.
6. The contours of the model must contain at least three levels.
7. The space must contain three figures.

Model Goals/Requirements

1. Each model must employ completely different levels of detail and approaches.
2. One model must emphasize the design of the bench.
3. One model must emphasize the flow of traffic through the space.
4. One model must emphasize the trees and other plantings.

Project 2

Using the form and contour models you created for Chapter 12, Project 3, integrate the two models and add entourage that is appropriate and properly scaled to the architectural form you created.

Appendix
Template Descriptions

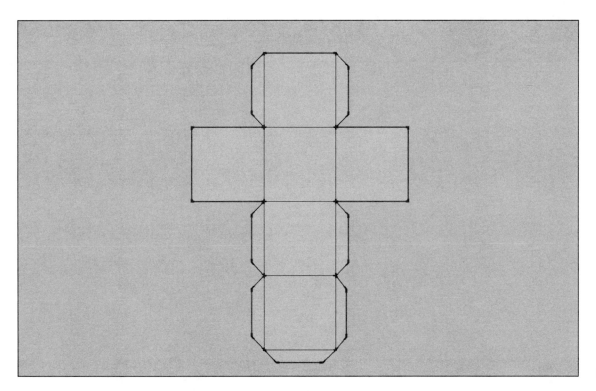

CUBE A cube is created by folding together six squares.

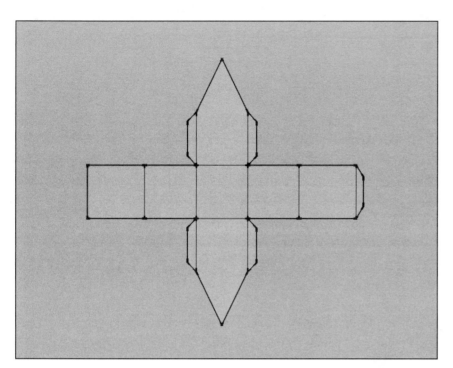

SIMPLE PITCHED-ROOF MODEL A structure with a pitched roof is basically a cube with a triangular volume on the top. Notice the template has seven sides, instead of six, like a cube.

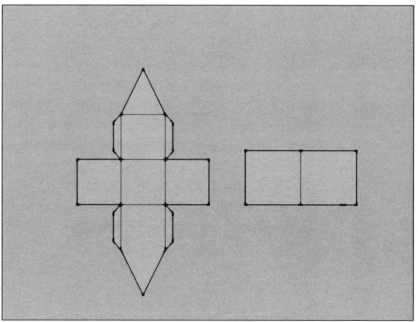

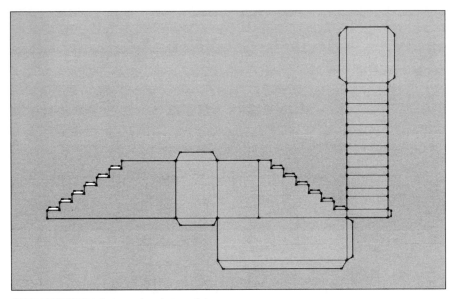

STAIR TEMPLATE A flattened stair template.

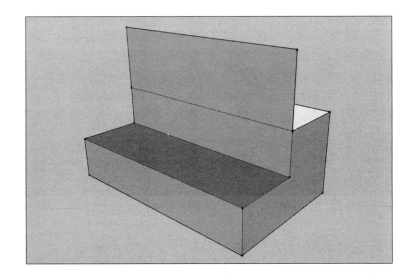

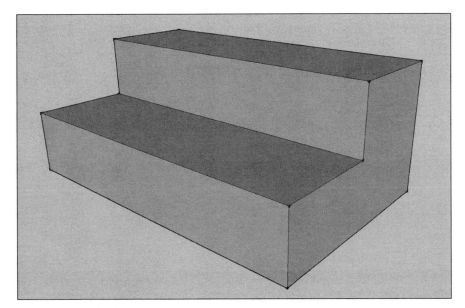

TWO STEPS, PERSPECTIVE A simple two-step solid in perspective.

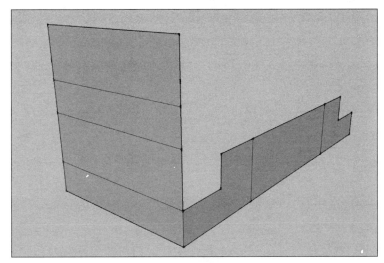

TWO STEP UNFOLDED The treads and risers are connected to each other.

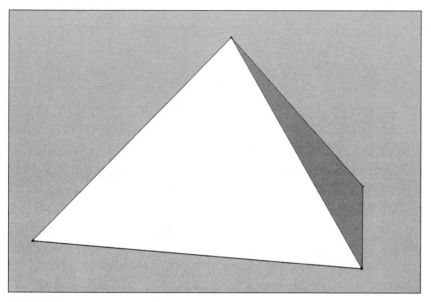

PYRAMID A pyramid in perspective.

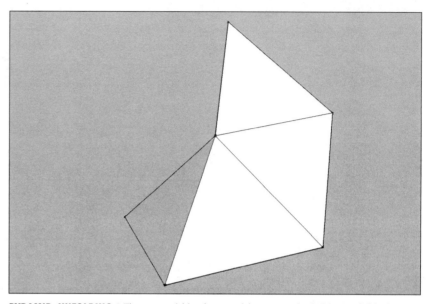

PYRAMID, UNFOLDING 1 The pyramid is shown with two vertical sides unfolded.

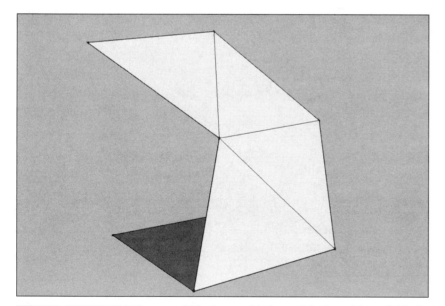

PYRAMID, UNFOLDING 2 The pyramid is shown with three of the four sides unfolded.

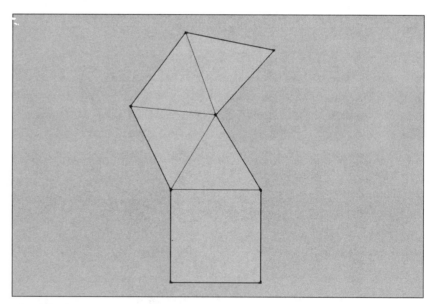

PYRAMID, TEMPLATE UNFOLDED Here, the pyramid is shown completely flattened, including the square base.

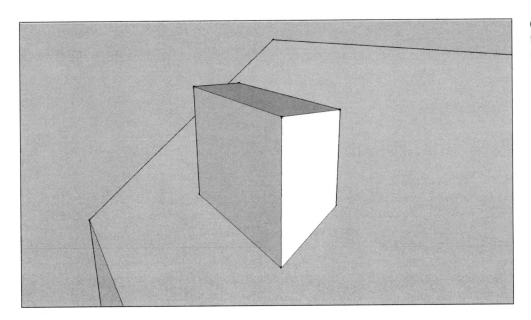

CHIMNEY ON ROOF, PERSPECTIVE Notice how the angles on the side of the chimney match those of the roof. The roof angle must be determined first.

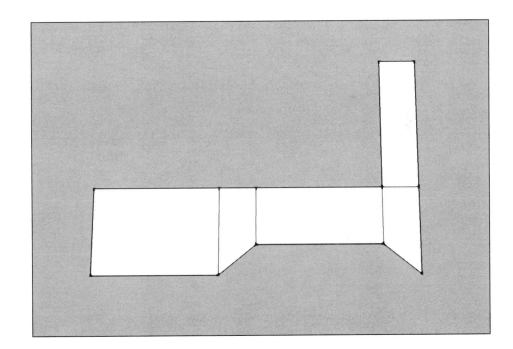

CHIMNEY, UNFOLDED A chimney, in its simplest form, has a top and four sides, if you don't count the roof upon which it sits.

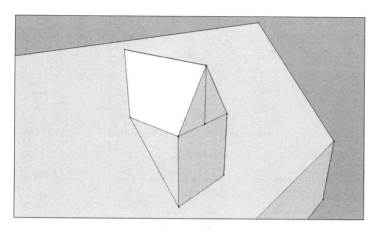

DORMER, PERSPECTIVE This is similar to the template created in Chapter 11.

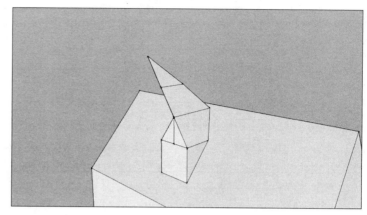

DORMER, UNFOLDED IN PERSPECTIVE The roof and dormer walls will be mirror images of each other.

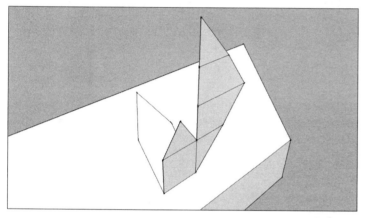

DORMER, UNFOLDED The lines on the roof indicate the location of the unfolded dormer template.

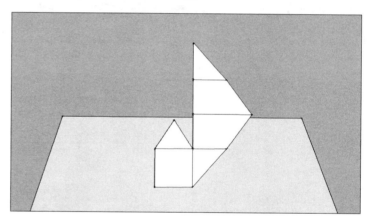

DORMER, TEMPLATE UNFOLDED ON ROOF This is an elevation of an unfolded dormer template in its location on the roof.

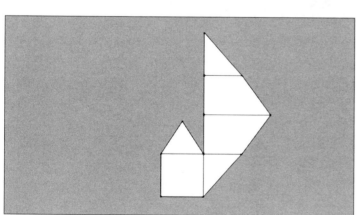

FLAT DORMER TEMPLATE A dormer template in its unfolded form. Remember, the angles of the roof must be determined prior to creating the angles of the dormer.

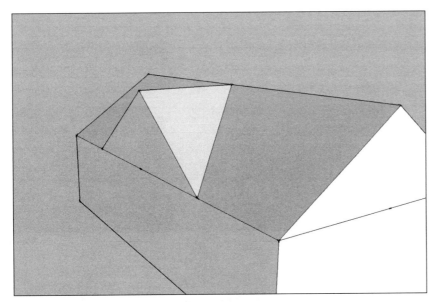

GABLE, PERSPECTIVE The gable roof in perspective.

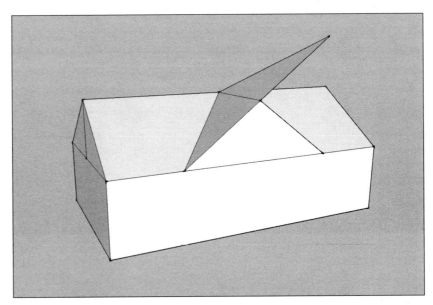

GABLE, UNFOLDING The sides of the gable will mirror each other.

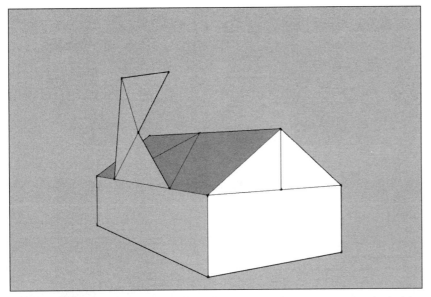

GABLE, UNFOLDING 2 The angles of the gable are calculated by measuring the height of the gable, its length from front to back, and the length shown on the roof's line.

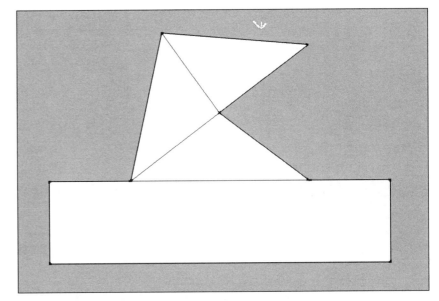

GABLE TEMPLATE, UNFOLDED An unfolded gable template.

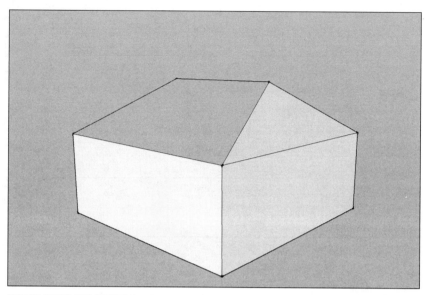

HIPPED ROOF, PERSPECTIVE A hipped roof structure in perspective.

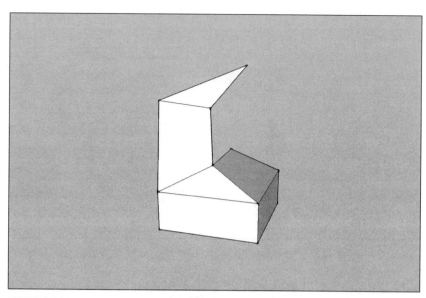

HIPPED ROOF, UNFOLDED 1 A hipped roof has very complicated geometries.

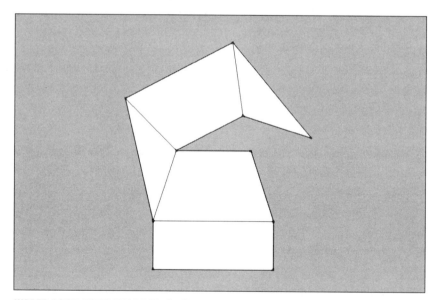

HIPPED ROOF, UNFOLDED ROOF The first two measurements you must obtain are of the ridge line and the eave line.

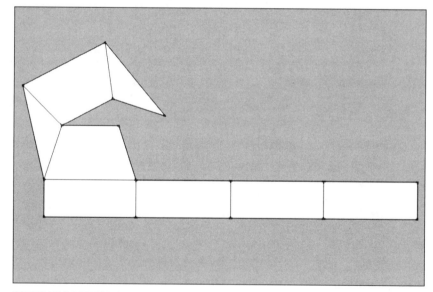

HIPPED ROOF, UNFOLDED STRUCTURE An unfolded hipped roof structure.

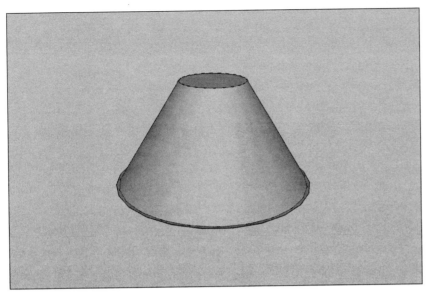

SIMPLE CONE, WHOLE A simple cone in perspective.

SIMPLE CONE, EXPLODED VIEW 1 These exploded views illustrate that templates for conical forms require numerous tapered planes to create a solid. This process is sometimes referred to as orange peeling.

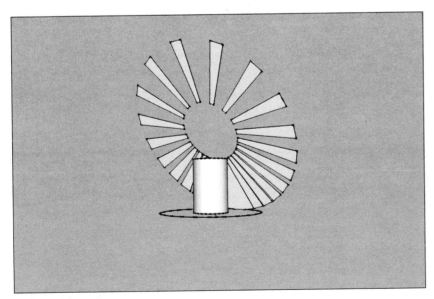

SIMPLE CONE, EXPLODED VIEW 2

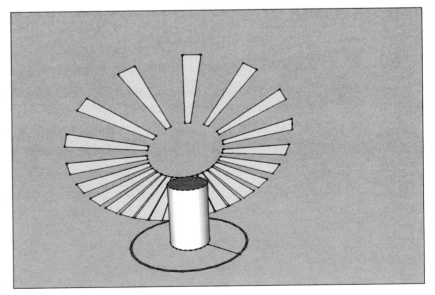

SIMPLE CONE, EXPLODED VIEW 3

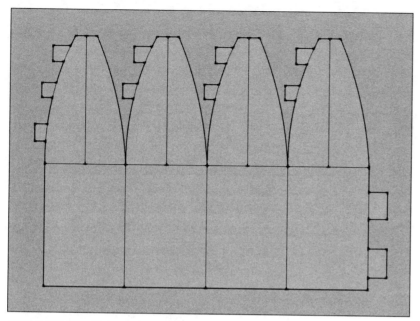

FOUR-SIDED CUPOLA A rough cupola can be created using only four sides for the lower portion and four orange peel sections for the domical portion.

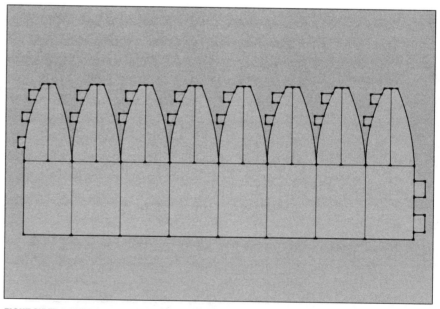

EIGHT-SIDED DOME The concept of a dome is similar to that of the cupola. The more sides, or orange peels, one uses, the rounder the object can become.

Glossary

acetate: A transparent sheet material that is available in a wide variety of colors. Most often used to emulate glass in model making.

acrylic: A transparent plastic commonly referred to by one of its brand names, such as Plexiglas.

anthropometrics: The study and measurement of the size and proportion of the human body.

archival: In model making, referring to any pure, acid-free material such as tape, board, or paper.

balsa wood: A porous wood that has the highest strength-to-weight ratio of any wood on earth. It is extremely soft, bends well with the grain, and is easily cut using a craft knife.

band clamp: A type of clamp used for clamping nonparallel surfaces such as triangles, cylinders, octagons, and so on.

bas relief: A sculpture that barely projects from its background. The faces typically found on coins are a type of bas relief. It is also referred to as *low relief*, or *raised relief*.

basswood: Basswood is harder and has a tighter grain than balsa wood, yet is still an extremely soft wood. It is easier to carve than balsa wood, yet harder to cut.

bozetti: A term primarily used by sculptors that refers to an early three-dimensional sketch. See also *study model*.

break-in period: As mold making is an imprecise science at best, molds typically require a few uses, or pulls, before they begin to function properly.

bristol board: A lightweight board, about 1/10″ thick, or thicker. The thickness and its description are dependent upon the amount of layers or plies of paper it contains. Although usually used for illustration, it differs from illustration board in that both sides of it are suitable for drawing. It is available with both hot- and cold-pressed surfaces.

burr: A raised deformation on the surface of wood or metal.

butt joint: A joint made by attaching two ends together, or butting them up against each other, without their overlapping.

cantilever: An unsupported horizontal object that projects from (usually) a wall.

capomaestro: A Renaissance Italian term that refers to a building site's foreman.

cardstock: Also called pasteboard, paperboard, or cover stock, it is often used for items such as business cards, playing cards, postcards, invitations, and so on.

cartoon: A preparatory drawing.

cartoon transfer method: A variation on a technique used during the Renaissance in conjunction with the process of fresco painting. It was a method commonly employed for transferring the master's original drawing, or cartoon, quickly and safely to a recently plastered wall.

cast: A solid object produced by the act of casting a liquid into a mold. Ice cubes, Jell-O, and cupcakes are all casts.

casting: The process of pouring a liquid into a mold and allowing it to cure or dry. After the material is solid, you may remove it from the mold. This three-dimensional copy of the original or pattern is called a cast or casting. Ice cubes are produced by casting water into an ice cube tray.

cementing: The act of attaching two pieces of material together (in this book, acrylic) using a cement adhesive.

chiaroscuro: An Italian word that refers to the juxtaposition of light and dark surfaces.

chipboard: A recycled, matte surfaced type of paperboard. It is typically grayish in color, and is typically used in study, contour, or massing models. It is utilized in many types of models, because of its unique color, and range of available thicknesses (1/32"–1/8").

cleat: A piece of wood that is fastened to something else to keep it from warping or hold it in place.

cold-pressed: Board with a rough surface, such as cold-pressed illustration board.

common throat: The part of the clamp that does the clamping.

compound miter cut: Also referred to as a compound mitered cut, it is a miter cut that is adjustable horizontally as well as laterally. This allows for a cut that is not only mitered, but beveled as well. These cuts are only possible when using a compound miter saw.

Computer Numerical Control (CNC): An automatic tool, oftentimes a router, used in conjunction with CAD programs to fabricate or mill parts. Although still expensive, these are extremely handy for creating topographic site models.

concept model: See *study model.*

concetti: A term primarily used by sculptors that refers to an early three-dimensional sketch model. See also *study model.*

context model: A model that shows the environment or context into which you will be inserting your design.

contour model: Any model that represents changes in elevation. These are normally associated with site models.

contractor's combination square: A woodwoking tool used for measuring lengths and angles, typically 45 and 90 degrees. Used to mark and measure wood. The word *square* refers to its ability to check the accuracy of right angles. A nice alternative to a metal triangle. Many metal triangles are made from nonhardened aluminum, and thus are not suitable for use when cutting. Combo squares can warp over time. *Try* means to check a surface's straightness, or to check for perpendiculars. Also called a combo square, machinist square, engineer's square, or try square (sometimes spelled tri-square).

countersink: A conical hole drilled into a surface, the purpose of which is to allow the head of a screw to be flush with the surface that the countersink bit was used on.

craft knife: Used in model building and other hobbies; often referred to as an X-Acto knife. Typically, it uses a #11 blade.

crosscut: A cut that is made at a right angle to the wood's grain.

daylight model: A model created for the purposes of exploring the effects of daylight upon a space; typically interior models.

detail model: Created to illustrate things such as molding connections and areas where two or more nonstructural materials meet.

dowel: Cylindrical wooden rods of varying widths.

dry fit: To preassemble and check the fit of pieces prior to gluing them in place. This technique is used to check the accuracy of various parts that will be joined together. In the case of contour models, it is used to determine if the sequence of the layers is accurate before the final assembly.

entasis: An effect first used in classical Greek columns where their centers gently swell outward.

entourage: Any element of a model that is used to indicate scale—trees, cars, and people, for example.

ergonomics: The study of the relationship among humans and their tools, machines, or workplaces.

faceted contour model: See *faceted site model.*

faceted site model: A site model in which irregularly sized, triangular facets join together to abstractly represent a building's site.

flap joint: A corner joint achieved by scoring the surface of your board, and bending away from the cut. This is a quick, suitable joint for use in study models.

floor flange: A type of plumbing fitting that attaches a pipe to the floor.

flute, flutes, or fluting: The vertical lines sometimes found on columns.

fold-down model: A model which has a wall or walls that fold down. Also referred to as a *fold-out model.*

fold-out model: See *fold-down model.*

Gatorfoam: Similar in construction to foam board, Gatorfoam is stronger, and available in a variety of thicknesses and colors.

glove molds: Used for casting objects in the round, such as entire buildings, furniture, cars, figures, and so on. Glove molds are typically made from a flexible material, such as silicone or latex.

grain: The visual appearance of the alignment or texture of fibers, usually referring to wood, but can refer to museum board, mat board, and so on, in model making.

honey bucket: Common use term for a portable toilet, a common sight on building sites.

hot-pressed: Board with a smooth surface, such as a hot-pressed illustration board.

illustration board: Similar in construction to chipboard, illustration board differs in the sense that it is faced with a white surface suitable for drawing.

industry models: Also known as secondary, or rough massing models, these models represent the next step in the design process. Although by no means final, these models are useful in depicting slightly more specific areas of the design.

interior daylight model: A model used to test the effects of natural light on an interior space.

interior model: A model that illustrates the relationships between the functions and scale of various interior spaces, to show furnishings, and to highlight the effects and composition of different nonstructural or finish materials.

intonaco: A smooth paste made from lime and sand, which, during fresco painting, provided a permeable surface for pigments, first absorbing them and then sealing them in the masonry as it dried.

jig: A template or guide that allows you to create numerous identical pieces.

kerf: The act of incising parallel grooves into a board in order to more easily bend or curve it.

Klingons: Jagged edges and tiny foam pieces left after cutting with a dull blade; very, very unprofessional looking.

layering: The successive buildup of different materials to create the effect of chiaroscuro or a juxtaposition of materials.

lazy susan: A rotating, usually circular tray.

low relief: See *bas relief.*

maquette: A term used primarily by sculptors that refers to an early three-dimensional sketch. See also *study model.*

massing models: Simplified versions of the overall form of your building or surrounding buildings. The lack of openings, details, and voids allow massing models to be quickly and easily constructed. The houses and hotels used in Monopoly are good examples of massing. Sometimes called solid/void models.

mastaba: The structure that covered early Egyptian underground tombs. Typically, these had sloping walls and a flat roof.

mat board: A type of paper-based board typically used for picture framing.

memory: After the board is cut, instead of curving down slightly in the direction of the cut, it retains its crisp edge. It also has an extremely smooth, white surface that is more resistant to dents than other foam boards.

mitered: Joined using a miter joint.

miter gauge: A protractor head that is attached to a metal handle. This is used to adjust the angle at which you will cross cut.

miter joint: A joint that is created when each corner is cut a mitered angle, usually 45 degrees, and attached together to create a crisp, clean, edge. Miter joints are usually found at 90-degree corners where they disguise the core and give a professional appearance.

modeling foam: Foam polystyrene or polyurethane foam are referred to as modeling foams. These are grain-free, high-density foams that can be glued, cut, carved, or sanded. These are available from a variety of online sources.

mold: An impression or inverse form of the pattern into which a casting material in its liquid state is poured. An ice cube tray, muffin tin, or cookie cutter can all be described as molds.

mortise machine: A machine capable of creating the female wooden joint into which a tenon will be added.

mother molds: A rigid shell or backing most often used in conjunction with a flexible mold. The mother mold is necessary to keep the flexible portion of the rubber from distorting.

mullion: Vertical and horizontal posts that subdivide a window.

museum board: An archival version of mat board. Typically the core of archival mat board will be a bright white, as opposed to the slightly yellowed core found in nonarchival mat board.

Mylar: A thin, clear, polyester-based film, often used for to represent glass in model making.

one-piece relief molds: A type of mold useful for making details that will later be attached to a façade or other flat surface.

open façades: A model that is missing one or more sides.

open top: A model in which the roof is intentionally left off.

overcut: A cut, usually the unintentional result of going past a corner when cutting a square or rectangle hole from a larger piece.

paradeigma: Full-size, wooden models employed as a design tool by the ancient Greeks.

part line: A line produced on the cast, the result of a small gap between mold parts. When the line is more substantial and must be removed, it is referred to as flash or flashing.

pattern: The original object, prototype, or sculpture from which casts or multiples will be made. A pattern can be made of nearly anything, as long as it is treated with a release agent.

pattern draft: A taper or bevel on the vertical surfaces of the pattern. Draftability, or any reference to something being draftable, are terms that may not actually exist in the English language, but have found their way into the lexicon of mold makers.

polyvinyl acetate (PVA): A glue used on porous surfaces.

presentation model: Also categorized as finished models, and are customarily employed after the final design stage. Detail, craftsmanship, and communication with the client are the goals of presentation models.

pull: Removing a cast from the mold. All molds have a finite amount of pulls before they deteriorate.

rabbet: An L-shaped groove that is cut into the end of a board. These model building tools were designed for creating a joint so that when joining two pieces of foam board together, the exposed edge will be disguised.

rabbet edge joint: In woodworking, this can also be referred to as a half-lap joint or a rebate joint. Part of the material, the thickness of which is equal to the piece it will be joined to, is removed from its edge. In model making, this technique is usually employed in order to avoid leaving an exposed edge in a foam board joint.

railroad contour model: An extremely realistic representation of not only the slope of a site, but its entourage as well. This type of model is most often used in presentation models.

raised: The process of stacking one layer of material upon another.

raised contour model: A model that represents consistent, horizontal, incremental changes in elevation/topography instead of a true gradient. See also *topographic model*.

raised relief: See *bas relief*.

reciprocation: The up-and-down motion of a saw blade; typically refers to reciprocal or scroll saws.

release/release agent: A lubricant that is applied to the mold and/or pattern. Think of it as a no-stick lubricant, such as Pam, that is applied to the mold as opposed to a frying pan. A mold release is typically wax or silicone based, but many other types do exist.

resist: A masking or other solution that prohibits a second solution, such as paint, from adhering to a surface.

rip: A cut that is made parallel to the woods grain.

rip fence: An adjustable rail that is used to guide the wood as it is being cut or ripped on a table saw. A table saw guide that runs parallel to the blade.

rough massing models: See *industry model*.

scale: In architecture, the proportions of a building or its parts with reference to a module or unit of measurement. In architectural drawing, the size of the plans, elevations, sections, and so on in relation to the actual size of the object delineated.

scale model: A model that is produced using exact, scaled-down proportions of a proposed or existing structure.

scoring: The scraping of the surface of a material in preparation for altering the size of said material.

scroll saw: A benchtop power tool useful for creating complex curves.

secondary model: See *industry model*.

section models: Created by cutting through the surface or any part of the model to show the interior or profile. This type of model will show the elevation of the interior rooms, while simultaneously showing the overall form of the building as well as the relationship of the sectioned rooms to the building itself.

site model: A three-dimensional scale representation of the context for your building or project. Other terms for, and varieties of, site models include contour models, topographic models, or context models.

spindle sander: A machine with an oscillating, cylindrical, sanding attachment. Useful for sanding both inside and outside curves.

spolvero: See *cartoon transfer method*.

stereo lithography apparatus (SLA): A computer-driven process by which a design can be fabricated in three dimensions. A laser is used in conjunction with a resin, whereby the object is constructed layer by layer until the final part emerges. This is primarily used in rapid prototyping, as opposed to architectural model building.

strawboard: A rough, yellow-brown board made from straw pulp. Strawboard has very little strength, but can be stiffened when its surface is made more rigid via the application of a semi-stiff veneer such as cardstock.

structural models: Focus more on how a building is constructed, as opposed to its aesthetic or formal character. Structural models focus on elements such as the framing or truss systems, connection details, or, in larger scales, can also be used for structural tests.

study model: A quick model that is used as a design tool.

thermal expansion: The change in volume of an object in response to changes in temperature. Things get bigger when hot, and smaller when cold.

throat size: The size of the space between the jaws of a wrench.

topographic model: A type of site model where the contours are represented using flat planes. Each level represents an equal increase in elevation/topography, instead of a true gradient. See also *raised contour model*.

Trabeation/trabeated: Post and lintel construction.

transfer method: One of any number of methods used to transfer an image from one material to another.

transfer paper: A graphite-coated paper which is used in one of the transfer methods.

transparent models: A model that can be seen through.

try square: See *combination square*.

undercuts: A taper on a pattern that will not allow a pattern or cast to be removed from the mold. If an ice cube were wider at the bottom than at the top, the frozen cube couldn't be removed from the tray. An undercut is sometimes referred to as a back draft.

utility knife: A heavy-duty knife, generally used by contractors, but useful to the model maker for cutting thicker boards.

V-groove cutter: A tool that incises a V-shaped notch or groove into a board; in this case, foam board.

vignette: A small portion or detail of a design.

whack-a-mole model: A model, such as that of St. Paul's, into which one's head can be inserted in order to see the interior.

working model: A type of study model that is used as a design tool.

References

Alberti, Leon Battista. *On the Art of Building in Ten Books.* Translated by Joseph Rykwert, Neil Leach, and Robert Tavernor. Cambridge, MA: MIT Press, 1988.

Buckles, Matthew. *Building Architectural and Interior Design Models Fast: An Easy to Follow Step-by-Step Guide to Constructing Design Studio Models.* Rancho Cucamonga, CA: Belpine Publishing, 1991.

Busch, Akiko. *The Art of the Architectural Model.* New York: Design Press, 1991.

Curl, James. *Dictionary of Architecture.* Kent, UK: Grange Books, 2005.

Dalby, Stuart. *Making Model Buildings.* Poole, Dorset, UK: Blandford Press Ltd., 1980.

Hohauser, Sanford. *Architectural and Interior Models.* 2nd ed. Rev. by Helen Demchyshn. New York: Van Nostrand Reinhold, 1982.

Janke, Rolf. *Architectural Models.* New York: Praeger Publishers, 1968.

Jetsonen, Jari ed. *Little Big Houses: Working with Architectural Models.* Helsinki, Finland: Building Information Limited, 2001.

King, Ross. *Brunelleschi's Dome: How a Renaissance Genius Reinvented Architecture.* Middlesex, England: Penguin Books, 2000.

King, Ross. *Michelangelo and the Pope's Ceiling.* New York: Walker and Company, 2003.

Koepke, Marguerite. *Model Graphics, Building and Using Study Models.* New York: Van Nostrand Reinhold, 1988.

Knoll, Wolfgang, and Martin Hechinger. *Architectural Models: Construction Techniques.* New York: McGraw-Hill, 1992.

Kurrent, Friedrich ed. *Scale Model: Houses of the 20th Century.* Translated by Gail Schamberger. Boston: Birkhauser, 1999.

Mills, Criss. *Designing with Models: A Studio Guide to Making and Using Architectural Design Models.* New York: Wiley, 2000.

Moon, Karen. *Modeling Messages: The Architect and the Model.* New York: The Monacelli Press, 2005.

Morris, Mark. *Models: Architecture and the Miniature.* West Sussex, UK: Wiley, 2006.

Neat, David. *Model-Making, Materials and Methods.* Ramsbury, UK: Crowood Press, 2008.

Pattinson, Graham. *A Guide to Professional Architectural and Industrial Scale Model Building.* Englewood Cliffs, N.J.: Prentice Hall, 1982.

Price, Brick. *The Model-Building Handbook.* Randor, PA: Chilton Book Company, 1981.

Porter, Tom, and John Neal. *Architectural Supermodels: Physical and Electronic Simulation.* Oxford, UK: Architectural Press, 2000.

Roman, Antonio. *Eero Saarinen: An Architecture of Multiplicity.* London: Princeton Architectural Press, 2002.

Smith, Albert C. *Architectural Model as Machine: A New View of Models from Antiquity to the Present Day.* Oxford, UK: Architectural Press, 2004.

Sutherland, Martha. *Modelmaking: A Basic Guide.* New York: W.W. Norton and Company, 1999.

Taylor, John. *Model Building for Architects and Engineers.* New York: McGraw-Hill, 1971.

Index

stereo lithography apparatus (SLA), 94
strawboard, 111
structural models, 21
study models, 11–12, *13*, *16*, 23–24
    furniture study models, 30–31

T

thermal expansion, 113
throat sizes, 68
tools (for model building), 57–73
    adhesives, 65–67
    circle cutters, 60
    foam board tools, 58–65
    hand tools, 67–69
    knives, 58
    paints, 67
    power tools
        fixed location, 71–73
        portable, 69–71

safety, 67
saws, 71–72
topographical models, 19, 105
trabeation, 115
transparent models, 29
TWA terminal at JFK airport, 6, *7*

V

Vassiliadis, Alec, 23, *24*, *30*, *38*, *39*, 45, *194*
V-groove cutter, 141
vignettes, 27
Vitruvius, 4

W

wall-mounted models, 105–6
walls (in models), 114–16
whack-a-mole models, 27, 29
William Zimmerman Architects. *See*
    Zimmerman, William

windows (in models), 117, 119–21, *122*,
    160–63
    adding a dormer window to a pitched
        roof (balsa/basswood), 167–77
wood. *See* balsa and basswood
working models, 12
workspaces (essential features of), 47–55
    safety, 54–55
    student workspaces at home, 53
Wren, Sir Christopher, xiii, 27, 29

Z

ZGF (architectural firm), 8, *15*, *19*, 192, 205
Zimmer Gunsul Frasca Artchitects LLP. *See*
    ZGF
Zimmerman, William, *13*, *15*, *26*, 43–44, *51*,
    91, *94*, *95*, *105*, *106*, *219*, 221